I

PET LIBRARY'S

Aquarium
Guide

PET LIBRARY'S

Aquarium
Guide

With 220 color plates

by Jim Kelly

England

THE PET LIBRARY LTD

The Pet Library Ltd.,
Subsidiary of Sternco In-
dustries Inc., 600 South
Fourth Street, Harrison,
N.J. Exclusive Canadian
Distributor: Hartz Moun-
tain Pet Supplies Limited,
1125 Talbot Street, St.
Thomas, Ontario, Canada.
Exclusive United King-
dom Distributor: The Pet
Library (London) Ltd.,
30 Borough High Street,
London S.E. 1.

© 1969 Jim Kelly
(England)

Printed in the Netherlands

ISBN 0-87826-005-6

Table of Contents

Cover picture: *Betta splendens*

Introduction

Over the years, in my capacity as professional aquarist, aquarium society official, as well as lecturer and author, I have constantly endeavored to help the beginner who wants to keep tropical fish. This book is an attempt to set down what experience in these matters has taught me. As an aid for a wider audience, it has been deliberately couched in simple terms, scientific nomenclature being used only where necessary.

I am not attempting to be the bearer of mysteriously acquired erudition; I regard myself as an exponent of common sense, which all scientists should be!

It would be a mistake to expect one book to supply all the information needed for this hobby. Any author making such an attempt — or claim — would be presumptuous. However, as a guide for the beginner, there are certain claims to be made, all of which are based on my own experience.

If the advice given in these pages is followed, the pitfalls awaiting the avid but over-anxious beginner will be avoided. To those hovering on the brink, may I suggest that no other hobby or branch of pet keeping can offer so many advantages.

Aquariums, if properly kept, emit no odors; they are reasonably cheap and easy to install. Their occupants make no noise; and, as fish can be left to their own devices, you need not worry about a caretaker during vacations.

No other hobby can offer — for so little outlay and effort — such interesting and educational side trips into the wonderful world of biology.

This present age is often regarded as a " neurotic" one. Its spate of sick jokes, decadent art forms, and a market flooded with self-improvement literature indicates that we need some form of escape, and keeping fish can be just that!

Whether you picked up this book out of idle curiosity, never dreaming you were on the brink of a " new" hobby, or because you are already seriously contemplating the thought of having a living picture in your home, come and join us — I promise you will never regret it.

Manchester, Great Britain   Jim Kelly

The Angelfish, *Pterophyllum scalare*. The bamboo sticks in the background are intended to receive the spawn.

I First Things First

A Short History of Aquarium Keeping

Those who cannot remember the past are condemned to repeat it!
These words of wisdom are to be found emblazoned on the wall of the
Aeronautical Museum, Terminal Building, at the John F. Kennedy
International Airport, New York. It is a reply to those people who
might ask why a book such as this should contain a history of fish and
the story of the men who kept and observed them.

Keeping fish in captivity is an ancient art, though how ancient, we
shall probably never know. However, records show that in early
China — long before the birth of Christ — the keeping and breeding
of Carp was a flourishing business. In fact "The Book of Vermillion
Fish" is credited to Chang Chi'en-te, a Chinese author who lived
more than one thousand years before our present western calendar
began.

The Greeks seem to have had a word for everything, so it is no
surprise that Aristotle (384-322 BC), called "The Father of All
Learning," set down and described many species of fish brought to
him. Lacking the benefits of Carl Linnaeus' principles for defining
genera and species, he used common names — common, that is, to
the fishermen of the Aegean Sea. Perhaps it was a good thing that
their numbers were limited to just over one hundred species!

Then for hundreds of years, men gave the subject little thought.
They merely parroted the Aristotelian teachings, adding little to our
knowledge. Archeologists have uncovered evidence that the Romans
kept fish in containers. However, I suspect that the Romans were
more interested in enhancing the pleasures of their cuisine than in
contributing to science.

A modern book about life under the Egyptian kings* quotes the
following:

> In the gardens at the Palace of Tutmosis the
> Third, were to be found huge ornamental
> tanks containing fish; they served the dual
> purpose of decoration and as a means of
> keeping down the mosquitos.

Across the ocean in the New World, the Spanish invaders under

*Cottrell, Leonard, " Life Under the Pharaohs."

Cortez were searching for the gold in "El Dorado." They found plenty of goldfish in the varied collection of fish and fowl in the gardens of the Montezuman prince, a collection that he had inherited!

The common goldfish (according to Duerigen) reached Europe about 1611 — the time Henry Hudson was embarking upon his last voyage. When the city of London burned in the Great Fire of 1666, the famous diarist, Samuel Pepys, was filling the pages of his journal with a description of "fishes kept in a glass of water"; across the English Channel in Strasbourg, Leonhart Baldner was acting like a Nero of the Middle Ages by passing his time "fiddling" with fish kept in glass containers.

Aquarium Societies

We could make numerous references to the history of this art. However, as this is but a guide for beginners, we will move on to more contemporary times and events by tracing the development of this hobby in the New World.

On March 12, 1893, the first American aquarium society, composed mostly of German immigrants, was called to order by its president, Baron von Schlichting. As was the custom in their homeland, they named the group after a mythical creature associated with the sea: Triton, the half-man, half-fish, demi-god son of Poseidon. A second society, Salamander, was formed barely a month later.

Three years later, both groups were replaced by the Aquarium Society. Despite the fact that they met at the German-American School Building in Jersey City, New Jersey, they soon changed their title to The New York Aquarium Society.

This group spawned many aquarists destined to become famous. One in particular, Eugene Smith, is worthy of mention, for, under his leadership, the hobby moved into the twentieth century.

Though aquarium historians are rare, many worthy men have participated in the formation and guidance of the hobby in the United States.

One worthy contender was Hugo Mulertt, overlooked by most authors because of the period of his activity (1870 — 1911). His first book on the subject of fishkeeping, "The Goldfish and its Culture," remained a textbook for many years. He also published a magazine called "The Aquarium." Aquatic trader, plant specialist, and author, he was active in all phases of the hobby. His contributions to the field were limitless and because of this, I am able to overlook another book he wrote, " How to Cook Fish"!

Enthusiasm for the hobby gradually increased, and, before long, reached a wider public. In 1853, the first public aquarium was built on the grounds of the London Zoological Gardens (England). It bore the high-sounding title of "Aquavivarium." Visitors showed a great deal of enthusiasm, but because of poor construction, it did not last long.

In twelve years at least a dozen other cities from Belfast to Berlin had followed suit and constructed their own public aquariums.

The use of the term "aquarium" first appeared in the works of the English naturalist, Philip Henry Gosse. His brilliant career took him around the world, and for a time, he taught school in Alabama.

The period from the turn of the century to the present is often referred to as the "Age of Discovery," and the art of keeping fish in captivity has improved along with man's expansion in the fields of science and technology.

Better communications shrank the globe. The time needed to cover long distances was drastically cut by the invention of the airship and the aeroplane. So the shipment of tropical fish became easier, and the markets of the world were flooded with new specimens at prices within the reach of the man in the street.

In the summer of 1936 the lighter-than-air ship LZ-129, the Hindenburg, flying passengers and freight for the German National Airline, *Deutsche Lufthansa,* included in its cargo "20,000 Tropical Neon Fish *(Hyphessobrycon innesi)."* It flew them from Lakehurst, New Jersey to Frankfurt, Germany.

In the technological fields, the production of better equipment and the common use of electricity solved the troublesome problem of keeping fish warm. Like the piano, everyone wanted a fish tank, and owning one became a status symbol.

Today, tropical fish are a big business. Airline companies, quick to realize the potentialities, devised better methods of carrying live fish and some even set up special sections within their companies to cope with the increased demand.

From the icy waters of the snow-draped Himalayas to the warm, crystal clear seas covering the Australian Barrier Reef; from the rivers and lakes of the "Dark Continent" of Africa to the steaming jungle tributaries of the mighty Amazon River; from the four corners of the globe, come an increasing number of new species to fill our fish tanks. The hobby's history is truly exciting and romantic!

The Basics of Aquarium Balance

One of the most difficult things we face in the process of growing up (though at the time we aren't aware of it) is learning to stand erect and *balance* ourselves on our two feet. As we get older, we probably savor the delights of the see-saw and learn yet more about the principles of balance, but our equilibrium is largely dependent on the weight of whoever occupies the other end of the see-saw. This interdependence applies to everything on this planet, and is especially important when striving to maintain a healthy environment for our fish.

The theory of the interdependence of plants and animals is not a new one. In the fifth century BC, the Greek philosopher, Empedocles, first recorded the universal and fundamental nature of the cooperation underlying group action — the interdependence of animals and members of the vegetable kingdom.

Espinas, a French scientist writing in *"Des Sociétés Animales"* in 1878, affirmed that no living being is solitary. From the lowest form of life to the highest, all are involved in some form of social existence.

Every day, plants release about 430 million tons of oxygen by making use of two raw materials — carbon dioxide taken from the air, and water taken up by their root systems. When you order a soda you order the same ingredients! Helped by chlorophyll — the green pigment in their leaves — plants use the energy from the sun to assemble complex compounds from simple ingredients.

The Magic Formula

$$6\,CO_2 + 6\,H_2O \xrightarrow[\text{Chlorophyll}]{\text{Light}} C_6H_{12}O_6 + 6\,O_2$$

one molecule of sugar

This action is called *photosynthesis (photo* = Greek for light, *synthesis* = a putting together), and it is extremely complicated. The formula above leaves out many steps of the actual complex process.

Fish, like ourselves, need oxygen to live. Through their gills they take the dissolved oxygen from the water, assimilate it into their bloodstream, and exhale carbon dioxide (the spent product of respiration); the aquarium plants do just the reverse so, theoretically, a balance is set up.

William Thomas Brande (1788 — 1866) in his "Manual of Chemistry" speaks of "the cycle of fish breathing the dissolved air, the latter being restored by the vegetables (plants) which give off oxygen and absorb carbon." Inspired by Brande's experiments, Robert Warrington read a paper to The Chemical Society of Great Britain in 1850, describing how he had kept fish and plants in an aquarium for months *without having to change the water!*

In our aquarium there are various forces always at work. One group of bacteria (aerobic) relies entirely on oxygen for its respiration; its opposite (anaerobic) does not need free oxygen at all.

If our tank water is clear and sweet, the fish healthy and active, the plants displaying good color and flourishing, then the factors favoring the aerobic are supreme. However, the amount of available oxygen can diminish. This could be the result of one or more of many possible factors such as: overfeeding, overstocking with fish, dying plants, and so on. In this event, the sulphur reducing group of bacteria (anaerobic) takes over and the tank becomes foul and unhealthy, giving off an odor characteristic of rotten eggs. This competition between the two factors is continuous, and holding a balance is decisive in maintaining healthy tanks.

For many years, aquarists persisted in the myth that plants were a necessary ingredient in a balanced tank. Today, using modern techniques, aquarists have proved that fish can live quite happily in tanks devoid of greenery, provided other considerations are met. The most important condition is the amount of water surface exposed to the air. The water surface is a very important factor in breathing, because a large water surface allows the spent gases (carbon dioxide) to leave the tank. We now know that what kills our fish is not necessarily a lack of oxygen, but a build-up of carbon dioxide in the water. When dissolved in water, this gas forms a weak acid (carbonic acid) which is poisonous to life when it exceeds a concentration of greater than ten percent.

Apparently, carbon dioxide is more of a limiting factor in the maintenance of our aquarium than is oxygen. Tests have shown that an excess of carbon dioxide can be present even when the water is saturated with oxygen. Under these circumstances, fish will not thrive. The gases in the aquarium are always in balance with the gases in the atmosphere above. However, oxygen enters the water from the atmosphere more readily than carbon dioxide leaves the water.

That is why it is important to have one's aquarium constructed to present to the surrounding air as large a surface of water as is possible. This is the reason manufacturers of aquaria usually choose the dimensions they do. The tank water, surrounded on five sides, has but one surface from which to throw off the harmful build-up of gas.

For a time, the Victorians had a fad of building what they described as Mantel tanks. These were deep, narrow aquaria, made to fit snugly on the drawing-room mantelpiece. They soon lost favor, as our readers will have guessed, because the fish died as a result of the small water surface, which was inadequate for a free exchange of gases. You can keep more fish (the volume of water being equal) in a container shaped like a saucer than you can in one shaped like a water glass. For years, aquarists bubbled air (aeration) through their tanks. They believed that the additional oxygen would have a balancing effect and would therefore keep the aquaria healthy — they did the right thing for the wrong reason! During aeration, the water is agitated and starts to circulate. This increased movement of water brings the heavier carbon dioxide charged water to the surface where the gas can escape.

Taking all this into consideration, you will see that most so-called goldfish bowls, if filled to their narrow necks, are unsatisfactory for aquatic life. What has probably saved the goldfish from extinction is the belief that water in fish bowls should be changed frequently (often, well-meaning owners do this with monotonous regularity). Consequently, this constant influx of fresh water never allows pollution to get a hold or harmful gases to reach a toxic level.

From these statements, the reader must not get the idea that plants aren't desirable. The many sound reasons for their being part of the aquarium are discussed in Chapter VI.

Aged or Old Water?

Though the terms "aged" and "old" might, at first glance, seem to mean the same thing, for the aquarist they have distinctly different meanings.

Freshly drawn water allowed to stand can be said to be "old" in time but not "aged." In an aquarium, water that has housed fish and plant life and has undergone certain chemical and biological changes can be considered "aged"; it can also contain excessive waste products of metabolism from the fishes and plants. That is why even in a well balanced set-up, it is extremely desirable to change a small amount of water (about one-third) regularly, to prevent this undesirable build up. The fresh water will be so diluted in the aquarium that you won't have to neutralize it by ageing.

Further, water drawn fresh from the faucet often contains chemicals to purify it for domestic consumption. Chlorine is widely used because of its disinfecting properties, but some areas also add fluorides in order to protect children's teeth. In certain strengths these chemicals can be harmful to fish, and though tropicals can tolerate widely varying water conditions, they won't take kindly to fresh water straight from the tap. Therefore, it is wise to let this water stand for a few days in open containers where the gases can dissipate naturally. Always store water in glass or plastic containers, never in copper or zinc as water reacts with these metals and can become toxic. Particularly dangerous are zinc bath tubs.

When setting up a new aquarium, wait for one week before adding fish to the newly-established tank (less if filtration or aeration is used). Gases can be removed by boiling and allowing the water to cool, but I don't recommend this because it also removes vital minerals and gases from the water. A better method of speedy de-chlorination is to use a neutralizing agent such as sodium thiosulfate (photographer's hypo). Add one grain (by weight) of the hypo to every gallon of water you wish to neutralize. Dissolve the crystals in a small amount of water before you pour the mixture into the tank. Don't add the sodium thiosulfate directly to the tank if there are fish in it.

II The Basic Requirements

Tanks

Obviously, the first piece of equipment required is a fish tank, and the two decisions regarding this are: what *type* (stainless steel, plastic-covered, glass, or other), and what *size* (gallon capacity)?

Choosing a tank is similar to buying a new automobile — which one would suit your taste and fill your requirements is a very individual matter. The Chinese had a saying, " One picture is worth a thousand words," and a little time spent viewing the tanks and stands available in your local store will be more valuable than a whole chapter on the subject. The following suggestions are to guide you in making a final selection.

Unless you already have a substantial base on which to place your tank, you will require a stand. The average ten gallon tank filled with water, gravel and rock weighs about 100 pounds. Sorry, but that beautiful ornate coffee table just won't do unless you want a " disaster area" in your home! Tanks with stand set-ups are worthy of consideration and allow you greater freedom of choice when planning a location for the aquarium.

Low-priced tanks may have a painted frame, but if your budget will allow, buy the best — stainless steel or a plastic-covered frame. These don't rust and simply need a wipe-over from time to time to keep them clean. Tell your dealer what you have in mind, how much you are prepared to pay, and be guided by him. Be choosy; select a tank made by a reputable manufacturer. Then you can usually receive satisfaction if later it proves faulty.

Where to place the tank in the home will be controlled by the space available and position of an electric outlet, but keep it away from drafts and cold locations. Try not to place the aquarium directly under a window or in a room with a southern outlook, as too much sunlight will stimulate the growth of green algae. You can make full use of artificial light, so a room with a north window is preferable. (See the section *Lighting the Aquarium.*)

Whatever the chosen location, it will attract visitors — perhaps some thoughtless ones. So remember, the result of dropping ashes into the fish tank can be disastrous! And do not allow anyone — child or visitor — to tap on the glass of the aquarium as the water within acts as a medium causing strong vibrations.

And if your house resounds to the patter of tiny feet, bear in mind that children, above all, will want to watch the fish, and many a set-up has been nearly pulled over by some anxious youngster trying to climb up the stand to view. If the stand makes the tank too high for the kiddies, put a small stool nearby for them to stand on.

Often, beginners automatically choose a small tank. This is not advisable, as it is easier to maintain a large aquarium than a small one. Choose a size (bearing in mind the surface area) that gives a nice, deep front view. Around 10 or 15 gallon capacity should be about right.

If you do not contemplate a manufactured reflector (tank cover/light holder), then cover the top with a piece of glass. This will help to keep out dust, cigarette ash, and small boys' fingers, and will stop your prize fish from committing hari-kari by leaping out onto the carpet. Glass covers will not restrict the air supply; oil was floated on top of an experimental tank and air pierced even that barrier!

The glass in your aquarium is held in place by special cement and, though strong, won't stand knocking about. Carry your container home as if it were some rare piece of Dresden china. If you put your tank on a piece of furniture, place it on a pad of felt or plastic to prevent furniture damage.

Other tanks made from a variety of substances are available — plastic, all glass, and so on. I have even witnessed dish pans and refrigerator liners pressed into service. The ingenuity of the aquarist knows no limits, but at the beginning stick to the recommended orthodox tanks — they are safer.

Lighting the Aquarium

Ever since the pronouncement in the Book of Genesis, " Let there be light!" fishkeepers have been hotly debating what sort of light to use. If your original purchase was a package deal, it probably included a reflector to house the lights. Reflectors manufactured today are well-made, rugged, and safe, and add a professional finish to one's set-up.

Bats, photographers, and tellers of ghost stories love the dark, but if we are to see our fish and encourage the plants to grow, we must light the aquarium. Natural daylight is fine, within limits, but some form of artificial illumination is still necessary. The latter has the added advantage of being controllable.

In their natural environment, fish receive light from above, so do

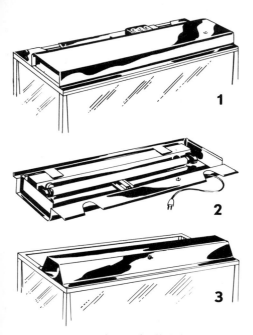

1

2

3

1 — Tank hood. Used to illuminate and also cover the aquarium. 2 — The underside of a fluorescent hood. A hood can conceal either fluorescent or incandescent bulbs, or a combination of both. 3 — Aquarium reflector. This too can be either incandescent or fluorescent. For best effect it should be kept on the front of the aquarium.

not experiment by lighting your tank from the sides or below — leave the confounding of nature's laws to the science fiction writers.

The amount of wattage needed will vary, but your pet dealer will advise you. A good formula for calculating the amount of wattage is:

$$\text{Wattage required} = \frac{\text{Length of tank in inches} \times 32}{\text{Number of hours the tank is lit}}$$

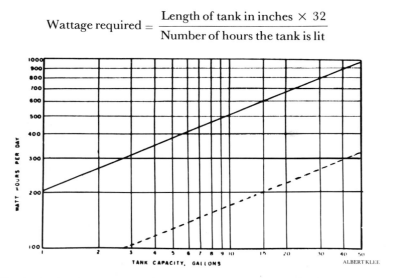

ALBERT KLEE

Graph showing how many watt-hours (bulb wattage x hours of illumination) of electricity per day is needed — approximately — according to the size of the tank. The solid line indicates incandescent lighting, the dotted line fluorescent lighting.

22

A COMPARISON OF THE TWO MAIN FORMS OF LIGHTING FOR AQUARIA

	Advantages	Disadvantages
Incandescent	Cheaper installation. Plants grow well under this light.	Heats water surface, can scorch surface plants. Bulbs fail before their rated time when used in aquaria. Light distribution not very even unless strip types used. Running costs high. Hot bulbs can pop if splashed with water; can also inflict nasty skin burns.
Fluorescent	Costs less per hour to use. Tubes run cool so can be placed near the water surface. Tubes can be purchased in long lengths, enabling one installation to light several aquaria. Tubes last at least 1,000 hours. Even light distribution.	Installation expensive; need starter, ballast and special fittings.

From experience, I recommend fluorescent lighting, but I choose the color of the tube carefully. Experiments carried out by leading authorities prove that fish do better under this type of lighting when the color tends towards the reds and yellows; under blue light some fish stop breeding. Blue light adversely affects fish eggs!

Reflectors serve useful purposes apart from being just lampholders. They can be home-made from hardboard, plywood, aluminum, steel and even plastic; but if you do construct your own, use non-toxic material since condensation settling on the reflector can carry the toxins back to the water.

Filters

Talk fish with any old-timer and he will tell you that to succeed in the "good old days" of the hobby, without the modern advantages of filtration, you *had* to be good. In fact, some of these senior aquarists still insist that filters are unnecessary, but so many aquarists have proved the worth of filtration that it is here to stay.

That it is possible to run a successful aquarium without the use of filters or aeration cannot be denied, but just ask the lady of the house whether she would prefer to go back to the old-fashioned broom instead of her vacuum cleaner, and you have your answer. Anything that helps to cut down on the work and make the hobby more pleasurable is obviously an advantage one should make full use of. What, then, is the function of filtration?

a) It helps to keep the water clean and give it that "good enough to drink" appearance by removing the floating debris.

b) It circulates the water in the tank, insuring a better exchange of gases and a better distribution of air.

c) By passing the water through media like activated charcoal, harmful waste products are removed. Bear in mind that no filter will remove waste products *dissolved* in the water; regular replacement by a partial change of the tank water is desirable even when filtration is employed.

Filter systems are many and varied. The more conventional ones usually take the form of plastic boxes hung outside or inside the tank and contain filter material such as glass wool, nylon floss, sponge or some man-made fiber. To facilitate the movement of water from the aquarium through the "sieve" and back again to the tank, they utilize an air lift and a siphon. The action of these conventional filters is largely mechanical and they are designed primarily to remove the particulate materials from the water.

Another type of filter fits underneath the aquarium gravel, and the action of breaking down the particulate material into gases (CO_2) and soluble nitrates is biological. That is, this type of filter circulates oxygen-rich water through the gravel. The oxygen encourages the growth of beneficial bacteria that break down the organic matter in the tank and thus helps to prevent pollution. This biological action is also present to a lesser extent in the conventional types. Remember, efficient as these filters are in removing debris from the water, they will not remove certain natural acids, oils or detergents.

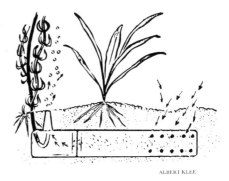

This is how an undergravel filter works. The airlift (left) draws the dirty water through the gravel (arrows) and through the holes in the filter, from where it is subsequently returned to the tank. The sediment which lodges in the gravel is broken down by aerobic bacteria into harmless substances such as carbon dioxide and water.

ALBERT KLEE

There are filters which can remove particles of colloidal size (substances which, though apparently dissolved, cannot pass through a membrane, such as bacteria, certain types of algae and protozoa). These are the so-called "water polishers." They are pad-like structures full of millions of minute, precisely sized holes, usually ten microns or smaller. To give you some idea of the minute size of a micron, approximately five hundred of them would just about cover a period on this page! These filters have just been introduced to the hobby, and at present are mainly used in industry for the sterile filtration of fluids.

No one filter system is perfect and each must be used correctly if maximum efficiency and utilization is to be achieved by the hobbyist. Your choice will largely depend on the funds available and the job you want it to do. Describe your aquarium to your dealer and seek his experience in these matters.

If you choose one of the conventional types that use filter media, remember that you must change or clean this frequently if the filter is to function properly. Some man-made filter materials can be rinsed under a faucet and be reused but they are so cheap and readily available, that is is hardly worth the effort. Poor quality glass wool has the nasty habit of letting tiny particles of the wool through the filter and into the tank. Mistaking these tiny fibres for worms, the fish may, with disastrous results, eat them. So be sure to rinse the wool free of loose particles before placing it in the filter. Preferably, use only the finest grade. Carbon also contains an appreciable amount of "dust" and here too "rinsing first" also applies. After use, carbon or activated charcoal becomes soiled. One simple way to reactivate it is to spread the charcoal on a tray and bake it in a warm oven to drive out the absorbed gases and adsorbed particulate matter.

Most of the "water polishers" are furnished with a stiff brush to enable you to scrub the filter pad free from clogging materials. Also available and very useful adjuncts to one's filter cleaning kit are long, flexible brushes. These filter brushes come in various sizes and are used to clean around the twists and bends of the plastic piping.

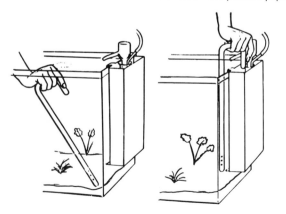

ALBERT KLEE

To start the siphon for an outside filter, immerse it completely in the tank so that it fills with water. Place your finger over the end as shown, then place it in the filter. Remove your finger, allowing the water to flow, only after the stem is in position.

Air Lifts

To lift the water from the tank, most filters now use a siphon tube, the end hanging in the tank protected by a perforated box to prevent fish from being sucked in, but even these make use of an "air lift" to return the water. An air lift is simply a piece of plastic tubing curved like the handle of an umbrella, the long end standing in the water, the short side ending in a spout. To work efficiently most of the tube must be immersed in the water. It should be no longer than eleven inches.

To provide air for operating these filters we require an air pump; these pumps are discussed at the end of this chapter.

Aeration

Aeration consists of agitating the water by means of a stream of air forced through a porous medium, such as an air stone. For best results, the stream of air bubbles should be neither fine nor coarse. After prolonged usage, the interstices of the stone can become clogged. A few minutes' immersion in vinegar and a brisk rub with a stiff brush will restore its porosity. Various ceramic aerator ornaments are available as substitutes for air stones, or you can have multiple sources of air bubbling in your tank by the use of a series of air valves. These can be made of metal or plastic, and can vary from a simple T-shaped pipe to more complicated affairs sporting an air control, screw valve, or other device.

Before connecting the aerator to the pump, blow gently down the tubing. There should be a free flow of air through the aerator. If effort is required, then re-check the tubing and the stones for blockage. If you regularly examine your system in this way, you will lengthen the life of your air pump.

Air tubing carries the air from the pump to the various parts of your filtration or aeration system. Manufactured from clear or colored plastic or rubber, the choice lies mainly in personal preference. If you want the tubing to be inconspicuous, then use a clear plastic, though this has a tendency to kink and harden when old. Rubber tubing, after prolonged immersion in the water of the tank, tends to rot and should be replaced *immediately*, as it can become toxic to the inhabitants.

Various clamps, either metal or plastic, are often attached on to tubing to regulate the amount of air passing through.

Heaters and Thermostats

Before discussing how to keep fish in the proper water temperature, let us examine the scales used to measure temperature. Too many writers assume that their readers "must know about that!" I have more respect for my readers than to take them for granted.

Two systems exist to measure temperature. The first (abbreviated F), propounded by Gabriel Fahrenheit and bearing his name, registers the freezing point of water at $32°$ F and the boiling point at $212°$ F. The second method, named after a Swedish scientist, Anders Celsius, registers the freezing point of water at $0°$ C and the boiling point at $100°$ C. The latter measure, usually called Centigrade (abbreviated C), is used by scientists and in countries utilizing the metric system. Fahrenheit is popular in the United States and Great Britain, and we shall use $F°$ temperatures unless otherwise indicated.

To meet the temperature requirements of each fish likely to find its way into our aquariums, our tank water would have to range between $65°$ and $85°$ F. It is best to aim for a happy medium, which experience suggests is about $75°$ F. Do not become a "thermometer worshiper," panicking if the thermometer registers slightly above or below $75°$ F. Fishes are amazingly adaptable and can withstand a gradual change of temperature provided it doesn't cover too great a range. Even a change of five degrees during the night will cause no harm, so do not worry over a thermometer reading anywhere from $73°$ to $78°$.

Thermometers come in various shapes and sizes. Cheaper ones have their column filled with colored spirit; the better ones use mercury, and some have a purely mechanical mechanism. Though the thermometer can be hidden away in the aquarium, it is usual to fasten it to the inside of the front glass. In this position a reading can be taken quickly and easily. Whatever sort of thermometer you purchase, have its accuracy checked first.

Heaters

Having agreed that the water in our tank must be kept at a fairly regular temperature, we now turn to the various ways of achieving this. In the past, gas and oil were employed but were messy and cumbersome. They filled the gap until the coming of electricity made

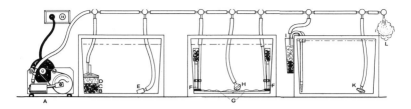

This is the preferred method for connecting a piston pump to a number of outlets in several aquariums. A — piston pump. B — bottom filter. C — charcoal. D — glass wool. E — porous airstone. F — airlift tubes for undergravel filter. G — undergravel or subsand filter. H — ball-type airstone. I — outside filter. J — metal air release. K — excess air lead.

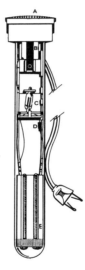

A heater-thermostat combination in one tube. A — temperature adjustment. B — bimetal thermostat. C — pilot light. D — condenser (to eliminate static). E — heating coil.

things much simpler and cleaner.

A heating unit consists of a coil of wire that becomes hot when a current of electricity is passed through it. The wire is protected and waterproofed by being enclosed in a glass or plastic tube. If the heater were allowed to heat continuously, the water in the tank would soon become too hot for our fish, so an automatic switch control is incorporated in the circuit — we call this switch a " thermostat."

Thermostats

Briefly, a thermostat is a switch consisting of two strips of metal welded together, each having a different coefficient of expansion. This bi-metallic strip expands when heated. As one piece of metal expands more than the other, the strip curves and in bending acts as a make-and-break switch. To avoid interference with radio and TV, a radio condenser is provided.

Though both heater and thermostat can be purchased as separate units, they are better combined into one. This is usually hidden away by hanging it from the rear top edge of the aquarium. Some units even contain a small neon indicator light — a visible reminder that all is well. As some manufacturers make their warning lights to show current flowing and others to indicate current off, check which type you have before installation.

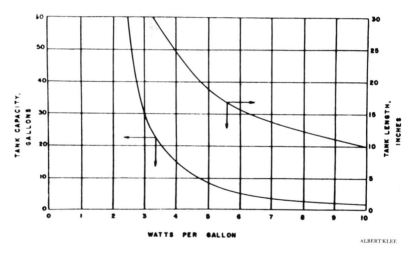

ALBERT KLEE

Graph showing the proper-size heater for your aquarium. The scale to the left is used for basing calculations on tank capacity in gallons, the scale on the right for basing calculations on tank length. The arrows show how each line is read. A 20 gallon tank for example, would have four watts per gallon, or eighty watts total.

For the heater size required, discuss the size of your tank with your dealer and let him advise the proper wattage. An approximate guide is to multiply the gallon capacity of the tank by five. For example, a 25 watt heater for a five gallon tank, 50 watts for a ten, and so on.

Thermostats are pre-set by the maker at around 75° F. Most have a small adjustment screw to adjust the setting. Don't play around with this adjustment more than is absolutely necessary. If you do have occasion to remove this piece of equipment from the water, *be sure to disconnect the power first.* The combination of electricity and water is like James Bond — licensed to kill! With proper use, accidents are rare. Safety is also due to the high standards now set by the manufacturers. Make sure all connections are safe, and if you don't understand electricity, get someone who does to do the job.

Gravel

As soil is to your garden, so gravel is to your aquarium. A good thick layer is needed to cover the floor of the tank, not only for decorative purposes but also to provide a rooting medium for your plants. Collecting your own gravel is fine, but not worth the risk of introducing parasites and infection. Gravel is usually cheap and can be bought in an assortment of colors to suit your taste. One pound covers an area of roughly 20 cubic inches, but if you are going to "landscape" your aquarium, it is better to have too much than too little. The actual area covered varies with the composition of the gravel and its mesh size. During discussion of the setting up of the tank, we shall go into detail about cleaning gravel. The gravel grains should be from two to three times the size of a pin head. Too fine a gravel, or sand packed too tightly, inhibits the circulation of water; too coarse a gravel allows particles of food to lodge in between — out of the reach of fish, scavengers and cleaning devices. This uneaten food can become a focal point for pollution.

Pumps

These are necessary to provide air for your filtration and aeration equipment. Though the cost will be a consideration when making your choice, get the best you can afford. Many beginners purchase a small output pump, sufficient only for their early requirements. Before long, they find that they need more air and either buy another small motor, or, as is usually the case, a larger model. Buying a more powerful pump at the start is both sensible and economical.

Pumps fall into two main categories: the vibrator, which relies on a make-and-break circuit to operate a diaphragm (similar to the circuitry used in an electric door bell), and the piston pump, which, as its name suggests, makes use of the air provided by a pumping action of a piston and cylinder. Some vibrators are apt to be low in output and noisy. What didn't sound loud in the hubbub of the store can drive you to distraction in the quiet of a room at home.

All types of pumps consume very little current and come complete, ready to connect. Some makes of pump, when stopped, allow the water in the tank to siphon back down the air tubing, which can ruin the pump mechanism, blow the electric fuses, and cause a mess on the floor! Play safe. Fit a check valve in the air tube between pump and tank or, better still, place the motor higher than the tank. Some manufacturers design their models to be hung from the rear wall of the aquarium. Follow the maker's recommendations regarding servicing, particularly for oiling. The more expensive "motor" type pumps include a bottle of special vegetable (non-toxic) oil for this purpose. Vibrator pumps are sealed and ordinarily require no servicing.

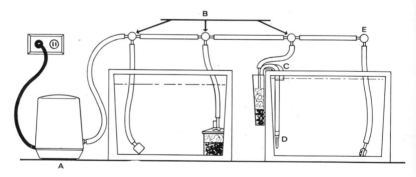

A powerful diaphragm pump, operating two filters and two airstones. A — Diaphragm pump. B — Three-way valves. C — Return stem. D — Intake stem. E — Two-way valves.

III   Making a Start

Floccinaucinihilification!

It's a perfectly good word meaning "setting little or no value on," from the Latin genitives *flocci*, a trifle, and *nihili*, nothing.

Now that you are in possession of the ingredients for setting up a tropical aquarium, you will no doubt be anxious to make a start. But, before you do, have another look at the word commencing this chapter and ponder!

Success comes before work only in the dictionary; for your aquarium to be a credit you must work. In reading this book you have already shown your willingness to learn the correct way of doing things, so don't spoil your efforts at this stage by being over-anxious.

Despite the desires of the family to see the aquarium in operation, you must resist the temptation to skimp on the preparations. To have a crystal-clear tank in the future, it must be carefully set up in the beginning. Too few aquarists realize that a little patience and forethought now can save hours of trouble in the future.

A Site for the Tank

The decision as to where to place the aquarium will obviously rest with you. But if the stand is placed near a wall, leave sufficient room to hang a box filter on the back of the tank as well as enough space to enable you to reach any electrical connections hanging there.

The next step is to insure that the tank and stand are perfectly level. If they are not, the water in the tank will be lopsided, and as a filled aquarium is enormously heavy and difficult to adjust, level it while it's empty.

And make no attempt to move the aquarium once it is filled with water (in the case of the large tanks, I doubt whether you could), but do give the site some careful thought: re-read "Tanks" in Chapter II.

Cover the immediate floor area with newspapers or, better still, the large plastic bags from the cleaners. This will protect the carpet and the floor, and earn you a pat on the back from the "Boss."

Now that we've taken care of the preliminaries, let's examine the tank. Clean it inside and out with salt and water, being careful not to use anything that will scratch the glass. Use no fluid detergents or soaps of any kind. (One soap advertiser used to proclaim, "If it is safe in water, it is safe in this product!" But he wasn't an aquarist.) Then rinse and wipe. Any small pieces of cement left by the manufacturer can be scraped off with a razor blade but don't trim too much; otherwise, on filling, you might find a leaking tank.

Washing the Gravel

Captain Queeg in "The Caine Mutiny" said, "You can't assume a thing!" and it applies equally well to the aquarium gravel. It may appear clean enough when you make your purchase but before new gravel can be placed in the tank it must be rinsed thoroughly under a swift flowing jet of water. Clean a small portion at a time and stir the gravel in a bucket continuously until the water flowing off is running clean. Only then is the gravel ready for the aquarium.

If the source of the gravel is doubtful (collected from outdoors), sterilize it by pouring boiling water over it; do not boil the gravel. Better still, lay it an inch thick on a baking tray and bake it in the oven (200–400° F).

Shallow gravel not only looks wrong, it doesn't provide a deep enough bed for the plant roots. It's cheap, so spread it thick. Rocks can be used to hold it together in pockets and if the rocks are left slightly protruding above the surface of the stones, they will appear more natural looking. Use about two pounds of gravel for each gallon of water. Extremely high tanks may require less.

Do not place a layer of peat below the gravel.

Experience has shown that advice to slope the stones from the rear of the tank to the front is a waste of time. After the aquarium is established the movement of both fish and water will level out the compost. The theory that this slope allows for the mulm and detritus to roll to the front of the tank where it can be easily removed is good, but in practice it just does not work out like that.

This doesn't mean that the floor has to be flat and uninspiring; careful use of rock will hold the gravel together and help undulate the surface. Try to emulate a natural contour to add character to the scene.

With all the gravel and rock in place, take a good close look at it. See how nice and clean it looks? Well, aim to keep it just like that in the future! Blackening of aquarium gravel is due to the reaction between small amounts of iron in the stones and hydrogen sulphide produced by anaerobic bacteria. If you feed the fish more food than they can eat, surplus food will drop to the bottom, where it will decay, causing an oxygen deficiency and pollution of the water. The first signs of this appear when the gravel starts to go black. If the process goes too far, then you have no alternative but to break everything down and start afresh. All the scrubbing in the world won't remove that dark film. To bring back the natural color, spread the stones outside in the weather for a few days.

Reminder: do not use soaps or detergents when cleaning tank or gravel!

Plants

Start by rinsing the plants you have purchased under a lukewarm tap. Subjecting plants to cold water only sets them back, and they take time to recover. Examine each plant for snails and any other small pests which often adhere to the stems and leaves. A quick dip in a strong salt solution usually makes them release their hold on the plant.

Buying plants from a dealer: be sure to carry them home carefully wrapped to prevent drying out. Make sure that they are never wrapped carelessly in plastic or paper wrap, or else on your arrival home you may find the plants broken or bruised. Even given optimum growing conditions it is doubtful if such injured plants could survive. Give the plants a chance. Take a large plastic bag with you when you make your purchases and insist that the dealer put your purchases in this bag *in water.* After all, they are aquatic life and should be treated as such.

After sorting the plants into groups according to size, fill the tank halfway with lukewarm water from a clean bucket. Pour the water gently so that the main flow is directed onto a saucer placed inside the aquarium, resting on the surface of the stones. If done this way the filling won't disturb the gravel. Though this isn't as important at this stage as the final filling, there is no point in breaking down what you have just built up.

Planting in shallow water is much simpler than planting dry; the water allows the leaves to rise and spread, giving a better idea of just how your decorative scheme is progressing. Start planting at the back and work your way forward. If you have to break off this operation, the water in the tank will prevent the plants from drying out, but in that event cover the unplanted plants with wet newspaper.

Planting: hold each plant firmly at the crown. This is located at the junction where the roots join the stem or main body. With one finger make a path in the gravel and slide the roots into this. On no account try to force the roots down or you will just break them off. Bury the roots and stem as deeply as possible; then, when in position, grasp all the stems together and gently tug upwards until the crown is just visible. When planting bunches be sure not to disturb any already set in place.

If you are fortunate enough to possess plants with good long root growth, you will find it much easier to wind the roots around the finger first; then with the loop still around the finger, push them all gently below the gravel. When the finger is slipped out of the loop the gravel will slide into place and hold the roots firmly.

Bunch plants come fastened together with strips of lead, wire, string, raffia or even rubber bands, without roots. You should bury the base of the clump just below the gravel; most of these will develop root growths later. If the bunch tends to float, weight it down by either sprinkling gravel among the leaves or fastening the clump firmly with small pieces of lead. Though this metal in strip form isn't toxic in the aquarium, bunches so fastened tend to rot where the plant comes into contact with the metal.

Set all but the floating plants in place. These are not placed on the surface of the water until after the aquarium is filled. Float them temporarily in a container of lukewarm water and they will come to no harm.

Installing the Equipment

With all the plants in place and the tank still half full of water, the heater/thermostat can now be affixed to the back frame. If placed near one end it can be easily camouflaged by the taller plants. If it is the kind containing a warning light, arrange the unit so that it is not obscured.

To function correctly the heater must be immersed in the water (when the aquarium is filled) for approximately three-quarters of its length, but the majority of manufacturers of this equipment include some form of fixing clip or bracket. *Do not connect to the power at this stage.*

If filters and/or aerators are to be used, it is also time to install them. In the case of box filter units, see that they are complete with filter media. If this includes charcoal, rinse by placing the charcoal in a coarse net and swirling it under a faucet. Charcoal sold in packets contains quite a lot of loose dust and this must be rinsed out before putting the charcoal into the filter box.

Appliances come boxed with full installation instructions; follow these recommendations and you can't go wrong. If the water is delivered to the filter by a siphon, it cannot be started until after the tank is completely filled.

Electrical Connections

The average aquarium requires power outlets for the heater thermostat, the reflector (lights), and the air pump or power filter. The plug supplying power to the heater must remain permanently connected, the flow of electrical current being controlled automatically by the thermostat; the reflector and air pump can either be switch-controlled or disconnected by simply pulling the plug from the outlet.

Aquarium appliances consume very little electricity and they come ready-wired, complete with a two-pronged plug. All you have to do is connect them to a power outlet. Don't drape wiring all over the tank as though you were decorating a Christmas tree. Loose, dangling wire is both dangerous and unsightly. Use tape to fasten it out of sight. But should the length of the wire supplied not be long enough, it is easier to fit a 3-outlet plug near the tank and run a single extension to the supply than to extend all the other wiring. Last, it is a good plan to mark the plug supplying the heater and warn all the family that it must never be disconnected without permission.

Filling the Tank

When all is in place — with the power still not connected — give the inside glass a final rinse and wipe away any scum that might have accrued from the previous operations. Siphon out the water you used to simplify planting, as it will no doubt be dirty. Give the inside glass another polish with a dry cloth and then proceed to fill the tank three-quarters full with freshly-drawn water warmed to around 80° F. This is the final filling and the one we must take the greatest care with; be careful that you don't disturb the tank. Allow the water to run ten to fifteen minutes before filling the aquarium. This is to eliminate the possibility of water picking up metals from the pipes.

One method enabling you to fill the tank quickly with a minimum of disturbance is to stand a large pickle or cookie jar on top of a saucer or plate in the aquarium; fill the jar with water and as you continue to pour, the stream will run gently over the sides down the outside of the jar via the saucer into the tank, the main force being taken by the jar. If you have a tap that allows you to mix both hot and cold water, then a simpler method and much faster way is to connect your garden hose to this and " trickle" the water via the hose onto the inside aquarium glass. Be sure the water is only lukewarm or you may run the risk of cracking the glass. Do not run in cold water and then heat up with hot — cold water chills the plants and sets them back.

The reason you do not fill the tank right to the brim at this stage is to allow replacement of the odd plant that may float to the surface during the filling operation or the setting into place of some final ornament. Under water both plants and rocks will take on quite a different aspect and any alterations should be completed now; do not wait until the aquarium is completely full. If you fill it to the brim, inserting your arm to make some alteration will, if you remember your Archimedes' principle, displace water all over the floor. This is a small point, yet it is amazing how many forget and end up with a ruined carpet.

When everything is ship-shape you can position the floating plants on the water and fill the tank until the water line just disappears behind the top frame of the aquarium. It is disconcerting to see so

ALBERT KLEE

The proper way to anchor a plant. Prepare a hole (center) and spread the roots in it as shown on the left. Rooted plants have a crown which should be level with the surface of the gravel.

many set-ups only partly filled with water. While those who follow this practice may put forth sound arguments as to why they do it, I like to see the tank full. It is a different matter if you are building a terrarium or vivarium; half filling with water then is not only logical but very necessary to the well-being of the inhabitants, but we are constructing an aquarium and need as much swimming space as possible for our fish.

Finishing Up

Place the reflector on top of the tank; if other lighting is being used and your tank is minus a cover, be sure to fit a cover glass. Keep the glass just above the rim of the tank either by using clips (purchased at your dealer) or else by running strips of plastic tubing or rubber weather stripping around the edge of the glass. If you have cut the sheet of glass yourself, smooth off the edges with a carborundum stone.

Before placing the glass or reflector in place, slide the thermometer down the inside front glass with the calibrations towards the front for easy reading. About halfway down is fine. Next, connect your heater/thermostat, lights and air pump to the power supply. Start your filter siphon and adjust the flow of air through the aerator.

Now you can stand back and survey the results of your handiwork. Pour yourself a cup of coffee and relax; you deserve it. While you refresh yourself, reflect upon the words of Albert Wendt, who wrote in " Aquatic Plants in Word and Picture": " The less we poke about in our tanks, the less we shall have to transplant!" Take a tip from him and leave well enough alone.

You must refrain from introducing fish to the aquarium for at least a week. Give the plants time to settle down and take root in their new home. Use this period also to check that everything is working correctly and that the water temperature is constant at about 75° F. Those who use incandescent bulbs for illumination will find that after long periods this type of lighting tends to heat the water. Don't mistake this for a malfunctioning thermostat.

A slight tendency towards cloudiness in the water is quite natural at first and is part of the balancing process. This cloudiness should disappear after a while. Let it alone and the aquarium will repay you by taking on a crystal clarity.

STAGES IN SETTING UP AN AQUARIUM

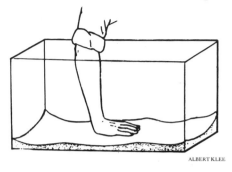

1. Add the well-washed gravel first, about 1 1/2 pounds per gallon, and smooth it into an interesting shape. It should be somewhat higher at the back and sides.

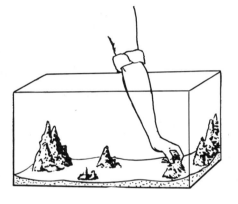

2. Now your artistic sense can begin to function. Add the non-living items of decoration, such as rocks and ornaments. Air lines leading to ornamental air outlets should be buried in the gravel, and a rock or some other weight used to hold them in place. The heater and filter may also be set in place, but not yet plugged in.

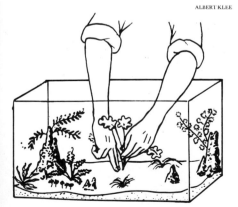

3. The gravel should be wet, and the plants are now added. Try for a variety in form, texture and color. Concentrate the tall plants to the rear and sides, low-growing plants in front.

4. Cover the gravel and plants with several layers of newspaper or brown paper. Pour water of approximately 75° F carefully onto this to avoid disturbing the setup. When the aquarium is half to three-quarters filled, lift the paper gently out by the edge and continue filling the aquarium, using your hand to break the fall of the water.

ALBERT KLEE

5. Another way to break the fall of the water is to use a piece of plastic or a dish, and to direct the hose upon it. Be careful when resting a bucket or a heavy object upon an aquarium, that it is capable of supporting the weight. If in doubt, don't take chances.

ALBERT KLEE

ALBERT KLEE

6. Now the heater can be plugged in and the filter and aerator started. Do not add the fishes directly to the tank. Float them for 15 to 20 minutes in a container, then introduce them by tipping the container so that they swim out.

41

IV Aquarium Management

Keeping It in Working Order

The dictionary definition of the word "maintenance" simply means to keep in a state of good working order. If the procedures outlined in the previous chapter have been carried out correctly, the water in the aquarium will soon become chemically and biologically similar to that found in natural conditions. "Natural conditions," however, represent an environment of ruthless competition in which things are not organized primarily for the well-being of the fishes found there. In the home aquarium we try to eliminate the detrimental factors and strive for the well-being of our fish.

Just as a clean and well-maintained automobile will repay us with hours of trouble-free motoring, so will a well-kept tank reward us with healthy fish and plants. How to keep the water clear and sweet is the next thing to learn. Many factors can disturb its condition, among them:

Overfeeding

This is probably the main cause of foul water. "Overfeeding" is usually confusing to the beginner and interpreted as the fish eating "too much food" with the emphasis solely on quantity. This is not true and has given rise to the myth that "one pinch of food per day is enough"! Breeders of fancy guppies feed as many as a dozen times per day and yet, despite this apparent overfeeding, their tanks are crystal-clear. The secret is to feed no more than can be consumed by the tank occupants in a few minutes. Any food left over after this will indicate that the amount used was too much. They can be fed either once, or several times a day. Surplus food simply falls to the bottom of the tank, lodging in inaccessible places. This enables the bacteria that produce unclean conditions to multiply and thrive, causing the "black gravel" referred to in the previous chapter. Most of our fish are diurnal and do not feed in the dark. The nocturnal ones such as catfish will learn to eat when fed, regardless of the light conditions.

The needs of our fish are few. They can live off nourishment stored in their bodies and survive long periods without feeding. This isn't to advocate starving them, but until you learn the correct amounts to give at each feeding, *under-* rather than *over-*feed. Too many fish are killed by well-meaning owners whose apparent kindness usually boomerangs.

Overcrowding

We have learned that fish breathe in oxygen dissolved in the water and exhale carbon dioxide which is liberated at the water surface where fresh oxygen is introduced. As long as this gaseous exchange can cope with the demands of the animals in the aquarium, all is well. But if we add too many fish we upset this balance and cause the animals to suffer. Aeration and filtration enable the hobbyist to readjust this, allowing more fish to be kept in a given area than if the tank were lacking these aids. However, don't make their use an excuse to crowd more fish into the water than it can support.

You must allow for growth and breeding. An approximate guide to the number of fish an aquarium can accommodate is to provide just under half a gallon of water in the aquarium for *every* fish one inch and under; half a gallon for fish one to two inches, and a gallon for each fish over two inches. These figures are for fully-grown specimens in an average planted community tank. When making your initial purchase of stock, tell the dealer the size of your tank and he can assist you in making your choice. (See chart, p. 44.)

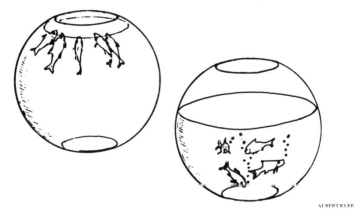

ALBERT KLEE

When fishes "hang" at the surface, something is wrong. Check to see if there are too many for the size of the container or if overfeeding has polluted the water. Bowls shaped like this should be filled to the widest point (right — correct), not to the top (left — incorrect).

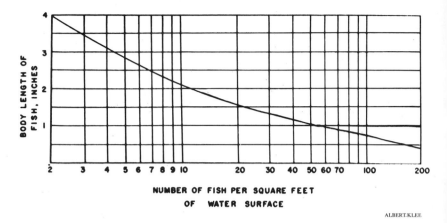

BODY LENGTH OF FISH, INCHES

NUMBER OF FISH PER SQUARE FEET
OF WATER SURFACE

ALBERT-KLEE

Another way to determine the number of fishes which your aquarium can safely support is by using this graph. Measure the surface area (length x width) of your aquarium in feet. The sloping line indicates the number of fishes of various body sizes which may be kept for each square foot.

Green Water

This healthy if somewhat unsightly water condition is caused by the presence of free-floating unicellular organisms called algae which require food and strong light to survive. The obvious way to eradicate green water is to deprive the algae of these two essentials. Unfortunately, it isn't quite so simple because these two ingredients are also required by other animals in the aquarium. The first step, if you are troubled by green water, is to cut down the amount of light. If the artificial light is already at a minimum, try shading the aquarium from the natural light by covering the tank back and sides, and increasing the number of plants in order to crowd out the green water organisms.

Various chemical cures are on the market. Some are quite efficient — the simplest being the chemical, potassium permanganate. Use one grain for 15 gallons of water. The purple color which results will fade by itself. Never try to eradicate this menace quickly. It must be done over a period of time, or other secondary symptoms will appear and further upset the balance in the tank. Changing the water will only add to the problem. For a short time the tank will be clear, but within a few days the problem will recur, stimulated by the fresh water.

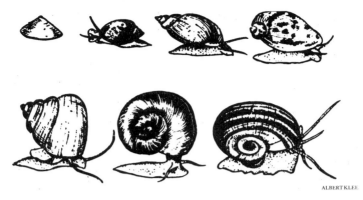

ALBERT KLEE

Common aquarium snails. Top (left to right): limpet, pond, Australian red, paper snail. Bottom (left to right): Japanese, red ramshorn, Columbian ramshorn.

Snails

The work done by snails as so-called scavengers has been overrated. For years we have been told that these creatures are a "must" to eat the food left over by the fish. Experience proves they contribute as much waste as they do away with! The decision to include them in your tank is purely personal and if you feel you would like snails, the most attractive are the red ramshorn *(Planorbis corneus)* and the Malayan burrowing or cornucopia snail *(Melania tuberculata)*. The latter spend a considerable time rooting about in the gravel keeping it well aerated. The mystery snail *(Ampullaria cuprina)* is also popular and as it is larger than the two other species it is less likely to be bothered by the fish.

Weekly Service

One of the advantages of keeping tropicals as opposed to some other pets is the lack of daily work involved — but do get into the habit of weekly servicing. Start by siphoning the accumulated detritus from the bed of the tank; cut away any dead or dying plant life and trim that which may be getting too long. Clean the inside glass with either a scraper or a piece of filter wool. Fill the tank with freshly drawn water brought to the correct temperature, to replace any which might have evaporated. Give the outside glass a good polish and before you can say " Jack Robinson," the job is done. A partial change of water is beneficial to the aquarium from time to time, and can be done in conjunction with the siphoning. Change about one-third of the tank every two or three weeks.

Lighting

The strength of light required and the length of time the aquarium should be illuminated will be learned by trial and error. Experiment at first by leaving the lights on for a few hours each night. If the water starts to turn green or if a heavy green algal growth appears on the front glass, this is an indication that there is too much illumination. First cut down on the time, then on the wattage in use. Poor plant growth or the appearance of brown algae indicates an insufficiency of light, so increase accordingly. Don't suddenly light up the aquarium. Fish, unlike humans, have no eyelids and suffer the consequences of suddenly being flooded with light. Rheostats to increase brightness gradually are available, but they should not be able to switch on a room light before switching on the tank light. Colored bulbs (where incandescent bulbs are used) may create weird and wonderful effects to the onlooker but they won't make for a healthy tank. Special fluorescent tubes emitting much red and blue light are sold under the trade name of Gro-lux. Though faults have been found with this type of lighting, aquarists generally give them a good name. They are available in wattages from 15 to 100 and in tubes up to 96 inches in length. Tungsten (incandescent) bulbs emit about 5% light and 95% heat and get very hot in use. Never attempt to change a bulb with the current on, or to clean bulbs that are hot.

pH — Hydrogen Ion Concentration

Chemical compounds in aqueous solution break up into tiny units that are either positively or negatively charged. These units are known as ions.

Imagine a seesaw with positively charged hydrogen ions (H +) on one side and negatively charged hydroxyl ions (OH-) on the other side. When the two balance, our aquarium water is said to be neutral. If there are more H + than OH-, then the water is regarded as acid.

This state of being either acid, alkaline or neutral is expressed as the pH reading (small p, capital H).

This scale was set down by the Danish biochemist Sorenson, who worked out the mathematics for us. In Sorenson's scale the figure represents a scale from 1 to 14, 7 being the neutral. One to 6 represents the acid range, 8 to 14, the alkaline.

The aquarist normally keeps his tank water around the neutral mark, though rarely does it come out at this, as most tanks maintain themselves just below 6.8. The pH reading will vary, so don't be too fussy about it. Changing fish from one tank to another will probably involve only a few tenths of a point difference, i.e., 6.8 to 7.2. Differences of more than two full points are likely to prove fatal to fishes.

Testing the pH value: The simplest method is by using special test papers. A piece is dipped into the water being tested and the pH, based upon the change of color, is read from a comparator chart. A fairly precise test is also obtained by coloring a measured amount of the test water with a special sensitive dye, Bromthymol Blue. The color change is compared with sealed color comparison tubes. Scientists and those requiring a quick and very accurate reading use an electrical device. With this, the reading is registered on a dial. Adjusting the pH: When making adjustments carry these out gradually. Don't subject your animals to rapid changes in pH value. To render the water more alkaline, small increments of sodium bicarbonate are added, re-testing after each addition; to acidify use either sodium biphosphate or peat water. It is difficult to maintain an exact pH reading for any length of time, as it constantly fluctuates.

It should seldom be necessary to alter the pH. Extreme fluctuations or excessively high or low pH indicates an unbalanced condition in the aquarium and had best be looked into. Once the condition is corrected the pH will almost invariably adjust itself.

DH — Degrees of Hardness

When we refer to the hardness of water we are talking about the amount of dissolved salts in water. This occurs in two ways: temporary or permanent hardness. The former can be removed by boiling. The bicarbonates of calcium and magnesium, for example, decompose during the boiling and leave chalk (calcium carbonate). Salts other than the mentioned bicarbonates cannot be removed by the process of boiling and, therefore, create permanent hardness.

One scale used expresses this hardness in terms of chalk concentration, the concentration in water given as parts per million (ppm). Another scale, DH (for "Degrees of Hardness"), is popular. One degree of DH is roughly equivalent to 17 ppm. Like pH, DH is usually not of concern to the beginner. Fish are very adaptable creatures and provided the water hardness is not excessive, they will come to no harm. After all, the hardness in their home waters varies considerably each time it rains! Soap solution hardness testing kits are available, but if it is just the hardness of your local supply you want, your water company will willingly give you this figure upon request.

The test kits utilizing soap are based on the fact that soap lathers with difficulty in hard water. A standard soap solution is added to a measured quantity of water to be tested. The number of drops required to produce a lather then gives the measure or degree of hardness. There are also more sophisticated hardness testing kits available which are somewhat more expensive but give a more exact reading.

Comparison Table, DH and parts per million

Expressed as DH			Type of Water	Expressed as ppm		
0	to	3	very soft	0		50
3		7	soft	50		120
7		13	moderately hard	120		220
13		25	hard	220		425
over		25	very hard	over	425	ppm

Peat Water

Rain water that has run through areas containing peat becomes acidic and very soft. This water is desired by aquarists for breeding certain of the "difficult" fish (e.g., neons). If this type of water isn't obtainable locally from natural sources it can be produced at home. Collect rain water from a clean, uncontaminated source in a glass container. Cover the water surface with a layer of horticultural peat until the peat is about three inches thick. The peat will float on the surface at first but after about three weeks of soaking it will fall to the bottom, leaving the water tinted an amber-brown with the qualities mentioned. In drawing off this water use the siphon; any attempt to pour it off will stir up the peat particles and contaminate the sample. Peat can also be added to the filter box but it is difficult to control. Peat water can be stored in glass bottles in a dark closet. Use it to adjust the water in the breeding tank to the desired degree of hardness and acidity.

V Those Extras!

Buying extras for the aquarium is rather like eating nuts; once started, one finds it very difficult to stop! Fishkeeping seems to foster a like attitude and, if allowed to go unchecked, can result in cupboards and drawers stuffed full with the abandoned impedimenta of one's zeal. However, some accessories are both useful and time saving:

Nets

Nets are used for catching and transferring one's finny charges. They are made from silk, cotton or nylon, with a wire or wood handle. See that the handles are slightly longer than your tank is deep, unless you want a soaking every time you use them. A net with too wide a mouth can be damaging to your plants.

In addition to the coarse nets used for catching the fish, you will need a couple having a very fine mesh for live foods such as baby brine shrimp and Daphnia.

Pipe-shaped glass implements were used at one time for catching small fry, but these have been replaced by plastic food containers available from the five and dime store. These containers are useful because they are transparent and the fish are not so alarmed when trapped.

When trapping a fish use two nets, one to drive the fish into the waiting "mouth" of the other net; or bend one wire handle until it is at right angles to the covered portion of the net. Slide the net under the fish to be captured; a quick lifting movement does the trick, but do not lift too quickly or you may flip the fish right out of the tank.

All a net requires after use is a quick shake, but if it was used for sick or diseased fish, make sure the net is dried thoroughly and exposed to heat before being used again. It is better to have separate nets just for this purpose. Then you won't unwittingly transfer a disease from one tank to another.

When catching the larger fish, especially if they are going to an aquarium show, use large plastic bags instead of a larger net; this insures undamaged fins and does away with the chance (under the net system) of the fish jumping to the floor during transfer.

Scrapers

Scrapers are long handles, at one end of which is fastened either a razor blade, a piece of hard felt or a sharp plastic edge. Scrapers are used to clean the insides of tank glasses, removing slime and algae.

Dip Tubes

If you place your thumb over the end of a length of stiff tubing, immerse it in the water, and then remove your thumb, a column of water will quickly shoot up the tube, taking with it detritus and mulm from the surface of the gravel.If the tube is stopped again, this water column is retained and can be removed from the tank. This, then, is the principle of the dip tube, useful for minor clean-up operations.

The simple tube has been improved by the addition of added chambers to trap the detritus and non-return valves to stop the sucked-up sediments from returning whence they came. Even with these improvements, the operation is a slow and tedious job.   -

Modern refinements have produced the equivalent of the household vacuum cleaner. Powered by air, hand or battery, it sucks

ALBERT KLEE

To operate a diptube, hold your finger over the open end and place it just above the dirt. Release your finger and the water will rush into the tube, carrying the dirt with it. Replace your finger over the end and withdraw the tube with the dirty water. Invert to empty.

up water and accompanying sediment, filters the sediment out, and returns the water to the tank through a cloth filter bag. This bag is cleaned quickly by rinsing under the tap. It works better than the hand dip tube and leaves the water in the tank. In the battery operated type keep the mechanism, which is in the handle, out of the water.

Power Filters

As described in a preceding chapter, filters are operated by air (via air lifts), but the past few years have seen the invention of filters which move the water by means of a mechanical impeller. This has resulted in more filtering efficiency. Though they are not cheap, the author has tried most types under trying conditions and found them excellent if the filter medium is changed often enough. Because of the faster flow the filter medium is quickly soiled. One drawback is that they do not provide any means of bubbling air through the tank. While the motion of the water does supplement natural aeration, it is not as effective for this purpose as an air-stone.

Planting Sticks

These are long, thin pieces of wood or metal having a "V" shaped notch at one end and the other end flattened like a spatula. They are useful for fixing plants in place in the tank and especially useful for reaching hard-to-get places such as in the middle of a clump of plants or between rockwork. Like chopsticks, they are easy to manipulate — once you know how! Personally, I much prefer nature's own planting sticks, one's fingers, as there is less chance these will slice off the delicate roots or leaves.

Rockwork

Rocks serve both for decoration and holding the gravel in place. The range of rocks available to the hobbyist from throughout the world is enormous. When selecting suitable pieces, remember that shape is more important than color. After prolonged immersion in a fish tank, rocks will become coated with natural aquatic growth. If you want to maintain a piece for its exceptional color or veining, then you must scrub it regularly with a toothbrush.

All pieces of rock must be cleaned by brushing hard and then placing them in boiling water before putting them in the aquarium. If you do the scrubbing in the kitchen sink, be sure to place the rock on a cloth or mat, as it may scratch enamel, porcelain or even stainless steel.

Not only will judiciously placed rockwork add to the natural beauty of your arrangement, but it will also serve to hold the gravel in pockets, providing shelter for shy species of fish. Try not to create any hidden pockets where the fish may hide and die unnoticed, thus causing pollution.

The most popular question raised after a rock hunt is, "Are the collected rocks safe to use?" If old and hard, the answer is usually "yes." If in doubt, seek the advice of your dealer, or soak the rock in water containing live Daphnia. If these creatures are still alive after a few weeks have elapsed, your fish will also be able to live with it. If the water in the tank is on the acid side, avoid rocks made of limestone, marble or gypsum. These will slowly dissolve, making the water alkaline and hard.

Petrified wood, rocklike in appearance, comes in many weird and interesting shapes and makes a beautiful decoration.

Ornaments

The intricate ceramic ornaments available today are a far cry from the old plaster archways which once adorned aquaria. The question of whether to use these "baubles" is still a hotly debated one among fishkeepers. If you want and like them, then decorate your aquarium with them; after all, it is *your* living picture. Some serve other purposes, such as hiding a filter or acting as an aerator. The latter operation would be dependent upon a supply of air from the air pump.

Though many ornaments are carefully designed and made, be careful. Don't use any into which your fish might swim and become stuck, and check to see whether or not the ornament was made for a tropical aquarium. Some years ago, trouble was caused by one that was not. It would have been fine for a cold water aquarium, but it became toxic at the temperatures found in tropical tanks. One national magazine once did a two-page spread recommending various ornaments for the aquarium, but some of those illustrated were definitely toxic to tropical fish!

Feeding Rings

Simple feeding rings are merely round or square shaped pieces of plastic tubing. They are floated or fastened at the water surface, and they keep dried food in one place so that it doesn't spread throughout the tank and cause pollution. More elaborate kinds contain a shelf or box which catch the particles of food as they fall. Make sure the feeder you choose is large enough to accomodate the number of fish you keep. If the community includes some small species or shy feeders, it is wise to have two feeding rings. This allows the fish to feed in peace and stops the greedy ones from getting the lion's share.

Worm Feeders

These are perforated bowls (usually made of plastic) placed at the surface of the water. They are used to dispense live Tubifex worms or white worms. The worms slowly work their way through the holes where they are eagerly snatched up by the waiting fish.

Large feeders include a miniature air lift for constantly flushing the "ball" of worms with clean water. The worms keep for longer periods in this type of feeder. Another type is made in the shape of a wine goblet. These float about the aquarium and have a flat platform underneath for catching the worms. The majority of feed rings are attached to the glass by small rubber suction discs. If these deteriorate, try bending a piece of lead plant weight into a "U" shape. Inverted over the tank frame and feed ring, this will do the job efficiently.

Siphon Tubing

A piece of tubing about five feet long with the diameter of a garden hose is extremely useful for emptying the tank, for changing small quantities of the water and for cleaning the surface of the gravel.

The operation is simple: holding the tube in a U shape with both ends up, fill it with water by holding it under a faucet or immersing it in the tank. Then pinch both ends tightly shut, and, placing one end into the aquarium under water, direct the other end into a bucket placed on the floor *below* the aquarium. When both ends are released, the water will flow out of the tank into the bucket. The flow can be controlled by squeezing the tube shut with the fingers.

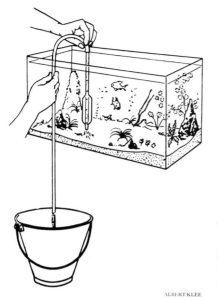

A siphon is useful for removing large quantities of dirt. A piece of clear plastic added to the rubber hose will give rigidity and make your siphon more maneuverable. You can control the rate of flow by pinching the hose.

ALBERT KLEE

By moving the tank end around just above the gravel, unwanted debris can be sucked away.

Some aquarists add a stiff piece of plastic tubing to the end immersed in the tank to give it rigidity. Though rubber tubing is quite good for your siphon, clear plastic is much better, as any obstruction can be quickly spotted and cleared. Snail shells can clog the tube. These are cleared simply by squeezing the siphon tube and crushing the shell into small pieces.

Note Book

This may seem a strange item with which to close our chapter on accessories, but time will prove its usefulness. Use a note book not only to record fish purchases, but also to record observations about the comings and goings in your aquarium. When your fish start to breed you can record dates of birth in the livebearers; in the egglayers — the time eggs were deposited and the length of hatching. It is amazing how one's memory fails in remembering little details. Should disease rear its ugly head, treatment and dosages and their effects can all be noted for future reference.

Sprinkle the notes with diagrams and don't worry if you are not a Leonardo da Vinci. No one need see your book but you. In time, this note book will be a valuable record of your hobby. This sort of observed experience is worth all the theory in the world.

VI   A Bit of Greenery

Introduction

In a way, setting up an aquarium is rather like painting a picture. In the artistry of the living picture one merely substitutes the colors and textures of fish, plants and rockwork for the artist's palette.

A planted aquarium performs many functions: the roots and leaves of aquatic "greenery" provide sanctuaries for the fishes and nurseries for their offspring; the vegetarians can browse on the green leaves; also, the leaves harbor whole colonies of microorganisms and tiny crustaceans that are essential to the well-being and balance of the aquarium as a functioning symbiotic unit. The plant roots and foliage absorb the waste products of metabolism and convert the chemicals in the gravel and water into valuable nutrients to help them grow.

Finally, plants provide that feeling of home and security for the fish, which respond by using the leaves of the plants as a place to lay their eggs.

If plants are to flourish, they require three things:

Light — in the correct amount for each species of plant;

Water — rich in organic content;

Temperature — right for maximum growth.

All these factors are controlled by the aquarist.

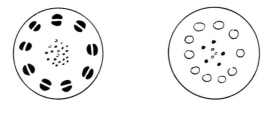

ALBERT KLEE

There are several differences between aquatic plants and land plants. The cross section of an aquatic plant (right) shows air holes or channels (the hollow circles) These provide the aquatic plant with the buoyancy needed to keep it vertical. The land plant, on the other side (left), needs solid reinforcements (black areas) to hold it upright.

We associate the growing of plant life with soil, and it is sometimes recommended that a layer of peat be placed underneath the gravel in the aquarium. Take my advice — don't do it! The plants will root just as well in plain gravel. Those beginners who do use peat soon find that the fish have rooted through the layer of gravel and stirred the peat, turning their crystal-clear tanks into mud baths. If the plants do require feeding, good fertilizers can be bought in trouble-free liquid or tablet form. You will find them at your local aquarium supplier.

Just as the plants in our gardens vary in growth, so do aquatic plants. Some boast long root systems and remain submerged, their growth stopping below the water surface; other types, with their ancestral swamp-like environment still fresh in their memories, send their roots down into the gravel and their heads and flowers soaring above the water.

Short, tall, thin, and bushy, like the rats that followed the Pied Piper of Hamlin, aquarium plants come in all shapes and sizes,

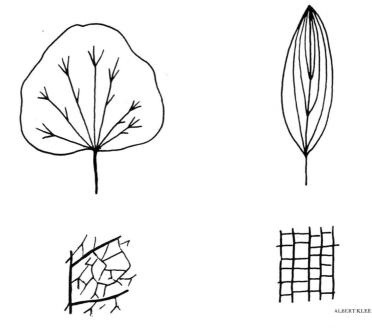

ALBERT KLEE

The majority of plants in the aquarium are of the flowering variety, although the flowers will not appear except under ideal conditions. They are made up of two general groups, that is, the parallel-veined plants (right) and the net-veined plants (left). The veins are best seen on the underside of the leaf. Practically all of the plants used for "center" plants are members of the parallel-veined group (*Echinodorus*, *Cryptocoryne*, etc.).

colors and textures. For the purpose of this book, they will be classified under the following headings:

Rooted: Usually planted singly in the aquarium and possessing long root systems. The larger varieties, like the Amazon Swordplant, make ideal centerpieces, while the long willowy forms like Vallisneria make ideal backdrops.

Bunched: Most of these come in bunches fastened together and are best left in clumps for planting. Some are without roots, but these quickly develop under the right conditions.

Floating: Drifting free on the top of the water, they send their roots down into the tank. Given good conditions, they soon carpet the surface and provide food and surface shelter for some fish and fry.

Availability of the different types of plants will vary according to the time of the year and the stocks carried by your local dealers.

At first, keep your choice simple and limited to just a few varieties. Don't expect your aquarium to look like those wonderful illustrations you see in the magazines. Plants take time to settle in, and until they do you will get little growth from them. Even if your tank looks bare at the start, leave room for the plants to spread.

Try to keep the right perspective, with tall plants in the rear and low growing bush varieties toward the front; a few minutes' planning on paper will save much frustration later. If you aren't artistic, then copy an arrangement you have seen. Public aquariums, stores and books will give you some ideas, but *keep it simple.*

Plant Names

Both the scientific and the common name (where possible) are used to describe the plants listed. If the particular variety is also known by another name in common usage, this too is included in the description.

For identification of each plant, the same system is followed: they are broken into groups according to family (name printed in capital letters), followed by the generic name (describing the genus to which it belongs), and then the common name. The families, as well as the genera, are listed in alphabetical order.

Forma and Hortulanorum

In our study of aquatic plants we shall come across the words "forma" (sometimes abbreviated "f") and "hortulanorum," occasionally shortened to "hort." Forma refers to the different shapes that a plant may take within each species, hortulanorum to the many varieties or sports that growers have produced over the years from the original plant form.

The list of plants that follows, though far from comprehensive, will serve to whet your appetite and give you a general picture of the vegetation available to help "paint" that living picture. Plants not deemed suitable for the tropical aquarium have been omitted.

Rooted Plants

Family ACANTHACEAE

Synnema triflorum — Water Wisteria: This is a very valuable aquarium plant, similar in appearance to Water Sprite (described further on in this chapter). The leaves differ in shape, varying from oval with tiny serrations on the edges to divided leaves with large serrations. The submerged leaves are pale green. A large plant, it is suited to aquaria of ten or more gallons.

Family ALISMATACEAE

Echinodorus grisebachii — Pygmy Chain Sword: Also commonly referred to as *E. intermedius,* this Lilliput among the Brobdingnagians hails from Cuba and Costa Rica. Very easy to grow, it will quickly cover the floor of the tank with plants. The leaves are similar in color and shape to its larger brethren, but reach only about four inches long. If you want this plant as a single or just a small clump, then pinch off the runners as they appear. Because of the soft nature of the leaves, it must be handled with care.

Echinodorus paniculatus — Amazon Sword Plant: This magnificent plant can grow to a height of 20 inches and form a beautiful eye-catching centerpiece in any tank large enough to accommodate its size. The translucent green leaves resemble lances protruding from the gravel. The plant propogates itself by sending out floating runners from the crown with new plants forming at intervals; these put out side-shoots which soon root in the compost. It likes moderate top lighting and should be left undisturbed after planting. Its leaves are often brittle and snap easily; because the leaf later rots at the break, remove a broken leaf at the crown. A fair amount of feeding is needed if the Sword Plant is to attain its maximum growth. It can reproduce by throwing up short stems capped by white flowers, though this is not a common occurrence in the home aquarium.

A close relative of the above, sold by many dealers erroneously as paniculatus, is *E. paniculatus* var. *rangeri*. Imported from South America, this broader-leaf version flourished in the deep, cool tanks of the Florida growers. This results in magnificent plants being offered for sale, but unless given ample room and clean water the crown of the plants tends to rot and the leaves become pitted with brown spots. Because of this, the true Amazon Sword is gaining a reputation which it does not deserve.

Excess dry fish food falling into the crown may rot there, and the mold will affect the leaf. Overfeeding may also result in polluted gravel which, in addition to other problems, can cause a rotting at the base of rooted plants.

If your tank is on the small side and thus unsuitable for the giant growth of these two previously-mentioned Echinodoruses, then try the *Echinodorus brevipedicellatus*. The leaves of this Sword only grow to about eight inches. Water, a little on the soft side, and careful feeding will soon have this junior Amazon flourishing.

Sagittaria latifolia — Giant Sagittaria: leaves can grow to a foot and a half in length and reach one inch across! Resembling the Eel Grasses in looks, the Giant Sagittaria comes from North America and parts of South America and is suitable only for the large, deep tank. It has no special water preferences, doing equally well in both acid and alkaline water. These cosmopolitan tastes also apply to the lighting requirements. Listed incorrectly as *S. sinensis.*

Sagittaria subulata forma *subulata* — Common Sagittaria: Probably the most common form of this family you will come across — its long, blunted, green leaves are very attractive. Grows about three inches smaller than *S. latifolia.*

Sagittaria forma *pusilla* — Dwarf Sagittaria: It is like the other species, but only grows to around two inches in length and about one-eighth of an inch wide. If the tank doesn't contain any fish that root around in the gravel, this dwarf will spread and create a lawn

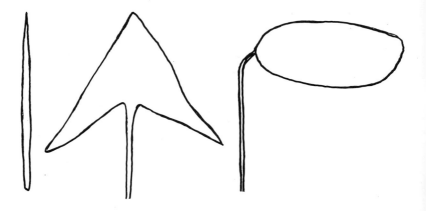

Many aquarium plants have different leaf forms, depending on their growing situation. A variety of leaves can even appear on the same stem. For example, these three leaf forms of *Sagittaria* show the submerged leaf (left), above water leaf (center), and surface floating leaf (right).

effect. Loves a good top light. Sometimes known as *Sagittaria microfolia.*

Family APONOGETONACEAE

Aponogeton fenestralis — Madagascar Lace Leaf Plant: This plant was once considered the status symbol of the " In" aquarium. Its large leaves, ovate in shape, are pierced, giving a skeleton-like appearance. Though these leaves look fragile, they are, in fact, quite tough. Unless snails are kept in the aquarium, the interstices of the leaves soon become blocked with algal growth. Not easy to cultivate in the home aquarium. Best purchased as a young plant or as a tuber.

Aponogeton undulatus: This is the most common of this large group of plants about whose nomenclature some doubt exists. It does best in slightly acid waters, and when conditions are right will tower to a height of 18 inches. Its habitat is the Island of Ceylon. The large, crinkly-edged leaves are found in various shades of green. Formerly *A. crispus.*

60

Family ARACEAE

Cryptocoryne: This large family of plants from the tropical areas of Southeast Asia is very popular with the aquarist because of its variety in shape, color and size. These plants will thrive and reproduce with less light than most aquarium plants, although they do require some light for growth. Because they are slow growing, they do not require a lot of attention. Change in water conditions can make the *Cryptocoryne* lose all their leaves, but if left undisturbed they will quickly produce fresh growth. Space permits but a short list of "Crypts." Choose from among the following:

Tall Growing:	*Cryptocory- ne cordata*	Deep red, heart-shaped leaves.
	C. griffithii	Broad, oval leaves, dark green.
	C. longicauda	Blistered in appearance, green.
Medium Growing:	*C. beckettii*	Broad elliptical leaves, dark green to reddish brown in color.
	C. var. *latifolia*	Broad elliptical leaves, dark green to reddish brown in color.
	C. willisii	The attractive leaf markings on the upper portions of the leaf make it desirable. Color varies through green and brown. Height nine inches.
Low Growing:	*C. nevillii*	Unless given optimum conditions, it will remain in pygmy form. Narrow, tapering leaves.

The variability and range in this large genus enables one to carpet the complete tank from front to back with the different kinds of Crypts. They provide variety in shape, color and texture.

Family HYDROCHARITACEAE

Vallisneria spiralis — Eel or Tape Grass: If "Oscars" were handed out to aquarium plants, this grass like species would have been an early recipient. Used in the aquarium since the beginning of the hobby, it found early fame when it figured with the goldfish in the experiments of Robert Warrington mentioned in Chapter I. Found widely in most tropical areas of the world, the slender leaves vary in color from light green to reddish brown. It propagates bisexually by sending up both male and female flowers which emanate from separate plants. In the aquarium, it commonly multiplies by means of runners, which extend along the surface of the gravel with new plants appearing at intervals. Because of its length, this plant has found favor as a background decoration.

Vallisneria, often abbreviated Val, is sometimes confused with Sagittaria species. Some aquarists even claim the plants won't live side by side, although in the author's experience this has not been found true. Unlike the Amazon, Val can be cut short to keep its length under control. The roots are gross feeders. Where the roots grow alongside the glass, the gravel is distinctly lighter.

Vallisneria spiralis forma *tortifolia* — Corkscrew or Twisted Val: Distributed throughout Nevada and California, this is a spiraled leaf variety. The " Cork" Val doesn't grow quite as tall as the Val.

Family PARKERIACEAE

Ceratopteris thalictroides — Water Sprite, Indian Fern, Sumatra Fern: This is a true aquatic fern from the tropical parts of the Old World, and does well either rooted or floating. Within the past decade a plant was introduced into the United States, named Water Wisteria (*Synnema triflorum,* see our listing under Family *Acanthaceae*). Similar in appearance to the Water Sprite, the two plants are often the subject of much confusion in aquarium literature. The Sprite has typical fern-shaped leaves (rather like the small plants you see in any woodland glade), light green in color. It does best in water a little on the hard side.

New plants form on the older, mature leaves, which usually break away from the parent and float to the surface where they soon grow into new plants. Allow the roots to form sufficiently before replanting in gravel. As a floating top plant they are used as a nesting site by the bubble nest building species of fishes. The plant leaves hold the nest together on the water surface. The Water Sprite will show its distaste for foul gravel and unclean conditions by breaking loose and floating upwards. Growth is rapid under moderate lighting. If you wish to speed up the propagation of this plant, remove a few large leaves and allow them to float on the water after bruising the leaves with your fingers. New plants will quickly grow where the old leaf was damaged.

Bunched Plants

Family CYPERACEAE

Eleocharis acicularis — Hair Grass: This is a submerged bog plant which sends up fine, grass-like, spiky shoots. It spreads by sending roots out under the gravel. Growing to a height of four inches, it tends to die back in the winter if given only natural light. When grown in thick clumps, it affords wonderful shelter for young fish.

Family FONTINALACEAE

Fontinalis antipyretica forma *gracilis* — Willow Moss: A finely leaved, dark green water moss which in its natural environment attaches itself to stones, wood, etc. It prefers cool conditions. If maintained at too high a temperature, its dainty leaves tend to shed. *Fontinalis* is usually bought without any roots, and fastened together in bunches. Don't open the bunch, but plant it as one would plant bunched plants generally. These plants are very prone to infestation by leeches and planarians (see Chapter XIII, *Fish Enemies*). To disinfect the plant, soak it for several minutes in a dark-red solution of potassium permanganate, or in lime water, for 15 minutes.

Family HALORAGACEAE

Myriophyllum hippuroides — Water Milfoil, Foxtail: Unless this plant receives good light, the long spiky leaves break off. Don't use floating plants which shade an aquarium containing Milfoil. Native to most of the United States, though usually green in color it is also available in red. It is excellent for hiding the fry of livebearers and receiving the spawn of egglayers.

Family HYDROCHARITACEAE

Elodea densa — Canadian Pond Weed, Anacharis: Dark green whorls on long-growing stems which must have plenty of illumination; otherwise, the lanceolate leaves turn brown and the plant rots away. It will tolerate hard water and is not very fussy over conditions. Planted in bunches, the stems are fastened together and buried just below the gravel. A coarse form, *E. crispa,* is more suitable for growth at low temperatures.

Family NYMPHAEACEAE

Cabomba caroliniana — Cabomba, Washington Grass: This plant is similar in appearance to Ambulia, but is a bright green. The fronds grow paired on opposite sides of the central stem. (The fronds of Ambulia grow all around.) Allow the cuttings to float for a short time before planting. Though listed as a bunched plant, it grows better planted singly than in groups. It likes cool, lime-free, soft water. It has at least six different leaf forms. The end of each stem forms thick crowns under the water surface; give strong top light.

Family ONAGRACEAE

Ludwigia mulertti hort: This is a South American bog plant with lancelike leaves, dark green on the surface and reddish tinged underneath. There is also a red leaved variety, as well as a rounded leaf form. The red extends into the stems as pink.

Ludwigia likes to grow above the water, and if left unchecked in the aquarium it will grow right out of the tank. If conditions aren't suitable, the leaves will turn brown and fall off. More correctly referred to as *L. natans*, it prefers soft water conditions and strong top light.

Family SCROPHULARIACEAE

Bacopa caroliniana — Water Hyssop, Baby's Tears (Europe): This plant has small oval leaves, leathery in texture, which protrude nearly horizontally from long, round stems. The fleshy green leaves are sometimes tinged with red or brown. Best planted in clumps; if given partial shade it will produce rich growth after emerging above the water. It is not popular with professional growers because of its slow growth. The leaves have a distinctive spearmint odor out of the water. In Europe, it is commonly called Baby's Tears, a name which is reserved in the United States for the bog plant Helxine.

Limnophila sessiliflora — Ambulia: With its divided leaves in whorls, this is a quick and prolific grower if given good, strong top light. It is usually purchased without roots, but these quickly form in the tank. Its habitat is Ceylon, India, and parts of Africa. It grows to fifteen inches. If kept under natural light only, it dies back in the winter months.

Floating Plants

True free-floating plants as opposed to some of the already described plants that will grow either planted or floating.

Family CERATOPHYLLACEAE

Ceratophyllum demersum — Hornwort: This plant has bristly, brush foliage, sending out offshoots from long, thin stems. It tends to break very easily and must be planted with care. In the fall, the tips of the plant stems thicken and drop to the aquarium floor, forming buds throughout the winter. Though not fussy about conditions, it prefers cool temperatures. It is usually grown floating, but if a section of the stem is pressed under the gravel it will put out tendrils which are not true roots, but " hold-fasts."

Family CHARACEAE

Nitella gracilis: The light green fronds remind you of a ladies' hair net, and sprout very sparsely from the plant stem. They can be planted in bunches, but don't worry if pieces break away and float; they will probably grow equally well on their own, as they don't form any true root system. Used in clumps and allowed to float, they are used by guppy breeders as a substitute breeding trap for sheltering young fry. On no account must this plant be allowed to dry out.

A much finer-leaved version is *N. flexilis*, sometimes referred to as *Chara flexilis* — a wonderful oxygenating plant.

Family HYDROCHARITACEAE

Pistia stratiotes — Water Lettuce: Large floating rosettes, not unlike lettuce plants in shape, the thick masses of roots growing down into the water are sought by young fish as shelter. The author does not consider this plant a suitable one for the home aquarium because it requires plenty of growing space above the water surface. When the tank is filled and covered by a reflector, the space is reduced and the plant is not seen in its full glory.

When incandescent lighting is used, the bulbs will burn the leaves. This plant is listed because it looks so attractive when viewed in the dealer's tank that the impulse is to purchase one. Unless you are able to provide plenty of space above the water, you had best not give in to the impulse. Suitable for outdoor pools and as a spawn receiver.

Family LEMNACEAE

Lemna minor — Duckweed: Everyone must have seen sunny ponds covered with this light green, ovate leaved plant. One identifiable characteristic is the single root suspended from the leaf. Found throughout the world, it forms part of the diet of many species of fish. Given good, but not too strong, top light, it quickly covers the water. It can cover nets, equipment, and one's hands when these are dipped into the tanks, and must be rigidly controlled in the home aquarium.

Family LENTIBULARIACEAE

Utricularia minor and *major* — Bladderwort: These Lesser and Greater plants have bladderlike organs adapted to capturing small insects or fry. The leaves have seven to twenty spikes and carry one to seven bladders. They are very hardy.

The Lesser *(minor)* is suitable for breeding tanks, its dense, tangled masses providing excellent cover; the Greater *(major)* should be avoided where the new-born fry of egglayers are present.

Family PONTEDERIACEAE

Eichhornia crassipes — Water Hyacinth: A striking plant. The leaf petioles, crammed with spongy tissue, act as buoyancy chambers and support the Hyacinth on the surface. The roots are violet, and the plant throws out lavender blooms having a bright yellow center. Though more spectacular in appearance than the Water Lettuce, the same advice about a large tank with plenty of overhead space applies. It is easy to grow. In some rivers in the state of Florida, its prolificacy has caused it to become a shipping hazard, as its dense growth clogs the waterways. The roots, which hang straight down, are aquatic and not to be planted. They are an old standby for goldfish breeding.

Family RICCIACEAE

Riccia fluitans — Crystalwort: Pale green, it floats as a mass. It propagates by dichotomous branching which resembles dozens of tiny "V" shapes. It loves the light and under good conditions will quickly form a carpet up to two inches thick. It has one drawback — if algal growths or Duckweed become entangled with the Riccia, it is impossible to separate them.

Family SALVINIACEAE

Salvinia oblongifolia: This rectangular, hairy leaved plant hails from Brazil. The under portions of the leaves are brown with thick root growth. Also called *S. braziliensis.* The species more commonly available is *Salvinia natans,* but this is better suited to the cold water aquarium.

Artificial Plants

Despite the fact that the mere mention of "artificial" foliage will draw sighs of protest from many plant growers and aquarists, imitation plants are becoming increasingly popular throughout the world. Reasonable in price and with a wide variety of shapes, sizes and colors to choose from, they have many things to commend their use to the fishkeeper. Made for the most part of pressed plastic, they discourage the growth of snail populations. Unlike living plants, they cannot be eaten or damaged by the attentions of snails and fish. Should disease strike the tank, they can be quickly removed and sterilized without any fuss. Interspersed between natural plants, they can add color and shape.

Aquarium plants available to the hobbyist are not usually what one would call colorful. Their foliage varies between the shades of green, red, and purple. Artificial plants, on the other hand, can be obtained in almost any color one desires and, if realism isn't essential, they fit the bill of decoration admirably. The majority on sale are non-toxic, but if you do purchase any from a source other than a bona fide aquarium dealer, check before adding them to the aquarium. Immersion for a few days with a few live Daphnia will soon tell you. After prolonged immersion in the aquarium, they do become covered with natural growth, especially brown algae. A good brushing with a stiff bristle and a rinsing under the faucet are all that is required to restore their original coloration. Like most soft plastic, they fade and become brittle after long immersion, but they are generally so inexpensive that it is simple to replace them.

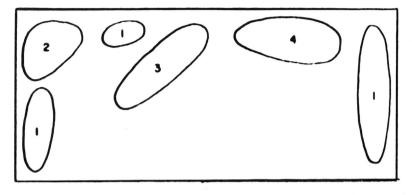

A suggested planting arrangement for a well-lighted tank. 1 — Dwarf Amazon Swordplant. 2 — Amazon Swordplant. 3 — Ambulia (*Limnophila*). 4 — *Hygrophila*.

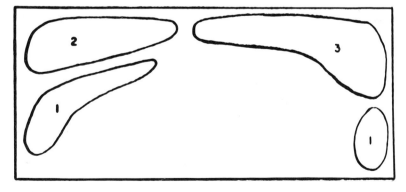

A suggested planting arrangement for a moderately-lighted aquarium. 1 — *Cryptocoryne nevillii* or *willisii*. 2 — *Cryptocoryne griffithii*. 3 — *Cryptocoryne affinis*. This arrangement would be especially suitable for killifishes.

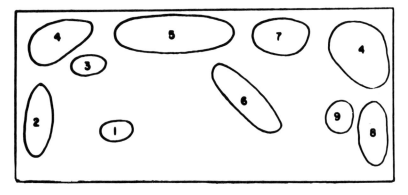

A suitable arrangement for an aquarium of 30 gallon capacity or larger. 1 — *Aponogeton fenestralis*. 2 — *Cryptocoryne nevellii*. 3 — *Hygrophila*. 4 — *Cryptocoryne griffithii*. 5 — *Cryptocoryne affinis*. 6 — Ambulia. 7 — Amazon Swordplant. 8 — *Ludwigia*. 9 — Water Fern.

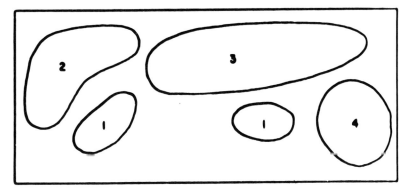

A special arrangement for a tank containing labyrinth fishes such as Gouramis and Bettas. 1 — *Bacopa*. 2 — *Hygrophila*. 3 — Ambulia. 4 — Water Fern.

MICHAEL YOUENS

1 — *Acorus gramineus*. 2 — *Anubias congensis*. 3 — *Anubias lanceolata*. 4 — *Aponogeton ulvaceus*. 5 — *Aponogeton undulatus*. 6 — *Aponogeton fenestralis*. 7 — *Azolla* species. 8 — *Bacopa caroliniana*. 9 — *Bacopa monnieri*.

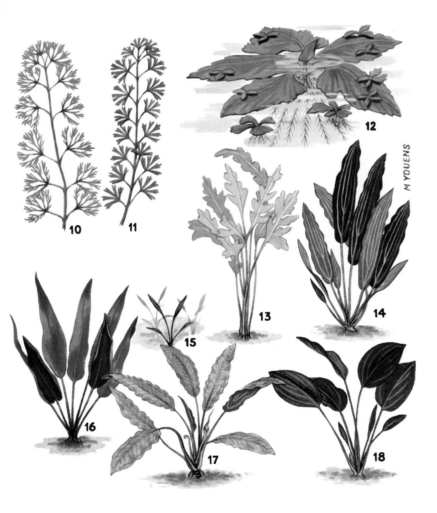

10   *Cabomba caroliniana.* 11   *Cabomba aquatica.* 12   *Ceratopteris cornuta.* 13 — *Ceratopteris thalictroides.* 14 — *Cryptocoryne affinis.* 15 — *Cryptocoryne nevillii.* 16 — *Cryptocoryne beckettii.* 17 — *Cryptocoryne willisii.* 18 — *Cryptocoryne cordata griffithii.*

19 — *Echinodorus paniculatus* var. *rangeri*. 20 — *Euchinodorus tenellus*. 21 — *Echinodorus cordifolius*. 22 — *Eleocharis acicularis*. 23 — *Eleocharis vivipara*. 24 — *Elodea densa*. 25 — *Hygrophila polysperma*. 26 — *Lagarosiphon major*. 27 — *Lemna minor*. 28 — *Limnophila heterophylla*. 29 — *Ludwigia natans*. 30 — *Marsilea hirsuta*.

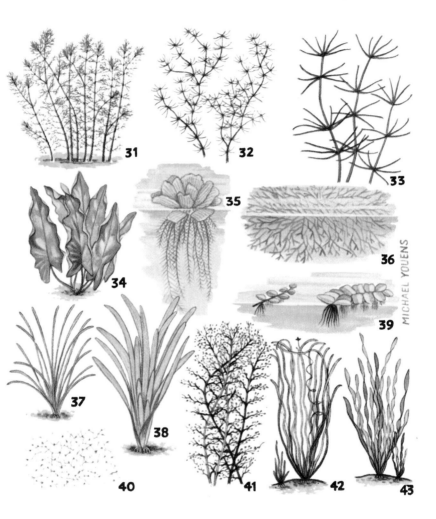

31 — *Myriophyllum elatinoides.* 32 — *Nitella flexilis.* 33 — *Nitella megacarpa.* 34 — *Nuphar sagittifolium.* 35 — *Pistia stratiotes.* 36 — *Riccia fluitans.* 37 — *Sagittaria subulata.* 38 — *Sagittaria latifolia.* 39 — *Salvinia auriculata.* 40 — *Utricularia gibba.* 41 — *Utricularia vulgaris.* 42 — *Vallisneria spiralis.* 43 — *Vallisneria spiralis* var. *tortifolia.*

VII   Feeding the Brutes!

The best food for fish is fish!

> Feeding his fish became an adventure fraught with
> significance and emotion; gastronomical discourse,
> a philosophical estimate on piscatorial mentality ...
> the fish were not simply fed, they were wooed with
> endearments ....

Those words were written to describe the affection held by the late Sir Winston Churchill for his pets; among this great man's many, many attributes was that of being a very experienced fishkeeper.

As feeders, fish can be separated into three groups: the *carnivorous,* who prefer the meaty, live foods; the *herbivorous*, who prefer a menu laced with vegetable matter; and the *omnivorous,* who will eat almost anything! This doesn't mean that the carnivorous fish won't touch vegetation, or that herbivores won't attack the Daphnia. In fact, very hungry fish will soon modify their eating habits.

The tales about the so-called "fussy feeders" seem to stem from a lack of understanding regarding how the fish like to feed. A bottom feeding catfish would have to be very hungry indeed to take his food in the open water in the middle of the tank, and a surface feeder such as the Butterfly Fish *(Pantodon buchholzi),* who likes his food served up on the water surface, would rarely venture down to the bottom in search of something to quell its appetite. Study the shape of their mouths and you will get some idea of how they feed best.

Carbohydrates

These provide the necessary energy for activity and warmth to the body. For the most part, they consist of the starchy foods such as bread and biscuit meals. The sugars also fit into this group.

Protein

A protein is a complex compound of carbon, hydrogen, oxygen and nitrogen. No living portion of the body is complete unless it contains protein! Even the tiniest bacteria boast some. Proteins are made up of various combinations of amino acids. Meat foods are high in protein, as are eggs, milk, and leguminous vegetables such as peas and beans. If our fish are to grow and if they are to replace the worn out tissues of their systems, protein is necessary.

Fats

Fats are similar in function to carbohydrates. They produce energy and can be stored up in layers in the body, against the time when food isn't available. The fish then draw from these reserve stocks.

Vitamins and Minerals

Not too much research has been done on the mineral and vitamin requirements of tropical fish. We can only assume that since these nutrient elements are absolutely necessary for most of the higher animals, they are necessary for fishes. A diet that is variegated and balanced will supply them. Many vitamins are destroyed in the process of cooking and drying, hence the need for live foods in the fishes' diet.

Live Food

" Man is what he eats!" Thus spake a philosopher of old, but the same can be applied to the fishes in our aquarium. A nourishing diet is just as important as keeping the environment right. The best diets are those that come as near as possible to what the aquatic animals feed on in their natural environment, but as we have already read, animals kept in captivity will quickly modify their feeding habits. We commenced this chapter with: The best food for fish is fish, and though smaller fish do form a major part in the diet of fish in the wild, they also eat small creatures, some of which can be purchased at your aquatic store or collected by the aquarist. These we now discuss as live foods.

In feeding live natural foods we must consider the relationship between the size of the food animal and the fish to which it is offered. It is no use giving the small ciliates to the large cichlids although they are ideal for newly born fry. Feeding a community of small tropicals with whole earthworms would be equally useless. The fish in both cases would starve despite the apparent " abundance" of food in the tank.

Newly born fish can take ciliates (infusorians), newly hatched brine shrimp, and micro worms.

Those live foods suitable for adult fish are adult brine shrimp, cyclops, Daphnia, fly larvae, fruit flies, and worms such as Grindal, white, or Tubifex. Earthworms are excellent, but they must be chopped for all but the very large fish.

Brine shrimp, Daphnia, cyclops, blood worms, glass larvae and Tubifex will last for several days to several weeks if kept in the refrigerator. The water should be changed daily and the container left uncovered, or at least perforated, for ventilation. Brine shrimp must be kept in salt water.

The foods which are described in detail below are listed alphabetically. The fact that brine shrimp heads the list and that it is considered the "ideal" food is purely coincidental. The reader must not conclude that the foods are listed in the order of their importance.

Brine Shrimp *(Artemia salina)*

These may be purchased as eggs which the hobbyist has to hatch out himself. The two major areas that provide these eggs are the salt flats around the Great Salt Lake in Utah, and the San Francisco bay area in California. A third major source is western Canada. Eggs from Utah are usually darker in appearance. There are two methods for hatching out the shrimp — the shallow pan and the hatcher, the latter depending on a vigorous air stream to keep the eggs agitated.

A hatcher can be constructed by inverting a large jug-type bottle. The bottom must be cut off by filling the bottle to a depth of about one inch with engine oil. Stand the bottle in cold water to a depth level with the oil. By inserting heated metal rods into the oil, the latter becomes hot and the glass bottle will crack at the oil/water level. Clean the exposed edge smooth with a carborundum stone. Insert a rubber stopper and then fill the upturned bottle with the following hatching brine solution:

To one gallon of water, add 6 tablespoons of non-iodized salt — cooking salt, sea, bay or kosher salt will do — and one tablespoon of Epsom salts (magnesium sulfate) and a pinch of bicarbonate of soda.

Place an air stone inside the bottle on a long stem and connect it to a pump giving a good flow of air. When the brine solution is bubbling fiercely, sprinkle brine shrimp eggs on the surface (enough to cover a

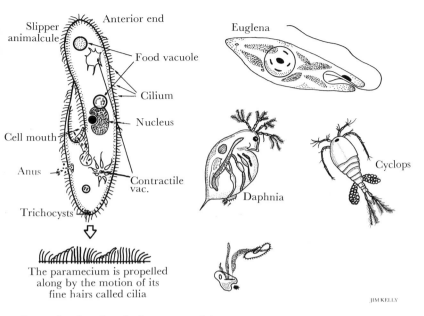

Slipper animalcule
Anterior end
Food vacuole
Cilium
Nucleus
Cell mouth
Anus
Contractile vac.
Trichocysts

Euglena

Daphnia

Cyclops

The paramecium is propelled along by the motion of its fine hairs called cilia

JIM KELLY

Some food animals (not to scale)

half dollar). The idea of using a bottle with a sloping neck instead of just any container is planned; as the eggs sink they are directed by the sloping glass sides into what used to be the neck of the bottle and into the main force of air, where the stone keeps them circulating around. If a flat bottomed container had been used the eggs would simply lie on the bottom and a poor hatching would result.

Place the hatcher in a suitable flower pot for a stand and locate the apparatus in a warm spot about 75° F. In about 24 hours the shrimp will have hatched out. The speed of the growth depends on the temperature of the mixture as well as the area from which the eggs were collected and their subsequent processing. So a temperature lower than 75° F would necessitate a longer period of growth. At a higher temperature this period is shorter.

To harvest, simply stop the aerator and place a low wattage light bulb over the hatcher. The egg cases will fall to the bottom and the newly hatched shrimp, attracted by the light, will swim to the surface. Siphon them out through a fine net or piece of muslin and rinse in the tank where they are being fed.

To grow them to adult size you must prepare a separate container full of the brine solution. Bubble air through this slowly. Feed the growing shrimp with either green water or cream a small portion of yeast into the brine. Don't overdo this feeding or you will foul the brine and kill the shrimp.

Artemia are disease and parasite free, and make a wonderful food at any size, although the nauplii are more nutritious than the adults. Constant feeding with shrimp will slowly increase the salinity of the aquarium water, but if the partial change of water is carried out as described under "tank maintenance" no harmful effects should be experienced. Many stores stock live adult brine shrimp.

Ciliates

Paramecium caudatum: Commonly called, because of its shape, the slipper animalcule, this is just one of a large group of semi-microscopic sized, one-celled protozoans that propel themselves through the water by means of tiny hairs called cilia. They can be collected from their natural habitats or bred in cultures at home. Because of their size, they are suitable for feeding the fry of only certain species. For years, aquarists have made infusoria cultures from a variety of things like hay, lettuce leaves and the like. These cultures were inoculated with ciliates and, hopefully, they bred. Lacking the necessary equipment for microscopic examination of his cultures, the fishkeeper often added them willy-nilly to his tanks and, in the process, added more bacteria than infusoria! Because of this danger, I much prefer to offer fry Euglena as their first food.

Euglena viridis: This is a tiny flagellum about 0.1 mm or less in length, found in profusion in freshwater ponds. In quantity, they form a greenish scum on the water surface. Euglena contain chlorophyll, the green pigment found in plants and, like the latter, give off oxygen and take in carbon dioxide, a point in their favor because they can live in the aquarium in large numbers without depreciating its oxygen content. To produce them in numbers one doesn't need intricate and costly laboratory equipment; in fact, most of what you need can be found around the house.

Boil half a pint of water in a small pan. When the water is bubbling vigorously, add a handful of wheat. Boil this for another ten minutes, then pour off the liquid. Place the wheat grains in a clean sterilized bottle with a narrow neck and add a cupful of cold water. Cork the bottle with a plug of absorbent cotton. Place this in a dark spot at room temperature for about two weeks, shaking the bottle daily to break up the surface scum that forms. At the same time remove the cotton plug for a few seconds, then replace it. If the plug gets wet, use a fresh, dry piece.

Collect your culture by skimming the green scum from a pond. If this isn't possible, certain biological supply houses will sell you an inoculation of Euglena. Add this to the liquid in the bottle. Now place it in a bright light and in a few days the contents will turn a bright green. Feed this liquid to your baby fish. Replace the quantity removed with fresh water and put the culture back in the light. This will insure a ready source of Euglena baby food with no foul odors and very little fuss.

Cyclops

Named after a mythological one-eyed giant, this small crustacean is often found in Daphnia cultures, where it is easily distinguished from the Daphnia with a magnifying glass. A little experience will enable you to differentiate its swift, jerky movements from the sedate locomotion of the Daphnia. It is frowned upon by some aquarists who claim it attaches itself to fish. I have fed mine cyclops for over twenty years, and I have yet to observe this phenomenon. The fishes seem to find the two tiny egg sacs that the cyclops tows, a rare delicacy. If Daphnia and cyclops are kept together, the former tends to disappear and one is left with a culture of cyclops only. Caught in ponds by using a fine net, they reach a length of 5 mm, which is suitable for the community aquarium.

Many kinds of fly and fly larva make good fish foods. The three shown here are mosquito larvae (thick bodied), blood worms which are the larvae of the chironomus fly, (red), and glass larvae (semi-transparent).

Larvae

Many species of fly larvae make good fish foods because they are found in abundance and are easy to net. The commonest used by the aquarist are the glass or phantom larvae *(Plumicornis corethra)*, blood worms *(Chironomus plumosus)*, mosquito and gnat larvae, and *Drosophila* or fruit flies.

Phantom Larvae: Also called glass worms because they are so transparent. They float horizontally in the water and propel themselves by sharp twisting movements. Adults reach up to $\frac{1}{2}$ inch in length and favor the surface areas of clear pools. Do not feed these if fry or eggs are present in the tank.

Bloodworms: Larvae of the midge, *Chironomus plumosus,* they are not — technically — a worm at all. "Blood" fits them because of their bright red coloration. Often found in Daphnia cultures, they are found abundantly in polluted waters — usually being prolific in waters receiving the waste from factories. There are reports of dead fish after they had eaten bloodworms; the *Chironomus* are said to have eaten their way out of the fish's stomach. However, many people find them to be an excellent and nutritious dietary supplement.

Fruit flies *(Drosophila fasciata,* formerly *melanogaster):* The tiny flies are eagerly taken by most fish, particularly the surface feeders. Breed the wingless varieties, though the broods aren't quite as large as those of the winged fruit fly. They are easy to keep in jars. Feed them on over-ripe fruit, such as ripe bananas. To feed the fish, simply shake some of the flies onto the surface of the tank. The Carnegie Institute of Washington sells a 52-page booklet, "The Drosophila Guide" (Demere **&** Kaufman), for fifty cents, and it is worth its weight in gold to the hobbyist, as it contains full instructions on the requirements and breeding habits of this nutritious animal.

Worms

The smallest of this family suitable for food are the **micro worms** *(Anguillula silusae).* Excellent for young fish, the fry of the livebearers will take them at birth. These worms, whitish in color, are cultured in a medium consisting of nine parts baby oatmeal, one part yeast, and enough water to make a loose paste. To this mixture add a starter culture purchased from your aquatic dealer. Kept in the dark in shallow dishes at a temperature around 73° F, micro worms are prolific and crawl out of the culture and up the sides of the dish. Two blocks of wood with two nails driven into them to act as feet are placed in the mixture. Across the top of the two blocks is placed a sheet of glass and the dish is covered with another piece of glass. The micro worms have an affinity for wet wood and will crawl up each block and cover the underside of the first glass. Feeding is achieved by rinsing this piece of glass in the aquarium. As cultures only have a limited life before they go sour, mix up a fresh oatmeal culture after a few days, and inoculate it with a spoonful of worms from the old set-up. Keep the culture in the dark when not in use.

Grindal worms *(Enchytraeus buchholzi):* Introduced from Sweden in 1949 by Frau Mortimer Grindal, hence their name. These small white worms fill the gap in size between the micro and the white worm. Fill a shallow wooden box with a mixture of peat and soil, moistened slightly. Place the culture of worms in a depression in the middle of the soil and cover it with either bread soaked in water (do not use milk for this purpose, as it quickly sours), oatmeal or moistened breakfast cereal. Press this down with a sheet of glass large enough to fit inside the box and cover this with a sheet of newsprint to keep out the light. Store in a dark place at room temperature. Allow the culture to stand for a few days. When the glass is lifted the worms will be seen congregating in clumps under the glass. Pick them off, rinse away the soil and feed to the fish. See that it is kept moist and that plenty of food is available, and the culture will last indefinitely. If the soil becomes infested with flies or larvae, eradicate them as follows: Remove the paper and glass and place the box in a bright light; after a short time the Grindal worms will have moved to the bottom of the box away from the source of light. When the top soil is clear of worms pass a flaming paper or blowtorch over it. This will quickly kill any flies, etc.

White worms *(Enchytraeus albidus):* Larger relative of Grindal, reaching up to one inch. Culture as for the above. Do not feed too many white worms to your fish, as the worms are very rich in fat and if fed too frequently the fish will become obese. Keep the culture a little cooler than for Grindal. A starter culture of worms can be bought, but a search around the base of trees, especially under rotting pieces of bark, will usually reveal enough to start with.

Earthworms *(Lumbricus terrestris)*: Though not strictly fed as "live" food, these worms are so easy to obtain and so nutritious that they should figure, where possible, in the complete diet. After a rain shower, you will find dozens of garden worms on the surface of the earth. These can be cultured under burlap sacks in the garden. Feed them kitchen scraps. The usual way to present these worms to one's fish is by chopping them up. This is not a method relished by most fishkeepers. Try this: first rinse the worms under the tap. Then place a handful of worms in a plastic bag and place this in the refrigerator for about fifteen minutes, just enough time to chill them but not long enough for them to freeze solid. Then, keeping the worms in the bag on a hard, flat surface, crush them into a thin layer. Return them to the refrigerator and freeze this solid. When needed, all you have to do is peel some of the plastic bag and break off a small portion, grating this into the aquarium. Like Daphnia, earthworms tend to be laxative, so feed sparingly.

Tubifex *(Tubifex rivulorum)*: There are several species and genera, including *Limnodrilus*. They are all thin red worms, up to one inch long, found in great numbers carpeting the beds of ditches and slow moving rivers. Burying the head portion in the mud, they wave their posterior parts about in search of food. They are obtainable from most aquarium departments, and are sold in live portions that resemble pieces of wriggling red meat. Tubifex quickly congregate into a ball and won't keep very long unless kept under running water. The best way is to place them on a shallow dish or saucer and keep under a dripping tap. Otherwise, the water covering the worms must be changed frequently or the worms will die. Do not feed any worms that have lost their color or are very thin and long. Feed to the

This freshwater Puffer, *Tetraodon fluviatilis*, is enjoying a meal of Tubifex worms.

aquarium inhabitants by dropping a few worms at a time into the tank, or use a worm feeder.

They are suitable for most aquarium fishes, but don't overdo the feeding. Surplus worms drop to the bed of the aquarium and form a mass, or even burrow into the gravel where it is difficult for all but the bottom feeders to reach them. They can be collected from the wild, but the process of separating them from the mud is messy and not worth the trouble. They are usually available all year round from your dealer. For the very tiny fish, chop the Tubifex by placing a lump of them into an *enamel* bowl with no water, and cut repeatedly into the ball of worms with the tips of a sharp pair of scissors. Another method is to place a portion on a wooden board and slice it with a razor blade.

Frozen and Freeze Dried Foods

Many foods such as brine shrimp, Daphnia, and Tubifex can be purchased as a frozen block. Treat these the same way as human frozen foods. Don't allow the complete pack to thaw out; break off a sufficient amount for each feed and quickly replace the balance into the freezer. If you wrap the pack in several layers of newspaper when bringing them home from the shop, they will not thaw out on the way.

Freeze dried foods, which look like small pieces of leather, are a new innovation in fish feeding. Such foods as shrimp, Tubifex, and liver are all available in frozen dried form. They are packed in plastic boxes, and feeding is simply a matter of sticking a small piece of the food to the inside glass of the tank where the fishes can pick at it. It is a good way to feed liver, but use only small portions at a time or you will cloud the water. Freeze dried products have an advantage in that they don't need refrigeration.

Dry Food

Though everyone generally agrees that live foods such as Daphnia, cyclops, Tubifex, and so on, are the best complete foods, dried packaged foods do have their use and act as roughage to aid the digestion. Manufacturers spend much time and money in research before their dried foods are put on the market, and today's hobbyist can take his pick from a profusion of packaged diets. In the cradle period of the tropical fish hobby, aquarists were perfectly satisfied to feed their pets on a monotonous menu of dried ant's eggs. In fact, some goldfish fanciers still do! These shriveled-up larvae and egg cases (usually to be had in the cheap range of packaged foods) add little to the intake of the fish but starch and bulk.

Dried foods have certain disadvantages. Food left uneaten will fall to the bottom of the aquarium, where it lodges in cracks and crevices. When the fish do not eat it, it goes foul very quickly in the heated water of the tropical aquarium. Bacteria feed on this decay and can multiply to such an extent that they form clouds in the water. Inspection of this cloud with a magnifying glass reveals that it is made up of hundreds of tiny creatures. Result? The oxygen in the water is rapidly used up, and the fish are found gasping atmospheric oxygen at the surface of the water. Even the use of aeration and filtration cannot relieve the situation when it has reached this stage.

Some foods lose an appreciable amount of their nutritional value during the cooking and drying processes to which most of these dried foods are subjected. Dried foods, particularly those cheap mixed foods consisting mainly of ground dog biscuit, occasionally become infested with tiny bugs and their larvae. Though these, for the most part, won't harm the fish if fed to them, they aren't very pleasant to have around the home.

Dried foods come in a profusion of varieties and grades, the three basic grades being Coarse, Medium, and Fine. Most of the finely powdered foods are suitable for feeding only to the very young fish; the larger species can consume fine foods only by sucking, and many will refuse to bother if the particles are too small. Crab and shrimp meal come in powder or coarse grade, but beware of the large package of shrimp offered at a cheap price. To sell at this figure the manufacturer usually has to grind up the complete shrimp, not just the meat. Consequently it contains fine shell which is less nutritious than the meat.

Flake foods are best purchased large, then rubbed down with the fingers to a size suitable for the fish. They are best when they remain floating on the water surface for long periods. Unless bottom feeders are present, be wary of food that sinks rapidly.

The secrets of feeding dried food are moderation and variety. Though not complete foods, they suffice where time is important to the hobbyist and the availability of live foods, either purchased or collected, is in doubt.

Vegetable Diets

Though most species will browse on the plants and green algae growths in the tank, there are some like those of *Metynnis*, some members of the *Cyprinid* family, and the algae-eating catfish who must have vegetables as an integral part of their diet. Lettuce leaves chopped into the tank have been suggested, but the author does not favor lettuce too often because the decaying leaves produce large numbers of ciliates. Spinach is better. Peas, when cooked, are excellent if the hard outer shell is first removed. Crush a quantity of cooked peas in the hand, squeezing out as much moisture as possible, then bottle the crushed peas and use when required. Sometimes floating plants like duckweed will be eaten.

Diet Deficiencies

It took man quite some time to connect certain human diseases like scurvy and beri-beri with a lack of certain essential vitamins. Now these ailments can be cured by the simple expedient of adding to the diet the missing substance. Fish are not excepted from these deficiency complaints. Frequently, this shortage is vitamin D. Guppies *(Poecilia reticulata)* and the Zebrafish *(Brachydanio rerio)* are particularly prone to this. Fish deprived of the vitamin through the ultra-violet rays of the sun (glass filters out these rays) need doses of liver or fish meal to compensate for the lack of vitamin D as well as calcium and phosphorus. The simplest way is to supplement their diet with fish oils like halibut or cod liver oil. The oil is mixed with the food. Mix only portions at a time. If left mixed for a long period, the oil turns rancid.

Making Your Own Foods

In preparing your own food mixes, there is no limit; but as many of these "home mades" don't smell too sweet, be sure to send the family on an outing before experimenting.

One good food that is both cheap and easy to prepare is beef heart. Purchase a small heart from the butcher and remove as many veins and sinews as possible, plus any fat or fibrous tissue. Grind the meat in a grinder or mixer, make up into small "pancakes" and freeze. Feed as for frozen foods.

A mixture that I like to use requires one pound of beef, four eggs, one-half pound of dog biscuit (the mixed meaty kind), and one teaspoonful of any fish oil such as cod liver. Grind the beef and mix the eggs, biscuit and oil, adding water slowly if necessary until the mixture is the consistency of a good pancake batter. Cook over a low heat until the mixture starts to bubble. Bottle in air tight jars, and refrigerate.

Most fish that humans consume is right for feeding in the aquarium. The snag is that cooked fish quickly breaks up into fine threads on entering the water. Be careful not to foul the water when feeding to fish!

Frequent Feedings

The average person eats three meals per day, and if he is in good health most meals result in clean plates. Imagine that one day you skip the first two meals. Arriving home in the evening, your wife sets the contents of all three meals in front of you. I doubt very much that even an appetite sharpened by a day's abstinence could face all that food at one sitting! Yet this is just what many fishkeepers expect their fish to do. Usually when the fish can be fed only in the evening, a large helping of food is tipped into the aquarium (all three meals at once). After a time our hobbyist wonders why his tank is never clean. Healthy fish consume food in small portions all day long, but they can eat only so much at a time. Feeding large portions is bound to cause problems.

Feed as often as is possible, but only what can be consumed by the occupants in a few minutes. If circumstances permit personal feeding only in the evening, either recruit the aid of the family to feed them when you are absent, or feed live foods that will live on in the tank for a long period of time.

Variety

I love strawberries and cream! No doubt you too have your favorite food. Yet if I were to eat strawberries and cream for breakfast, dinner and supper, I would very quickly hate the sight of them. For fish too variety is the spice of life, and this does not mean just a change in brand names. Too many fishkeepers buy one brand of food, feed it meal after meal until it is gone, and then switch to another brand, thinking they are feeding a varied diet. Most emphatically, they are not! Variety means varying the diet daily, feeding *all* the different types of food mentioned in this chapter.

When you return home with foods that are packed in perishable containers, either empty them into screw-top glass jars or buy yourself some of those little plastic boxes with tight fitting lids from the dime store. Mark the date of purchase on the outside. This date will help you to keep an eye on the age of the food in the boxes. Don't indiscriminately mix different foods together; some foods can affect others. Liver spoils very quickly and can send " off" any other food it is mixed with. Throw away any foods that emit a musty odor, have developed fungus growths or have become riddled with insects or larvae. The smell of these foods attracts insects, so keep the lid tight at all times when not in use.

VIII   The Fishes

Mention the word "fishes" to most persons and they immediately think only of animals that live submerged in water. But that is not strictly true. What about the whale? He lives in water, yet isn't a fish. Aristotle was well aware of the difference between the fishes and aquatic mammals over two thousand years ago.

Like human beings, fishes have backbones and are therefore classified as belonging to the "chordates." In point of fact, with more than 40,000 separate species on record, they form the largest group of the animals with backbones or endoskeletons. Of these, we primarily maintain in our aquaria those coming under the heading of the Teleosts.

Fins

Fin function provides some of the power to propel the fish through the water, contributing to steering and stability. As the number and shape of these fins help in identification, it is well to learn their names.

The majority of fishes have seven fins: three single fins called *dorsal* (top), *caudal* (tail), and *anal* (under); and two paired sets referred to as *pelvic* (under) and *pectorals* (breast). In some fishes the top dorsal fin is divided into two; the rays at the front of this fin are known as hard or spinal, and their numbers are expressed by *roman* numerals; the remainder of the rays are soft and designated by *arabic* figures. Where these spiny and soft rays occur together in one fin *(Percidae,* etc.), the fin count can be expressed thus:

$$D.VI/12-13,$$

meaning that the dorsal fin in this particular fish contains six spinal rays and twelve to thirteen soft rays. Occasionally, a comma is substituted for the diagonal as a divider.

Skin

Fish skin consists of two layers, a thin outer layer (epidermis), made up of simple cells which are constantly being worn away and renewed, and a thicker inner layer (dermis) consisting of a complicated mingling of muscle fibers and blood vessels. Mucous glands permeate both layers to produce a protective coating over the body of the fish. This "slime" not only helps to streamline the fish, it protects it from attack by bacteria, parasites and fungi. Never use dry hands or dry nets when handling fish, or you may damage this layer, leaving the fish open to infection.

Scales

The scales overlap each other like the shingles on a house and consists of four kinds: cycloid, ctenoid, ganoid, and placoid. (Some phyla such as marine mollusks are devoid of scales and possess an outer shell or exo-skeleton.) Scale counts are used to identify the different species of fish, particularly in closely related genera. There are two ways to count scales. The first is along the lateral line. The second is the transverse count — count the number of scales running obliquely from the dorsal to the anal fin.

In appearance, scales are not dissimilar to the cross section taken through a tree trunk for, like the latter, they possess "rings" which give a guide to age. As each fish scale develops, it forms a circle. During the winter when growth slows down, irregular circles, called annuli, are formed. Counting these will give the approximate age. This method obviously is not applicable to tropic zone fishes where there is no seasonal change.

Muscular System

If you remove the scales and outer skin from a fish and expose the flesh beneath, you will observe zig-zag lines running transversely around the body. These are the *myotomes* connected by the tissue *myosepta*. Imagine a series of paper cups fitting one within the other. These provide the muscle action used in propulsion. The gill arches, jaws and operculum are actuated by other, weaker muscles.

Eyes

The spherical lenses in the eyes of fish enable them to see in the semi-darkness of the water. Having monocular vision, fish can see in two directions, but are incapable of focusing both eyes on the same object at the same time. When stationary, objects up to a foot and a half away can be brought into accurate focus, but fish are aware of objects much farther away from them than this. One of the oddities concerning unusual vision in fish are the *Anableps* species. These creatures live half-submerged in water. Their eyes are divided into two parts, enabling them to see both above and below the water at the same time and on two sides, as well.

Gills

These may be called the " lungs" of the fish. Water is taken in through the mouth and passed over the gill filaments, where an exchange of gases takes place: the oxygen is extracted and the spent gases of respiration (primarily carbon dioxide) are expired. In the labyrinth fish *(Anabantidae)*, as well as in a few other genera, there is an extra respiratory organ enabling them to breathe at the water surface and, in the case of the climbing perch, even to live out of the water! The gills are protected by a movable outer cover called the *operculum.*

Mouth

The mouth is usually large and comes in many forms, each reflecting the eating habits of that particular species. Teeth too are intimately connected with diet, varying in location, shape and function. Some teeth are positioned on the jaws, tongue, or the palatine bones of the mouth; the actual mastication of the food is performed by the pharyngeal teeth in the throat. If the jaws are equipped with strong teeth then the pharyngeals are weak or absent altogether, and vice versa. Some species have mouths modified into a sucker, enabling them to cling to rocks or the glass sides of the aquarium. Many of the catfish *Plecostomus* from South America have this ability.

Nostrils

Fish perceive odors through sensory tissues in the nares (nostrils). The stimulation so received is passed via the nerves to the *olfactory* portion of the brain. Smell plays a very important part in the identification of food, particularly in the case of the Blind Cave Fish *(Anoptichthys jordani),* deprived of the sense of sight.

Lateral Line

The lateral line is visible as a series of dots along each side of your fish. This actually consists of a series of sense organs called *neuromasts* which extend from behind the head to the base of the caudal fin. Via a sunken canal, they are connected through pores in the scales. The lateral line is sensitive to low pressure waves and supplements the sensory systems of the olfactory, visual and auditory senses.

Swim Bladder

This is similar in function to the ballast tanks aboard a submarine that are filled with water to submerge the boat. In the air bladder of the fish a combination of oxygen, nitrogen and carbon dioxide is used to inflate or deflate the swimming bladder. This organ adjusts the weight of the fish in relation to the amount of water its body is displacing, allowing it to rise or sink. Sometimes intestinal troubles give rise to malfunction of this organ, and as a result, the fish cannot control its movements. It loses its balance and usually lies on its side, swimming up only with an effort. Some fishes, such as the South American *Corydoras,* lack this useful organ and so usually spend their time on the bottom.

Endocrine System

Glands produce fluids which pass through ducts, as, for example, the salivary glands. Some glands lack ducts, however, and allow the fluids to seep through the surface of the gland. We call these ductless or *endocrine* glands. Their function is to manufacture hormones which regulate and integrate certain body functions. The main difference between the endocrine glands of the higher vertebrates and those of the fishes is that whereas in the former they are distinct organs or form part of some other organ, in the fishes they are diffuse structures.

If the endocrine system is likened to a factory, the pituitary gland is the managing director because it has a direct influence on all body functions. Found on the under surface of the brain, it is divided into four regions, the functions of each not being fully distinguished. The pituitary influences growth, dispersion of pigment in the skin, balance and the activities of other glands.

Among the other glands are the thyroid, adjacent to the heart and concerned with metabolic activity; the pancreas, which among other functions produces insulin associated with the metabolism of carbohydrates; the mucosa lining, which controls secretions from the pancreas; the interrenal tissue, which has two functions, the first concerned with water and mineral metabolism, and the second with carbohydrate control; and the pineal gland, whose function is not known.

Do Fish Feel Pain?

Whether they do or not is a very debatable and controversial point among everyone from angler to ichthyologist. We have read that fish have an elaborate system of nerves and sensory organs and the presence of these suggests that they feel something. Experiments have proved that some species are more sensitive than others, but not whether these feelings include pain. Only another fish could speak authoritatively on this subject! However, it has been observed that when fish experience internal stimulation such as when they are feeding or spawning, their sensitivity to external stimuli is reduced.

Do Fish Sleep?

The absence of eyelids, so that their eyes cannot be closed, leads many people to conclude that fish in the aquarium do not sleep. Observations, however, have proved that fish go into a state of suspended animation akin to sleep. Even when the tank is plunged into darkness, many of the fish will lie motionless on the gravel or plant leaves and in some cases even flat horizontally in the water, remaining in this trance-like state for long periods. The exceptions to this are the nocturnal animals.

Why Cold-blooded?

The temperature of the human body is around 98.6° F. Man is a homeothermal animal in that he maintains a constant body temperature independent of the environmental temperature. On a cold day, we wrap up against the cold, but our body temperature, though it does fluctuate slightly (in sickness it usually rises), still remains within the region of 97 to 99.5° F.

Fishes, on the other hand, have a body temperature controlled by the temperature of their environment. If the temperature of the water in the aquarium is increased, then the metabolism of the fish is quickened and they eat more and become more active. Find the right temperature range to suit the species you keep, as increasing the temperature too much will shorten the life span of the fish. A drop in temperature slows down the body functions, making the fish listless, without appetite, and subject to disease. Unless the condition is corrected the fish will die; 75° F is considered a good median temperature.

Evolution

To study the evolution of the fish we have to go back a long time; just how long is best illustrated by this example:

Look at a clock face. It is numbered from 1 to 12. Let us imagine that these twelve hours represent the history of this planet, twelve o'clock representing modern times, one o'clock the genesis. For every hour that elapses on this clock a period of 100,000,000 years has elapsed in actual time!

At a quarter after eight the ancestors of the fish are swimming in the sea. Just after ten the earth resounds to the heavy tread of the dinosaurs. Yet not until our time clock is just about to strike twelve, one and a half seconds before, in actual fact, will *Homo sapiens* make his appearance, and not until just one tenth of a second before those two fingers are upright will recorded man come on the scene. On such a scale, it makes us, compared to fish, " new boys" indeed!

How life actually began is still a mystery, but many scientists agree that life first began in the primeval soup of the early seas. In the Cambrian Period, about 500,000,000 years ago, life did exist in the waters of the world. There was no sign on life on the land. Some of the commonest creatures inhabiting the sea were the Trilobites; they looked something akin to the modern wood louse. Averaging about three inches long, some specimens did grow as long as 18 inches. In the Silurian Period (300,000,000 years ago), the sea scorpions took over, but they were short lived. Within the inland lakes and rivers, creatures were evolving who were streamlining their shapes and developing fins so they could move more easily in their watery environment. The first fishes were beginning to take shape. These split into two major groups: those having cartilaginous skeletons, the sharks, rays, etc., are called *elasmobranchii,* and the rest, the bony fishes, are called *teleosti.*

Nomenclature

"It's all Greek to me!" is the usual outcry when the fishkeeper comes up against the Latin or Greek scientific names of the fishes. Why bother with the difficult-to-pronounce, hard-to-spell scientific names? Why not use the common name of "guppy," rather than the hard-to-remember *Poecilia reticulata (Poecilia* = many colored; *reticulata* = netlike)? The answer lies in the fact that scientific names serve several useful purposes and simplify identification of species — and, like it or not, they are here to stay!

In the United States of America, for example, several ground squirrels, at least twenty other rodents, a snake, and a turtle share the common name of Gopher. However, each of these creatures has a separate and distinct scientific name, enabling us to distinguish one from the other. These names also explain the relationship of various creatures, one to another.

Just as most civilized humans have two names, so do fish. Let us look once more at the Guppy, *Poecilia reticulata. Poecilia* is the family or generic name. It can be applied to many related fish just as we have many Smiths and Joneses; *reticulata* refers to the specific species, and because it is not quite so important, we omit the capital letter.

Guppies are live-bearing fish just like Mollies, Platies and Swordtails, to mention but a few, and all these come under the family name *Poeciliidae* — the live-bearing toothcarps. Finally, one may come across yet another name following these two; this is the name of the person who first described and classified this particular species, for example, *Poecilia reticulata* Peters.

The confused beginner can take heart in the fact that the scientists themselves often find it just as difficult.

IX The Family Game—Breeding

As opposed to merely keeping fish in an aquarium, breeding them is an enterprise requiring planning, preparation and attention to certain conditions. The hobbyist must learn about the requirements and conditions conducive to the mating of his particular fishes. Knowing this, he can create in his aquarium an environment which simulates — as nearly as possible — the necessary "natural" conditions that encourage fish to breed. Other than that, there are no "secrets" to fish breeding. Simply pay attention to the last detail, making sure, of course, that the chosen pair are male and female — ready to spawn.

Stimulated or triggered by the influence of internal secretions and external environmental conditions, spawning is just a part of the natural life cycle of the fish. The breeding cycles of temperate zone creatures are influenced by seasonal lengthening and shortening of the daylight hours. Fortunately for us, the majority of fishes kept in an aquarium are not seasonal, and they will breed throughout the year if conditions are right.

Basic Principles

Concerning water conditions in the breeding tank, they should be similar to those found by the fish in their home waters. If they came from soft acid waters, there is no use expecting them to breed in tanks containing hard, alkaline water. The salts causing the hard, alkaline conditions would merely destroy the outer casing of the eggs and render them infertile. Probably one of the main reasons why we still tag fish "difficult to breed" is that we lack knowledge regarding their natural environment.

It goes without saying that the fish in question must be a pair. Though this may seem an obvious condition to the beginner, further aquatic experience will prove just how hard some species of fish are to sex successfully. Always try to breed fish that have paired off naturally in the aquarium and are displaying the behavior associated with the mating act.

Reference has been made to a separate "breeding tank." This doesn't imply that fish won't or can't be bred in the community aquarium. In the case of some livebearers it would be difficult to stop them, but a separate tank enables the aquarist to carefully control the environment and also to adopt methods of saving the eggs from the cannibalistic tendencies of the tank inhabitants. Just as we humans class "caviar" as a desirable food, so do fish! Nothing is more disheartening to the would-be breeder than to see the results of his carefully laid plans — the precious eggs or fry — being consumed by adult fish.

Take suitable precautions after the production of fry or eggs to see that the resultant young fish are raised properly. Feeding is critical in their first few days of life, and the breeder has to provide sufficient food for their wants but not so much that it fouls the water.

Methods of Reproduction

[a]   Viviparous — giving birth to *live* young that have developed from eggs within the body of the mother and have been nourished from her bloodstream.

[b]   Oviparous — producing eggs which hatch *outside* the mother's body, expelled by her and fertilized by milt from the male during spawning.

[c]   Ovoviviparous — producing eggs that hatch within the mother's body. They are unlike viviparous species in that the eggs do not receive nourishment from the mother's bloodstream.

Therefore, we can divide our fishes into two major categories: *livebearers* and *egglayers*. The latter, which form the larger group, are further subdivided according to the methods employed in spawning:

[i] *Egg Scatterers:* The female drops her eggs all over the tank, willy-nilly, and the male fertilizes them with a covering of male sperm or milt.

[ii] *Egg Adherers:* Fishes which drop adhesive or semi-sticky eggs that are "anchored" to various sites; the parents have no further interest in them once they are ejected and fertilized.

[iii] *Egg Tenders:* Similar to [ii] but after (carefully) depositing the eggs on a pre-determined site the parents (carefully) look after them.

[iv] *Mouth Breeders:* After spawning takes place the eggs are picked up in the mouth by one of the parents (which parent depends on the species). Here they incubate and are expelled as free-swimming fry.

[v] *Bubble Nest Builders:* An elaborate surface nest of bubbles sometimes including bits of plant and tank debris is

constructed. The eggs are deposited in the nest, after which they are looked after either by the male alone or by both parents until the eggs hatch.

[vi] *Substratum or Egg Buriers:* Probably the most unusual and interesting method of all is the one in which the eggs are buried in mud.

Commencing with the livebearers we shall briefly describe each method in turn, but as this is a beginner's book, only the basics will be covered. Readers wishing to pursue this fascinating part of the hobby should consult the more advanced books on the subject. Among them is The Pet Library's "Advanced Aquarist Guide" by Dr. F. N. Ghadially.

ALBERT KLEE

Sexing livebearers. The arrows point to the anal fins. In the adult male (left) this modifies as he matures to form the gonopodium, a structure used for sperm conveyance. The dark spot on the female (right) is the so-called "gravid" spot.

Livebearers

The majority of fishes found under this heading belong to the family *Poeciliidae*, probably the first fish the beginner will breed. I use this term with tongue in cheek! So often one hears the boast that an aquarist has *bred* such a fish, when in actual fact all he can take credit for is providing intentionally (or, in many cases, unintentionally) the suitable conditions. Guppies, Platies, Swordtails and Mollies are a few of the commoner species belonging to the livebearing group suitable for the aquarium. Because they generally make good community occupants livebearers usually figure in the first choice of fish, and the fishkeeper will soon witness the antics of the active males chasing or "courting" the females.

This male "dance" is wonderful to watch, particularly in the Guppy. Yet, a strange fact is the apparent disinterest and lack of concern displayed by the female toward the sex act which apparently causes the male to attempt to mate at every opportunity.

Copulation is achieved by the anal fin of the male which at puberty rolls up rather like a tube, thickens and forms the organ called the gonopodium. Through this he "shoots" the male spermatozoa into the genital opening of the female.

The incubation period varies with the tank temperature but on an average lasts for about a month. During this period, the developing fry can often be seen, especially in the Guppy, through the walls of the peritoneum. This black area on the female is called the gravid spot.

At birth the fry are delivered speedily tail first, and after a short dash to the surface to gulp air which activates their swim bladders, they are free-swimming and capable of eating newly-hatched brine shrimp or fine-grained food.

It is quite common for adult fish to eat their own kind. Because of this very few young escape alive when they are delivered in the community aquarium. In fact, as a general rule fishes of extremely disproportionate sizes should never be kept together.

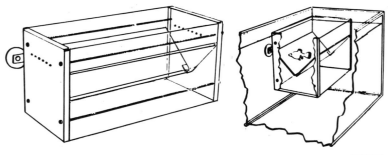

ALBERT KLEE

The V-type of breeding trap is the most common. Right: the trap in use.

Breeding Traps

A wiser practice is to isolate the pregnant female in a breeding trap. This piece of apparatus allows the fry to fall through a small aperture or a mesh net to safety, away from the cannibalistic habits of the adults. Breeding traps are made from a variety of materials: plastic, netting and even stainless steel mesh. They either float or hang on the side of the tank. If used in the community aquarium there must be a lower compartment to keep the eggs or fry away from the eager appetites of the rest of the fish. These traps are available commercially; the larger sizes are preferred. A simple home-made trap is illustrated, constructed from a small tank (the size is immaterial), a piece of glass and three rubber suction cups. The glass sides of the tank are painted black outside, as is the cover glass. This gives the female a feeling of security.

As the young fish are born they roll down the sloping glass, through the slit formed by the rubber disk to the safety of the rest of the tank. Having used this trap successfully for many years, I can recommend its use. The pregnant female is placed in the small compartment above the sloping glass; this serves the dual purpose of keeping the female inactive and allowing the darkness to provide her with the security she requires during labor. Fish have been kept in this for up to a week without suffering any harmful effects — feeding during this period should consist of young live brine shrimp as this nutritious food won't foul the water and any shrimp penetrating into the large compartment will provide food for the young fry as soon as they are born.

Size of Brood

On an average, from ten to fifty young can be expected from each birth, although some species will produce more, the record brood being in three figures! One unusual feature of the livebearing female is her ability to have up to five more successive broods (after the lapse of the appropriate gestation period), without being further inseminated by the male. The sperm is stored in the female's body, available to fertilize newly developing eggs. This raises a question important to breeders: if it is desired to re-mate a female after she has delivered a brood, which male will be the father of the subsequent brood? The latest studies on the subject indicate that the fresher sperm is more viable and is therefore more likely to fertilize the developing eggs. Many beginners, purchasing just females and experiencing this successive birth of young fish, apparently fatherless, have claimed " parthenogenesis," or virgin birth, when in actual fact the fish was merely " doing what came naturally"!

Certain "highlights" appear in any undertaking. In keeping

tropical fish, the first is the aquarist's first view of his tank, but a close second must surely be his discovery of a brood of newly born livebearers swimming around the tank; this sight never fails to interest the younger generation. If you want to raise a batch of fry in the community aquarium, be sure to provide plenty of plant cover, particularly the floating kind. The young can hide there and escape the predatory instincts of the larger fish or other tank occupants.

Sexing egglayers. As a general rule the female (left), when in spawning condition, is plumper. Often, the anal fin of the male (right) is concave. A very good way to sex egglayers is to look *down* on the fish. The female will be noticeably rounder.

Egglayers

Eggs expelled by the egglaying female may be either pelagic (floating) or demersal, those that sink in water. Each egg consists of a central nucleus surrounded by a cortical membrane. In this outer covering is a small opening or entrance (micropyle) through which the male sperm enters. This opening is so fine that only one spermatozoon can enter. The egglayers are the largest group of fishes available to the aquarist, but because of the minute size of the egg plus the difficulties involved in raising the fry their breeding is often spurned by the newcomer. In my book, to warrant the term "fish breeder" the aquarist must have achieved success not only in the fairly simple breeding of the livebearer but must also breed the more difficult egglaying species. Because of their variety and different methods of spawning, we shall discuss them separately under the headings previously suggested.

Parental care differs from species to species; some fish make loving parents, tending to the eggs, cleaning them and in some cases even fanning the eggs with their fins to insure that they receive a liberal supply of freshly oxygenated water and to keep them free of debris. Newly born Discus fish actually feed from the body secretions of the adult. A rare sight in the aquarium is that of an adult Discus accompanied by her free-swimming host of newly born youngsters. Yet another sight to behold is the behavior of the mouth breeding species. They carry the eggs in the mouth. This means that the parent fish can take no food and, as a consequence, she or he often becomes very emaciated.

The concern displayed by these parents is offset by those fish who just scatter their eggs and leave them to the mercies of predators and other hazards. What, then, is parental care? What is its purpose? Perpetuation of the species is ruled out as the sole reason, because we know that some fish show complete indifference to the future of their brood and yet the species survives. To fishes, breeding is a biological necessity and their actions can best be summed up as instinctive.

Egg Scatterers and Egg Adherers

In this group are the majority of characins, some catfish, barbs and minnows. The eggs are just scattered all over the tank; some are adhesive, adhering to plants by means of tiny fibers, other, non-sticky types fall on the floor of the aquarium. One thing both types have in common is a complete disinterest (apart from their attraction as food) in the eggs once they are fertilized. Some of the eggs hatch in just a few hours; others take up to a week.

Use a medium size tank and for egg adherers, plant it thickly with plants so as to afford attachment places for the eggs. For the species that scatter non-adhesive eggs, cover the floor of the tank with glass marbles; the eggs will fall into the interstices and safety. I have had similar success when spawning the Danios by substituting broken brick or well-washed smooth pebbles. Keep the females separated from the males until the former fill up with eggs, then introduce the males. The spawning act goes on right through the day. When you see the adult fish paying attention to the eggs, remove them.

The fry are supplied with their first food in the form of a yolk sac, but this doesn't last very long and ciliates must soon be supplied (see Chapter VII). After about a week the fry should have grown sufficiently to be able to eat newly hatched brine shrimp or micro worms. The Danios form good subjects for the first breeding attempts with an egglaying species.

ALBERT KLEE

A typical spawning sequence of a cichlid. Left: the prenuptial " dance." Top right: after laying their eggs on a flat surface, either or both of the parent fish care for the eggs, fanning them with the pectoral fins to aerate them and to keep dirt away. Bottom: after hatching, the fry are moved to another site by the parents, who still guard their youngsters.

Egg Tenders

Among this group we find most of the aquarium "giants" — the cichlids. As sexing is often difficult and the fishes show preferences in selecting their mates, it is best, if possible, to raise a few together and let them pair off naturally. After a vigorous courtship that often includes much sparring, the pair will select a suitable site (usually a flat stone) and after cleaning it thoroughly, deposit the eggs. This action is aided by a small tube which protrudes from the female's body adjacent to the anal fin, called an ovipositor. Most of the fishes in this group make excellent parents, tending and cleaning the eggs. They are almost clinical in their efforts to keep bacteria, fungus, and drifting debris at bay.

Adult Dwarf Cichlids prefer some suitable hiding place in which to lay their eggs. The addition of small flower pots to the breeding tank is much appreciated. Boil the pots in water to insure they are perfectly clean before introducing them into the tank. They are laid on their sides in conspicuous areas.

The community "top of the pops," the Angelfish, chooses a large plant leaf on which to lay its eggs but will use strips of slate or glass just as readily. One breeder uses strips of stainless steel, 12 inches by 3 inches, bent into the shape of a " U." These stand upright in the tank, and both Discus and Angelfish make use of them. With this the incidence of eggs developing fungus is lowered.

Aquarium literature notes that up to two thousand eggs may be deposited at one spawning, but generally the number is only a few hundred, the laying spread over a couple of hours. Depending on water temperature, the eggs hatch in about a week. When hatching, the eggs appear to be growing a tail out one end and a head out the

Angelfishes spawning on a vertical slate. The eggs are clearly visible as the male fertilizes them. These fishes always start at the bottom and work up.

other. For several days the brood resembles a quivering mass of jelly. When they are free-swimming, the parents frequently take the young fish in their mouths (in the case of cichlids) and after apparently cleaning them, spit them back out into a depression which they make in the sand. It is uncanny how these fish display an awareness of the dangers from debris floating about in the water and settling on the eggs. Their young are frequently moved from pit to pit. The parents alternate in swimming back and forth so that all the youngsters are under surveillance constantly.

If suddenly frightened, the parents have been known to eat both eggs and fry, so avoid any sudden movements around the breeding tank. With their built-in mechanisms, the parents can sense when the lights are going out and will chaperone their young around them into a "safe" area. Never plunge the tank suddenly into darkness and take the fish unaware, for any young still swimming about the tank outside this safe area are likely to be gobbled up. Professional breeders remove the parents as soon as the eggs are deposited and rear the young artificially. However, when parents are left in the tank, their actions are so interesting that is is almost worth the partial loss of a brood.

Mouth Breeders

The spawning act is much the same as for the preceding group and, with a few exceptions such as a mouth breeding Betta, this group belongs to the cichlids. The pair of fish, after cleaning a suitable area, circle each other head to tail, while the eggs are deposited and fertilized. Then one of the parents, usually the female, picks them up in her mouth, where they remain until the fry are free-swimming. It takes a period of up to two weeks. Which parent undertakes the task is not a matter of discussion by the participating parents, but is pre-determined by the species' inheritance. Because of the "enforced" fast the brooding parent becomes very thin, and it is essential for the breeder to have plenty of food ready for her immediately after the young become free-swimming, or she may just satisfy her hunger by eating them. This method of incubation not only insures complete protection for the eggs, but also gives them the benefit of a built-in "air-conditioning" system with the incubating parent mouthing the eggs frequently much as a brooding bird revolves her eggs. When free-swimming, the fry always keep within easy swimming distance of Mother, and at the first whiff of danger scuttle back to the safety of her mouth. Usually the female performs this function, but in the case of the mouth breeding Betta (a relative of the Fighting Fish), it is the male who looks after the eggs. Average broods vary from two to three dozen fry.

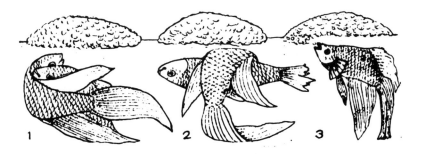

The spawning of the Betta is typical of the "bubble-nest builders." 1 — The male bends his body around the female in a typical embrace. This takes place immediately below the nest. 2 — The pair roll over together, at which point the female releases her eggs and the male fertilizes them. 3 — The male retrieves the eggs and blows them into the bubble nest. When spawning is completed he will stand guard over them.

Bubble Nest Builders

This group *(Anabantidae)* includes the popular Fighting Fish *(Betta splendens)* from Siam, the Dwarf, Thick-lipped, Kissing and Moonlight Gouramis, and the Paradisefish. The fry of anbantids are among the tiniest we encounter in aquarium fish. The male bubble nesters are more colorful than the females, having longer, more pointed fins — particularly the anal and dorsal. The females bulge just behind their pectoral and ventral fins; distinguishing sex isn't difficult.

The breeding tank for the bubble nesters should be about 15 gallons capacity. Use soft, aged water to a depth of only six inches. The bottom should be clear to allow the male to find any fallen eggs or fry, but sink a good clump of plants in one corner, weighted with a lead strip, to provide shelter for the female.

Taking in mouthfuls of atmospheric air at the water surface, the male of this group (although at times the female assists) breaks the air into tiny bubbles, coats each one with saliva, and aided by this sticky mucus builds a floating nest. This mound of bubbles very quickly becomes an egg receptacle which may be half an inch high and up to three inches across.

During the nest building the female should be placed in a small jar or breeding trap and floated in the tank to stimulate the male. When satisfied that his preparations are complete, the male will turn his attentions to the female, and at this stage she should be released into the tank. The male promptly chases her below the nest, and wrapping his body around hers appears to squeeze the eggs out of her body. As they appear he covers them with milt. The eggs of some species, being demersal, start to sink, but the parents break off the nuptial embrace, catch them up in their mouths and spit them into the bubbles of the nest. On the average, from three to seven eggs are extruded each time. When the female is empty she flees from the male, whose attitude now changes to one of belligerence. He takes up a position as guardian underneath the nest. The female should be removed at this point or the male may kill her.

Once spawning has taken place, never plunge the tank into complete darkness. Illuminate it faintly through the night by substituting one of those low-wattage warning bulbs that glows red. This consumes very little electricity and will light the nest sufficiently for the male to discover any fry unlucky enough to fall out and return them to the bubbles.

The eggs hatch in just over a day and the fry hang vertically in the nest. In two days the young fish will be free-swimming and the male parent should now be removed.

Drafts of cold air across the top of the nest can add up to failure. Avoid this by covering the breeding tank with either a glass cover or hood. Temperatures around 80° F are best. The mechanism for breathing atmospheric air is not fully developed in the fry. After several days of maturation each tiny fish must rise to the surface and gulp a bubble of air.

The first feeding for the fry must include ciliates or finely powdered dry foods. The breeding habits of the bubble nesters are extremely interesting to watch, and they are not difficult to breed if the female is full of eggs and the male constructs a good-sized

Substratum or Egg Buriers

If you could take a walk through the flood plains of Argentina, South America, or certain sections of Africa about the end of winter, you would be amazed to see the ditches which were dry just a few weeks ago filled with rainwater and teeming with life!

The reason for this apparent spontaneous appearance of fishes is due to the spawning habits of certain of the killifishes. At the end of autumn, just prior to the dry season, they spawn and bury their eggs in the mud. As the pools and ditches dry up, the adults perish but the eggs remain. At the time of the spring rains they hatch out.

Courtship commences when the male swims around the female, spreading his fins and generally showing off; then he quickly dives headfirst into the muddy bottom accompanied by the female who positions herself below him but twisted to one side.

This action brings the folded anal fin of the female into contact with the anal of the male and copulation takes place. After the eggs are fertilized, the female unwraps her fin with a snap-action that sends the eggs deep into the muddy bottom of the pool.

In the aquarium we substitute a layer of peat into which the fish deposit their eggs. This peat (best placed in shallow plastic trays about three inches deep) is then removed, squeezed gently until just damp and then stored in polythene bags in a temperature of between 74° to 76° F for periods ranging from two to 36 weeks! (the latter in the case of *Pterolebias zonatus*).

Despite the annual nature of these fish, they are firm favorites with aquarists. The colors displayed by these usually long, tapering, almost torpedo-like specimens are some of the brightest seen in the home aquarium, with the exception of tropical marine fish. While other killifishes such as the *Aplocheilus* and *Aphyosemion* genera are long and tapering with the fins set well back on the body, many annuals such as those of the genus *Cynolebias* are more deep-bodied.

If the eggs are kept at temperatures in excess of 76° F, or if the peat they are stored in is too damp, the fry could be "belly sliders" — a term used to denote imperfectly developed fry.

After storing for the required period, the eggs and peat are placed in a tank and covered to a depth of not more than two inches with soft, acid water. Any depth greater than this would make it hard work for the newly-hatched fry to force their way through the peat to the surface to gulp air. Water depth may be increased after three days.

Summation

There are no short cuts to successful breeding. Some breeders are able to produce broods of fish at their first attempt; others try for ages before being blessed with a hatching. The basic principles requiring attention are:

[a] Choosing fish that are a matched pair and ready for spawning.

[b] Stimulating them to mate.

[c] Supplying them with the correct conditions (pH, hardness, and so on), and with a breeding tank suitably prepared for their particular method of breeding.

[d] Feeding and rearing the young fish.

Most of the eggs, with the exception, perhaps, of those of some killifish eggs which become covered with peat, are reasonably easy to spot, but the newly-hatched fry are not. It is best to look for them with projected light such as a flashlight rather than under normal illumination. The fry are small and transparent in most cases, and I have known instances where hobbyists have unknowingly destroyed young fishes because they hadn't detected them in the breeding tank.

Suitably sized food for the fish in question must be on hand; generally the first food for the young egglaying species consists of ciliates, but the livebearing species can take newly-hatched brine shrimp and micro worms at birth. The fry of cichlids, killifishes, the larger barbs, and characins can usually bypass the infusoria stage.

If the eggs or fry are transferred from one tank to another, be sure that they are moved into similar water conditions and at the same temperature. Transfer them in a quantity of their own water if possible.

Young egglayers are supplied with a small store of food at birth in the form of a yolk sac. Until this is consumed they will show little interest in other food, so don't be in too much of a hurry to feed them. Watch their movements carefully, and when the egg yolk is absorbed and they seem actively engaged in searching around for sustenance, they should receive it. Feeding should be done in small amounts several times a day. The stomachs of fry are tiny, and when too much food is introduced at once the excess decomposes and remains to pollute the water. On the other hand, the demands caused by their rapid growth require that food be available frequently if the fish are not to be stunted.

X Genetics and Reproduction

There are folk who think the production of wonderful fish is simply a matter of organization, who quote authority as the final arbiter of their arguments; yet this organizing ability isn't what keeps the fishkeeper in his fish-house until the early hours, watching the miracle of birth, when other people are enjoying less practical dreams.

We can approach the study of life from two distinct points of view. We can ask the questions, "How do all organisms function here and now?" and "How do these same organisms change over a period of time?"

Our studies of anatomy, physiology, ecology and morphology seek the answers to the first question, while evolution, genetics, and embryology probe the second.

Unless the newcomer to the hobby has had previous training in biology, the study of genetics is a complicated matter. Most authors assume a pre-knowledge and fill their books with mathematical formulas, sprinkled with X's and Y's. "X" usually marks the spot where the beginner's interest flags.

Unfortunately, to condense the science of genetics into a few pages is not an easy task. To retain clarity, it is necessary to make statements that to the trained geneticist are, because of over-simplification, untrue or, at best, only half-true.

The application of genetics to fish breeding can be made complicated and even contradictory by just the use of proper phraseology! Yet, if we are to breed fish successfully, even if we only wish to follow the current aquatic literature intelligently, we should have some knowledge of the basic principles.

An understanding of genetical laws doesn't help us to achieve success so much as it helps us to understand our failures!

Mechanisms of Heredity

Nature has many methods of reproduction. With fishes we are concerned with the spermatozoon (sperm) from the male fish contacting the *ovum* of the female. The product of such a union is called a *zygote*. In the livebearing species the sperm of the male enters the female, where they unite with the eggs within her body. In the egglayers, the female discharges the eggs from her body, and these are then fertilized by being covered with milt (sperm) from her partner.

The two germ cells, now brought together as a zygote, consist of a nucleus surrounded by a watery substance enclosed in an outer case or membrane. When these two cells form a zygote they merge their part into a single cell called the "nucleus," which contains the genetic materials that pass on the hereditary characteristics from both parents to the new fish.

Chromosomes

Think of a string of beads. Each individual bead is a *gene*, and the complete string containing many "gene beads" is the *chromosome*. The latter simply means "colored body" because scientists found that under a microscope they stood out clearly when treated with special dyes. Though chromosomes are visible in the body cells, we are only concerned here with those contained in the sperm, egg and the result of the union (zygote), as only these have any bearing on inheritance, forming the link between an individual and his parents.

Chromosomes are arranged in pairs, each species of animal having a characteristic number of them to each cell. In man, as in the Guppy, the chromosomes number 46 (23 pairs). Note that most chromosome totals are divisible by two.

The chromosomes in the male sex cell or sperm are not paired; therefore, this cell has only half the number of genes normal to the species. The female sex cell or egg has the full complement of chromosomes, but in preparation for fertilization these divide along the line of pairs, half being discarded as a "polar body." Thus, the union of the sperm and the egg restores the normal number of genes to the zygote or gamete. In the case of the human, the sperm has 23 chromosomes, the egg the same number, providing the union of the two (the zygote) with 46 single or 23 pairs of chromosomes, the same number as for the body cells.

Genes

These are the single "beads" on the string, too small to be seen even under the microscope. They are the basic building blocks of heredity.

They consist of complicated chemical parcels which have the ability to make more packets similar to or even identical with themselves.

They affect such factors as color, shape, finnage, etc. They work together in pairs, one from the father and one from the mother.

If both genes carry the factor to produce "red" in the fish, then the fry will probably be red, but if one gene carries red and the other black, then the fry might just be black — the outcome here depending on the concept of a "dominant" black gene.

A *dominant* gene is one whose effects will override the other.

A *recessive* gene, conversely, is one whose effects will not be apparent if paired with a dominant. If we brought together a black gene and a gold gene in one zygote (as with a cross between a half-black and golden guppy), the fish would be black in appearance but would carry the gold gene; the dominant black overrides or masks the "recessive-to-black" gold gene.

Genes, then, are rather like computers programmed with the potentiality to develop, in the new fish, characteristics inherited from both parents and thus to resemble them. This way, stored information is passed on from one generation to another.

Summary:

Chromosome —	Thread-shaped bodies occurring in numbers in the nucleus of animals; they occur in pairs, several to each nucleus.
Genes —	Single units of inherited material, numbers of which together make up a chromosome; indivisible, they are able to duplicate themselves.

Male or Female — the Determination of Sex

The chances of young fish being male or female are theoretically fifty-fifty. An explanation of what determines the sex is best given by referring back to the number of pairs of chromosomes carried by a human being — 24 pairs; of these, 23 pairs are termed autosomes, the remaining pair are the sex chromosomes. In the human *female* (as in fish), these two are similar and known as X chromosomes; in the *male* we find one X, similar to the female's, but the other one is smaller and of different shape, which we refer to as the Y chromosome. Consequently the sex chromosomes in the female are designated (XX) and in the male (XY).

The male sperm can carry either an X or a Y, and depending on which makes contact with the female's X chromosomes, the sex of the future progeny lies.

If it contains a Y, then this pairs with the female's X and we have a male (XY). If it carries an X, then this pairs with the female's X and we have a female (XX). As the possible combinations of X and Y with X and X are: XX, XY, XX, XY — the chances of the young fish being either male or female are equal.

Mendelian Laws

If we are to breed fish successfully, and in so doing attempt to improve upon their parents, we must have some knowledge of the invisible organization that controls the passing on of qualities from one generation to the next.

The study of inheritance owes much to Gregor Johann Mendel (1822 — 1884). An Austrian monk working in his monastery gardens at Brunn, Mendel combined his inquisitive mind with his great love of nature. In his leisure time, he worked with the pea-plant, studying the inheritance of certain characteristics. Thusly, he experimented with the possibilities of inherited units, establishing mathematical rules for their operation in simple systems. He formulated two generalizations commonly termed the "Laws of Inheritance."

The Law of Segregation. During maturation (when the chromosome divides) each gene pair separates so that each egg or sperm (gametes = sex cells) contains but one gene from each pair. When two gamets come together at fertilization we have two genes for each trait brought together again in the offspring.

The Law of Independent Assortment. The distribution of one gene pair is completely independent from the distribution of any other gene pair — that is, if the pairs of genes are on separate chromosomes. This law is not universally applicable..

Mendel experimented by crossing pea plants and noting the results. We can produce similar conditions by tossing coins! If we tossed two coins in the air simultaneously many times and noted how they fell, we would find that half the time they would land head side up and the other half tails; one quarter of the time we should have two heads, and the other quarter two tails — a ratio of 1 : 2 : 1.

This is what Mendel found in his experiments with peas. His laws demonstrated that the genes in both sperm and egg act as units and are distributed to the future progeny according to this ratio.

Basic Facts: When dealing with genetical computations, one truth that seems to be missed by most beginners, and at times even by people who should know better, is the fact that all genetical reasoning based on Mendelism can only be worked out on the basis of factors that differ from each other in *one characteristic only*. To help clarify this statement, let us take as a basis for experiment two Guppies: a plain, gold-colored, round caudal female fish, and a spotted, gray, swordtail male.

On paper we can record all the possible combinations of this cross as follows:

Plain	Gold	Roundtail	Spotted	Gray	Swordtail
Spotted	Gold	Roundtail	Plain	Gray	Swordtail
Plain	Gray	Roundtail	Spotted	Gold	Swordtail
Spotted	Gray	Roundtail	Plain	Gold	Swordtail

Now let us pair up factors:

[a] Plain	pairs up with	Spotted.
[b] Gold color	pairs up with	Gray color.
[c] Roundtail	pairs up with	Swordtail.

The common denominators within our groups are:

(i)	body pattern	[a]
(ii)	color	[b]
(iii)	caudal shape	[c].

We have reduced our original six factors: gold, gray, plain, spotted, roundtail, swordtail, to three, each of these three differing from any of the others in *one characteristic only*.

Now let us see what happens when we cross a gold female fish with a gray male. The first parent generation is given the symbol (P), and in our drawings we illustrate in the circles below each fish the genes they carry — two *plain* circles denote the gold and the two *black* circles the gray.

The youngsters born from this mating we call the (FL) generation (from the Latin *filia* — daughter, and *filius* — son); though they all appear gray in color they are made up from one gene for gray and one for gold. The reason they appear gray is that the gold gene is recessive to the gray gene.

We illustrate their genes by one plain circle (gold color), and a black circle (gray color).

These siblings grow up, and we choose a male and a female which we cross (brother to sister) to give us the (F2) generation.

In this next brood we see the 1:2:1 ratio of Mendelism showing itself, because in every group of four fish we now have one gold (two plain circles), one gray (two black circles), and two which, though gray in appearance, carry the genes for gold (one black, one plain circle).

Looking at this brood in the aquarium, the observer would see one gold-colored fish to three gray; this is the Law of Dominance manifesting itself.

If the gold-colored fish were crossed with its gold sibling (or crossed back with the gold parent), the fish produced would breed true gold.

A similar thing would happen if you crossed the pure gray (two black circles) with the pure gray; the fry would be all pure breeding gray fish but the hybrids (one black, one plain circle) would simply produce the results we observed in the (F2) generation.

These theoretical proportions do not necessarily appear in each brood, but are average for the combined proportions of many broods.

How can the fishkeeper make use of this knowledge? For an exercise, assume that we have obtained an albino Guppy female* and despite our search we cannot obtain an albino male. How would we set about breeding to obtain albino fish?

We now know that if we crossed the albino female with a pure-bred gray male, all the fry born in the first generation would be all gray-colored, i.e., no albinos.

If a pair of *these* fish were bred together, brother to sister, we would have in the next batch of fry one albino and three gray fish in every four fish in the batch.

It is now a simple matter to cross these F2 albinos together or to cross one of these F2 albinos (male) with the original albino female — the result would be all albino fish!

In fact, breeding albino fish isn't quite as simple as this, not only

An albino is a fish lacking in black color. The eye is colorless, but appears red because the color of the blood is seen through the tissues.

because they have a higher mortality at birth, but also because their lack of pigment seems to make them more attractive and many are cannibalized. The ratio, therefore, in practice is not 1:3 but nearer 1:53. Still, this doesn't alter the mechanism we have used — the laws of heredity can help us in our fishbreeding.

Heterosis — Nature's Supercharger

Ever since man has become a part-time "home aquarist," he has been trying to get the edge on nature by improving on her methods. Systems of development that she has taken thousands of years to bring about are much too slow for him.

One such possibility of improvement is by means of heterosis or "hybrid vigor." This is the conditon in which the first generation hybrid shows more vigor than either of the parent strains.

One good example of this is the mule, which is the result of a cross between the horse and ass, the product of which gives us an animal that magnifies some of the useful qualities of each parent.

Heterosis has been utilized in another way known as inbreeding-outbreeding. An excellent example of this is "hybrid corn." Two separate strains of corn are inbred for seven generations. The two strains are then crossed to produce the eighth generation, which is larger, stronger, and more productive than either of the two original strains. However, whatever factor produces this desirable hybrid, it is apparently not inheritable, for the progeny of this eighth generation reverts to a weaker strain. Therefore, in order to maintain hybrid feed corn, the separate strains must be continued separately in their own purity for the ultimate cross to be satisfactory.

However, not every cross produces vigorous offspring. Many hybrids, while displaying desirable characteristics, lack vigor and are infertile.

The botanist has produced plants with hybrid vigor by simply crossing one kind of plant with another. The resultant hybrids have added many new varieties to the plant kingdom, the rose growers alone having used this method to produce thousands of varieties for our enjoyment.

But don't get the idea that producing hybrids is a simple matter. In her march of time, nature has taken many precautions to prevent her populace from becoming a hodge-podge of creatures of highly varied ancestry.

Hybridization in fish comes under two headings:

Intergeneric: The parents are from different but very closely related genera, viz.: crossing *Poecilia sphenops* with *Heterandria formosa*, both livebearing fish. It is impossible to cross a livebearer with an egglaying species.

Interspecific: Fish from the same genus but from two different species. This is the easier to bring about, and has resulted in the many and varied hybrids of the *Xiphophorus* genus.

As a final note, the majority of young produced from these crosses are sterile. Mother Nature in all her wisdom is saying, " So far — but no farther!"

Try to improve your fish, but do it by good selection and breeding practice. Couple this with the correct environment and a suitable diet that will enable the fish to grow and flourish.

Mutations

New features in fishes aren't always inherited. On occasion chromosomes and genes change, not only in their distribution ratio during maturation and fertilization but also in themselves. If these changes can then be inherited, they are referred to as mutations.

Mutations are mistakes, and the majority of them are either degenerative or lethal. Almost any change affecting the normalcy of the body's chemistry usually upsets the delicate balance of the entire organism with disastrous results. But sometimes a mutation works for the good, resulting in a new variety. The hi-fin Swords and Platies are examples. They are similar in form and color to the normal varieties but have long, flowing fins. In the Angelfish, mutations have resulted in change of finnage and color, and a black Molly was produced that sported a lyre-shaped tail — all welcomed by the hobbyist as new additions to the aquaria.

These changes, when they occur, don't often announce themselves with banner headlines. They might manifest themselves in just the odd fish in a brood that differs ever so slightly from the normal. Here the observant fishkeeper knows his fish scores, and by planned breeding procedure can use this change to produce something new.

Not all mutations occur by accident. Artificial changes can be produced by bombarding the fish with Gamma and X-rays, others by treatment with certain chemicals. Even subjecting fishes to extremes of temperature has caused these changes.

Selective Breeding

To improve your strains of fish do some selective breeding. Choose where possible superior fish to sire the progeny. Cull the resulting brood ruthlessly, removing all runts, malformed fishes and sickly specimens from the tank. They must be kept from interbreeding at maturity.

Sometimes an undesirable trait in one or the other parent cannot be seen because it is recessive, but if and when it shows up in a second or third generation, the parent fish as well as the offspring should never be bred from again.

This is why it is wise to keep accurate records of parentage, source, etc. Though the word "pedigree" isn't often associated with fishkeeping, we must have these facts for selective breeding. The specialist breeder is already proving the worth of accurate genetical knowledge. Fish specialists studying the Guppy, Killifish, Goldfish, and many other species have, over the years, greatly advanced our knowledge. The devotion displayed by these enthusiasts has proved that to breed fish successfully one doesn't have to be a professional or have academic training. Most of today's improved aquarium species have been produced by amateurs.

If all this sounds like a lot of hard work, I can assure you that it isn't. Don't be discouraged by early failure. The joy of raising your own fish is worth any effort; and, if you are fortunate enough to produce a new mutant (and reproduce it), the sky is the limit!

A well planted, well stocked aquarium.

XI Selecting the Fish

With most of the ingredients of our "living picture" now ready, we arrive at what I consider to be the *"pièce de résistance"* of the whole recipe — selecting the fishes and stocking the tank with them.

Exactly how many fish to choose will depend on the amount of money available, the size of the tank, and even the species you choose. To clarify the last statement we must bear in mind that most fish offered for sale are young specimens. They are all probably about one inch in length, but their adult sizes can vary from two to ten inches, depending on the species. Whatever your choice, you must allow them room to grow and not commence by stocking the tank to its capacity. Don't go by the amount of fish seen in the dealer's tanks; he usually overcrowds for economic reasons.

The old rule of allowing one inch of fish to each gallon of water is quite a sound one. Because this calculation tends to confuse the beginner, it may be better to explain to the dealer the size of your tank and let him recommend the number. He is in the advantageous position of being able to calculate adult size, recommending amounts based on his experience in these matters. Fish are measured from the nose tip to the end of the body or caudal peduncle; sizes given do not include the length of the tail.

The term "community aquarium" implies a varied collection of fishes. This isn't really necessary. Some of the nicest aquariums I have seen contained but one or two varieties.

The following notes will help you when stocking the tank:

(a) **Environment:** Most stores, through lack of tank space, tend to keep more than one type of fish in their tanks. Tanks containing two, three, or even more species are common. Fishes in these tanks usually have similar water and temperature requirements. Avoid the fishes which require special conditions such as extreme acidity or high temperature. A pH range of between 6.8 and 7.4, plus temperatures from 72 ° F to 78 ° F are fine for most.

(b) **Disease:** Healthy fish will be active, show good color, and have clear, clean finnage. Certain diseases like ich and fungus can be seen as either white spots or cotton or wool-like growths on body and fins. Examine the fish carefully, and refuse any specimens not up to par.

(c) **Individual Species:** Be fair to the person whose job it is to capture the fish you choose. Most dealers will permit you to point out the particular fish you want; in that way he gets a satisfied customer. But don't expect him to single out one particular fish from a tankful of fast, schooling swimmers. Netting just one fish in that case can be quite a feat!

(d) **Size:** Find out just what size the fish will grow to. The Oscar or Velvet Cichlid *(Astronotus ocellatus)* is a beautiful and attractive specimen at one inch but, fully grown, can reach up to ten inches. Such fishes are not for the community aquarium. Leave the "monsters" for the specialist, or be prepared to give them individual aquaria.

(e) **Balance:** Though all fishes may be found all over the tank from time to time, each species will generally frequent particular "layers." These fishes can be separated into classifications of top, middle, and bottom dwellers. Consider this in your collection and try to include some from each group. For example, Hatchetfishes of the genus

Carnegiella prefer the surface area, while *Corydoras* catfish are more likely to be on the bottom.

(f) **Sexes:** Most of the specimens for sale will be young, and because of this, except for the livebearers, they will be difficult if not impossible to sex. Nevertheless, try to create a balance of males and females; in the case of the livebearers, two females to each male will insure that one female can rest from the attentions of the active male. Never mix male Fighting Fish *(Betta splendens)* together. One male per tank is enough.

(g) **Imported or Home-Bred?:** Both of these categories will be included in the fishes for sale, and with today's improved methods of transportation, imported specimens soon settle down and become acclimatized. The advantage of locally bred species is that they have been born and raised in water similar to that existing in your tank.

Bringing the Fish Home

Most aquatic establishments will pack your fishes in either plastic bags or wax containers. So long as the fishes aren't overcrowded and there is twice as much air as water in the container, the fish can remain in these apparently confined spaces for quite long periods.

Seeing the dealer fasten the neck of the fish bag seems to cause concern to most beginners, and the question arises, " How will they breathe? Don't worry! Remember, fishes breathe the oxygen which is dissolved in water. The air above the water will allow a gaseous exchange for quite some time. Many dealers today express the air from the bag and replace it with pure oxygen. This enables the fishes to remain in the bag for longer periods of time. The containers of fish can be carried home in just a paper sack, but if a long journey is necessary, and particularly if the weather is cold, it is better to put them in a strong cardboard or styrofoam box insulated with newspaper. In the car, do not put the fish bags in the direct air flow of the car heater, as the water may get too hot and the fish die.

On arrival home, float the containers in the tank for a few minutes to let the two water temperatures become equal. Never subject fish to more than a two-degree rapid change of temperature.

Now, gently tip the bags and allow a little of the tank water and that in the container to intermix. Then, holding the mouth of the bag open, allow the fish to swim out. *Never dump the fishes into the tank!*

Given this freedom, the fishes will usually make a bee-line for cover, but their curiosity soon gets the better of them and out they come to investigate their new home. A little live food introduced at this stage will quicken the acclimatizing process.

Quarantine precautions are almost unnecessary with the first batch of fish, but future purchases should be placed in quarantine. This will allow you to examine them and check on whether they are harboring any disease.

Bullies

Every tank will soon boast its "king" when the fish develop an order of precedence called "pecking order," and, as in human society, a bully may manifest himself from time to time. At the worst, this aggressive action reveals itself in torn and ripped fins. Don't tolerate this type of behavior. Remove the offender immediately and float it in a jar until you can give it to a friend, or sell it to the dealer who can place it with bigger fish that will compensate for its actions. But don't confuse bullying with the vigorous courting procedures displayed by some species.

The best time to look for bullying behavior is about an hour after the evening feed: turn out the tank lights but leave a light on in the room so the tank is barely illuminated. These are the conditions the "bully" loves and he will soon start his antics.

Some species, like the cichlids and Fighting Fish, choose a particular area of the tank and regard this as their domain, defending it against intrusion from other fish. Though this defensive pose may look like bullying, it is usually only a flurry of movement and often does no harm to those concerned.

Pictures of the following 19 fishes are included here for identification purposes. These fishes are not in the Catalog, but are included in the Index by common name, and details of their characteristics may be found under the "Index by Scientific Name." They are listed alphabetically.

Alestes longipinnis — Longfinned Characin.

Alestopetersius caudalis —Yellow Congo Characin.(Female above.)

Aphyosemion cognatum — Redspeckled Killy.

Barbus ticto — Two Spot Barb, or Tic-Tac-Toe Barb.

Copeina arnoldi — Spraying Characin.

Corydoras elegans — Elegant Corydoras.

Corydoras paleatus — Peppered Corydoras.

Dermogenys pusillus — Halfbeak (albino
female).

Doras hancocki — Talking Catfish, or
Spiny Catfish.

Heterandria formosa — Mosquito Fish, or Dwarf Top Minnow. (Female left, male right.)

Hyphessobrycon callistus — Serpae Tetra. (Male left, female right.)

Hyphessobrycon roberti — Robert's Tetra. (Female left, male right.)

Hyphessobrycon rosaceus — Rosy Tetra, or Black Flag Tetra. (Immature specimens; female above, male below.)

Misgurnus anguillicaudatus — Japanese Weatherfish.

Osteoglossum bicirrhosum — Arowana.

BRAZ WALKER

Pimelodella gracilis — Slender Catfish.

Synodontis angelicus — Polkadot Catfish.

Aequidens portalegrensis — Porthole Acara. (Female left, male right.)

Xenomystus nigri — Black Knife Fish.

XII   Fish Catalog

Between 1500 and 2000 species, subspecies, and varieties of fishes have passed through, or are being kept in tropical fish hobbyist's aquariums throughout the world. Obviously, it is beyond the scope of a beginner's book to list and fully describe all of these species. Many of them are rare, others are difficult to keep, while still others lack color, have bad habits, or for other reasons are not popular.

In this catalog of fishes the author intends to list and briefly describe those fishes which are most suitable for the home aquarium and most likely to be available to the hobbyist. For the convenience of the hobbyist the Families are listed alphabetically although scientifically it is not usually done this way.

The descriptions are necessarily brief and incomplete. However, the author believes that they will be of value to the hobbyist since they emphasize those details which will be most useful in recognizing the fish and in differentiating it from similar species.

The discussion of care also is limited to those features and requirements most likely to be of use to the hobbyist in maintaining and breeding the species. The sizes given are the maximum known for the species. Many will breed at considerably smaller sizes, and in many cases, the sizes given are applicable to fishes grown in a natural state; fishes grown in aquariums often mature at a considerably smaller size. The sex distinctions given are not necessarily the only ones, but those most likely to be noticeable to the hobbyist.

In general, sexing is done by an experienced observer on the basis of the overall appearance of the fish. With time and practice, it becomes almost intuitive. The author knows many old time aquarists who glance at a fish and say it is either a male or a female but, when pressed for a reason, they are honestly unable to specify.

In addition to this catalog of fishes and in order to extend the usefulness of this book, the author has prepared a chart listing some common varieties of fishes and their outstanding characteristics.

While some of the material may appear redundant to that given in the catalog, the purpose of the chart is to provide a ready reference of information which is quickly available in a very limited space. The catalog is designed for more leisurely and more detailed reading.

It is arranged alphabetically according to family, genus and species. It is supplemented by a list of common names and their scientific equivalents at the end of the book.

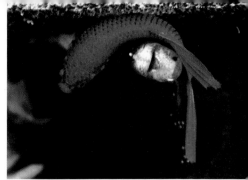

Betta splendens — Siamese Fighting Fish. Shown here in the mating embrace, the eggs are clearly visible as they drop.

Family ANABANTIDAE

Labyrinth Fishes

The anabantids are found both in Africa and southern Asia. They are distinguished by a special structure in the head which serves as an accessory breathing organ, from which they derive their name of "labyrinth fishes." This special adaptation permits labyrinth fishes to exist in waters which are deficient in oxygen. The most common illustration of this is the row of "Betta jars" so frequently seen at tropical fish dealers. These jars may hold anywhere from three ounces to a quart of water, and within each one is an individual Siamese Fighting Fish, not at all perturbed by the lack of surface area or the closeness of its quarters.

Every few minutes they rise majestically to the surface, leisurely gulping a mouthful of air; as they slowly sink, the exhausted air may be seen emerging as a bubble from their gills.

The majority of anabantids are so-called "bubble-nest builders." Sometimes the male, sometimes both parents, build a raft of bubbles at the surface. Frequently, this is free-floating, but many species prefer to anchor it to the plants. The eggs are deposited within this nest and usually guarded by the male, although occasionally the female will participate. As a rule, the female had best be removed, particularly if the male shows any signs of belligerence. Commercial breeders remove both parents in order to insure maximum hatching and rearing. However, for the aquarist one of the delights of tropical fish-breeding is watching the care and attention lavished on the young by the parent. After all, our aquarium is being kept primarily for pleasure, not for profit.

Most of the anabantids, originating as they do in hot, humid climates, prefer temperatures above 75° F, perhaps closer to 80° F. Their aquarium should also be well covered to establish a warm

129

humid area above the water surface. With the exception of the Siamese Fighting Fish *(Betta splendens),* the majority of anabantids we are likely to encounter are fair to good community fishes and may be kept together. However, when they begin to show signs of pairing off, the happy couple had best be removed to a separate aquarium for breeding. The size of the aquarium, of course, is determined by the species. For example, *Colisa lalia,* or Dwarf Gourami, will feel perfectly at home in a five-gallon aquarium, while *Trichogaster trichopterus,* or Three-Spot Gourami, will require at least a fifteen to twenty gallon aquarium. Some of the signs of spawning are increased color, a tendency to frequent one corner of the aquarium from which other fishes are being driven, and, of course, the building of the bubble-nest. Once the bubble-nest is built, the normal procedure is for the male, using a combination of enticement and drive, to bring the female underneath the nest where the eggs are laid and fertilized during the embrace. Certain anabantids, such as the Dwarf Gourami, lay eggs which are lighter than water and will float up into the nest. It is interesting to note that those species which lay these light eggs will always maneuver so that they are directly under the nest during the embrace. The eggs of other species, such as the Betta, are heavier and will sink to the bottom.

The female floats torpidly after the embrace, the eggs being gathered up by the male and spat into the nest. The embrace may be repeated a number of times over a period of hours. Egg-laying completed, the parent which is to do the guarding takes up its position under the nest and drives off all intruders. At a temperature of 80° F, hatching usually occurs within approximately thirty hours. The young hang vertically under the nest, absorbing their egg yolk. In another twenty-four to forty-eight hours they become free-swimming, at which time they require the finest of fine foods such as rotifers, algae, and other single-celled organisms. There are several commercial dried foods on the market prepared specifically for this type of fry. In another two or three days, the young should have grown enough to have graduated to newly-hatched brine shrimp, microworms, strained Daphnia, etc.

Care should be taken not to disturb the parents during the breeding period, as otherwise they may forget their parental duties to the extent of eating the eggs or young. Temperature is also important during this period, as the fry are particularly sensitive to chills. Suprisingly enough, the fry are not born with the labyrinth. Its formation takes place several weeks after hatching, and until the time it is fully developed and activated the fry is dependent upon water absorbed through the gills, just as are the fry of other fishes.

One other point of interest regarding the anabantids; for a long time it was believed (and still is, by some people) that because of the labyrinth the anabantid is restricted to breathing only atmospheric oxygen. That is not true. An anabantid, cut off from the surface, has no problem surviving.

A magnificent specimen of the *Betta*.

Betta splendens — Siamese Fighting Fish

Originally imported from Malaya and Thailand, the Siamese Fighting Fish has a body length not much over two to two and one-half inches. The full magnificence of the Siamese Fighting Fish or, as it is more usually called, the *Betta,* is in the intense coloration and magnificent finnage which adorn a show specimen like the sails of a full-rigged ship. The original *Betta* was a dark purplish red fish, although occasionally a few color variations, noticeably the Cambodia (red fins on a white body), have been found. Today, almost all the hues of the rainbow are being bred ranging from a cellophane *Betta,* which is white with clear fins, through reds, blues, greens, lavenders, purples, and up to an almost black *Betta.* The female, however, unfortunately does not carry either the extreme coloration of the male nor his finnage. She resembles, even in spite of all the

131

efforts of breeders, the original wild *Betta,* although she has increased slightly in size.

The name " Fighting Fish" is somewhat of a misnomer. While it is true that this fish will fight other males of his own species like a gamecock, he is relatively peaceful and slow-moving when kept in a community aquarium and rarely bothers other fishes. In fact, he is more often sinned against than sinning, his gorgeous draperies furnishing a target for some of the nippier fishes. Nor will two male fighting fish, as a rule, fight to the death. Usually, the fight ends with the loser fleeing. Of course, in a small aquarium there is no place for him to hide and he may eventually be killed. In their native home of Thailand, they are used for sport, wagers being laid on the outcome of a fight. In Bangkok, the capitol of Thailand, almost every tourist stop has a hawker offering to show tourists the Fighting Fish in combat for a fee. His fish are not really select specimens, but nondescript fishes picked up just for the purpose of entertaining the tourists. The show they put on usually leaves much ferocity to be desired.

GENE WOLFSHEIMER

Two *Bettas* in swirling combat.

Breeding takes place as given in the general description for the anabantids, except that the male and female should not be put together except for breeding purposes. At other times, each male should be isolated or just one male kept in the community aquarium. The females, which are not belligerent, may be kept together or with other fishes.

Siamese Fighting Fish display their finest colors during breeding or when facing another male. Owners of these exotic fishes put a small mirror in the aquarium when they want their fish to display their finery.

Colisa fasciata — Giant Gourami.

Colisa fasciata —Giant Gourami or Striped or Bearded Gourami

Hailing from India and Thailand, this interesting and lovely Gourami is misnamed — he is not really a giant. Seldom reaching a length of five inches, he will breed at only three inches. A deep-bodied fish, the anal fins like those of related genera, *Osphronemus* and *Trichogaster,* are elongated to form long thread-like feelers which serve as tactile organs. Unfortunately, this is one fish which does not show at its best until it has been established in an aquarium for some time. Typically, in a dealer's tank, it appears to be basically a silvery fish, perhaps with some light-brown or bluish vertical barring. However, kept in an old, established aquarium and fed a nourishing diet, the stripes become alternately dark blue and brown with a brilliant sheen. The eye gleams bright red. This is a deep-bodied fish. The sexes may be distinguished by the longer and more pointed fins of the male.

Colisa labiosa — Thick-lipped Gourami. Shown here in the process of spawning, this species prefers to anchor its bubble nest among floating plants.

Colisa labiosa — **Thick-lipped Gourami**

Coming from southern Burma, the Thick-lipped closely resembles the Giant Gourami in shape and coloration, but it is considerably smaller, attaining a length of only three inches. Like the Giant Gourami, it suffers from a misnomer. The lips are not actually noticeably thicker than that of other fishes of its type, although they do have a black ring which gives them an appearance of thickness. A somewhat retiring fish requiring high temperatures, under proper conditions the Thick-lipped becomes a deep gorgeous blue-black, making it one of the most attractive fishes in the aquarium.

GENE WOLFSHEIMER

Colisa lalia — Dwarf Gourami.

Colisa lalia — **Dwarf Gourami**

In the author's opinion, the Dwarf Gourami and the Honeycomb Gourami must certainly vie for honors as the most beautiful of the anabantids, and certainly among the most beautiful of the aquarium fishes. However, where the Honeycomb reveals its coloring only under ideal conditions, the Dwarf Gourami consistently shows his alternately red and green vertical zig-zag stripes. This, together with a brilliant-blue breast and a gentle disposition, make him a must in almost any collection of mixed fishes. The female, unfortunately, does not display quite the brilliant coloring of the male although she is quite attractive in her own right. A deep-bodied fish, the Dwarf Gourami only reaches a length of two to two and one-half inches.

Colisa chuna — Honeycomb Gourami.

Colisa chuna — **Honeycomb Gourami**

A fairly recent introduction from India, the Honeycomb is somewhat slimmer than the Dwarf Gourami, but approximately the same length — two to two and one-half inches. Beautiful, even when not displaying, the male is a dark brownish-red with a blue throat and chest, the color of which extends into the anal fin. Under ideal conditions, which include a high temperature and a well-planted aquarium, the red becomes a brilliant golden-red, and the blues glow with an electric quality which must be seen to be believed.

Helostoma rudolfi — Kissing Gourami

Helostoma rudolfi — **Kissing Gourami**

Ranging extensively through southeast Asia, the Kissing Gourami reaches the rather large size (large, that is, for a popular aquarium fish) of up to ten inches. They are not very colorful, being a uniform light-pink or flesh-colored, with black eyes. The main reason that they are kept is the odd habit which gives them their name. Two kissers will pucker up and apparently osculate, sometimes holding that position for several minutes at a time. However, two males will indulge in the practice as will two females. In fact, it is even doubtful as to whether they are kissing, transferring food, or engaging in a kind of combat. It is interesting to watch, and the fish is fairly hardy if the water is kept at 75°F or above. Further, they do clean algae from the aquarium and are peaceful. For these reasons alone, they are well worth a place in our community tank.

A closely related species is *Helostoma temmincki,* or Green Kissing Gourami. These are imported from Bangkok and are a lovely pale-green with a black vertical band outlining the caudal peduncle.

A. VAN DEN NIEUWENHUIZEN

Macropodus opercularis — Paradisefish. (Both males.)

Macropodus opercularis — Paradisefish

Although several species of *Macropodus* have been kept in the aquarium from time to time, the red Paradisefish and an albino version are the only ones which have achieved any degree of popularity. One of the earliest, if not the first, tropical fish kept in an aquarium, the Paradisefish is hardy and interesting. It is one of the few anabantids which doesn't mind a low temperature, frequently surviving as low as 40°F. They are ideal parents, breeding in typical anabantid fashion, both caring for the fry. The author has frequently seen aquaria in which several broods of young have been raised, and it is interesting to watch both parents caring for a nest containing eggs while the preceding, free-swimming batch swarms about.

Unfortunately, however, the male Paradisefish only shows his beautiful blue and brick-red colors during breeding, being rather drab at other times. Also, he is inclined to be belligerent with smaller fishes although this belligerency has been exaggerated. All in all, however, it is a fish worth keeping by the beginner with adequate room. The fins of the male are extremely long and pointed, the anal and caudal in particular, extending into trailing filaments.

Chocolate Gourami.
Sphaerichthys osphromenoides —

A. VAN DEN NIEUWENHUIZEN

Sphaerichthys osphromenoides — Chocolate Gourami

A rather attractive fish from Sumatra and Malaya, the Chocolate Gourami may reach a length of three inches. The color is variable, usually a chocolate-brown with several narrow ivory or yellow vertical bands. They are rather delicate in captivity, being especially susceptible to velvet infection. There is some question as to whether they are bubble-nest builders, or mouth-breeders. One report in the literature cites them as building a bubble-nest, whereas several others claim they have been seen carrying eggs or young in the mouth.

Trichogaster leeri — Pearl or Mosaic Gourami

One of the few larger fishes which may be safely kept with almost any size neighbour. Coming from southeast Asia, the Pearl Gourami reaches a length of almost five inches, but will breed at three. When in breeding colors, the male exhibits a deep orange breast which has caused it, at times, to be called the Red-breasted Gourami. Basically, the body color is a light-lavender with an overall opalescent or pearl

A. VAN DEN NIEUWENHUIZEN

Trichogaster leeri —
Pearl or Mosaic Gourami.

gleam. A fine black zig-zag line extends from the mouth, through the eye, ending in a black spot at the base of the tail. The entire body and into the fins is covered with a series of dark reticulated markings from which it derives its name, Mosaic Gourami. Both parents frequently participate in caring for the nest and young. The fins of the male are extremely elongated, particularly the anal and dorsal.

GENE WOLFSHEIMER

Trichogaster microlepis — Moonlight Gourami. (Male above — female below.)

Trichogaster microlepis — **Moonlight Gourami**

This is a fairly recent introduction from Thailand which reaches a length of almost six inches. In spite of its large size and its rather quiet coloration, it is a uniform smooth silvery gray-blue. The Moonlight Gourami appears destined for popularity. In spite of its size it is quite peaceful.

GENE WOLFSHEIMER

Trichogaster trichopterus — Three Spot Gourami. (Male above — female below.)

Trichogaster trichopterus — **The Three-spot or Blue Gourami**

A long-time favorite, this is another fairly large importation from southeast Asia, reaching a length of six inches. The coloring is a rather dull, medium-dark gray-blue. The name was given because there is one spot in the center on the body, one at the base of the tail, and the eye forms the third. At one time quite popular, it has largely been replaced by aquarium strains such as the Blue Gourami, which is similar in size and shape but a much more colorful blue.

The Blue Gourami. (Female left — male right.)

The Opaline or Cosby Gourami is merely a sport or mutant originating from the Blue Gourami. It resembles the Blue Gourami in size, form, and breeding behavior, the major difference being the dark blue, somewhat iridescent markings which overlay the basic blue body coloration.

Opaline or Cosby Gourami. (These are immature fish and the fins have not yet developed sufficiently to indicate their sex. At this point, they both look like females.)

Abramites microcephalus –
Marble Headstander.

Family ANOSTOMIDAE

Abramites microcephalus — **Marble Headstander**

A rather large (up to five inch) fish from the lower Amazon, with a distinctive nose-down swimming posture. Poorly defined, broad brown-gray and light ivory-yellow bands are found over the body. It is a fairly hardy fish, but is apt to be quarrelsome, particularly with others of its species.

BARRY PENGILLEY

Anostomus anostomus — Striped Anos-tomus.

Anostomus anostomus — **Striped Anostomus**

This slim five inch fish has three dark stripes, running the length of the body, which are interspersed with lighter lines. The fins are bright-red in good specimens. Although not usually quarrelsome, it is a large fish best kept with others of equal size. Its habitat is near the headwaters of the Amazon.

Chilodus punctatus — Pearl Headstander.

Chilodus punctatus — **Pearl Headstander**

Ranging throughout northern South America, this is a medium-sized (up to three inch), attractive and peaceful, although unfortunately, somewhat delicate aquarium fish. The ground color is a pearl to light-purple. The scales are large, each scale being marked by a dark-brown spot, which gives the fish an unusual appearance.

Leporinus fasciatus — Banded Leporinus.

Leporinus fasciatus — **Banded Leporinus**

This is a very attractive fish with its broad, alternating bands of black and yellow. It is widely distributed in South America, although there is some difference in shading according to the locality where it was collected. Small specimens tend to be delicate, but larger ones grow to thirteen inches and are very hardy. This fish is a great leaper and has been known to rise from the water with such force that it injured itself by striking the aquarium cover. Large specimens will eat plants.

Leporinus striatus — Striped Leporinus. Widely distributed in northern South America, east of the Andes, immature specimens are similar in appearance to *Anostomus anostomus*. As it has been known to reach a length of ten inches it is suitable only for larger aquariums.

141

Family CALLICHTHYIDAE

Armored Catfishes

This family is restricted in distribution to the northern two-thirds of South America. Characteristic of the family is the presence of heavy, overlapping scales. Bottom dwellers, the *Callichthyidae* have an adaptation permitting them to breathe atmospheric oxygen with which to supplement that absorbed through the action of the gills. By far the greatest number of varieties in the family are found in the genus *Corydoras*. These droll little fellows are usually known as dwarf catfishes because few of them attain a length greater than two and one-half to three inches. It is interesting to watch them dart to the surface and gulp in a mouthful of air. Unlike the anabantids, whose breathing organ is located in the head, the *Callichthyidae* swallow the air and absorb the oxygen as it passes through the intestine. Because the *Callichthyidae* have been called "scavengers" and frequent the bottom layer of the aquarium, it does not mean that they do not require careful feeding. No catfish can eat droppings, or waste matter from other fishes; in fact, they create their own. Their value as scavengers lies in the fact that they grub ceaselessly over the bottom, searching for those bits of food overlooked and uneaten by other fishes which, if left to rot, would provide a focal point for contamination of the aquarium. Two Corydoras should be kept to each five gallons of aquarium water. They will, by digging actively into the upper layers of the gravel, even root out and remove Tubifex worms which have established themselves. These hide in the gravel and cannot be reached by most fishes.

Sexing Corydoras. The male is on the left.

ALBERT KLEE

A word of caution when handling catfishes: the leading spine of the dorsal and pectoral fins is extremely rigid, sharp and strong. The fish can erect and lock these fins into place, and a jab from one of them can be quite painful, the pain persisting out of all proportion to the extent of the puncture.

Corydoras have been bred in the aquarium, although spawning is not frequent. After a characteristic dance, the male embraces the female, who then places several large eggs against a flat surface such as the aquarium glass or a rock. While apparently there is no parental care, the adults do not destroy their eggs unless hungry. The eggs hatch in five to eight days in an average temperature of 70°F.

One member of the *Callichthyidae, Callichthys callichthys,* builds a bubble nest which is looked after by the male.

Albino varieties of *Corydoras aeneus* or Bronze Corydoras and *Corydoras paleatus* or Peppered Corydoras have been developed and are frequently available to aquarists.

A. VAN DEN NIEUWENHUIZEN

Corydoras aeneus —
Bronze Corydoras. (Male)

Corydoras arcuatus —
Skunk Catfish. (Male above.)

Corydoras aeneus — Bronze Corydoras

This is a plain, greenish bronze *Corydoras,* and one of the hardiest of its genus.

Corydoras arcuatus — or Arched Corydoras

One of the prettiest of the *Corydoras.* The body is clear-ivory varying to light-beige in some specimens, but the distinctive mark is a black band which begins at the tip of the head and follows the arch of the back to the root of the tail. Here, it joins a transverse bar on the caudal peduncle and then continues along the lower edge of the tail. It is reported to be somewhat more delicate than other members of the genus.

Corydoras elegans — Elegant Corydoras

One of the smaller *Corydoras,* seldom reaching two inches in length, *elegans* is also slimmer than most *Corydoras.* The sides are light-yellow to light-gray, with the upper portion somewhat darker. It has a dark band along the side, with another lighter band below in a row of dark spots. The gill cover is a shiny, bright blue. It is notable for the oddity of its markings rather than for any particularly pretty coloration.

Corydoras hastatus — Dwarf or Pigmy Corydoras. (Two females.)

Corydoras hastatus — Dwarf or Pigmy Corydoras

This is the smallest of the *Corydoras,* growing only a little more than an inch in length. In fact, to those unfamiliar with the species, it doesn't seem to be a *Corydoras* at all, as rather than remaining on the bottom, it swims freely about the aquarium with a dainty darting motion. One characteristic is the stripe running from the gill cover and ending in an oval blotch at the root of the tail.

Corydoras julii — Leopard Corydoras

This species derives its popular name both from its markings and

Corydoras julii —
Leopard Corydoras. (Male above.)

from its former scientific name of *Corydoras leopardus*. The body color is a light silvery-gray varying to lavender; the tail is barred. There is a stripe consisting of a series of dots along the lateral line, numerous small dark dots all over the body and head, and a prominent dark tip to the dorsal fin.

Corydoras melanistius — Blackspotted
Corydoras. (Sex indeterminate.)

Corydoras melanistius — Blackspotted Corydoras

Superficially, this fish resembles the Leopard Corydoras. However, it may be distinguished by the following: the dorsal fin is more triangular and does not have the black tip, there is a black blotch on the body just below the forward edge of the dorsal fin, and a black vertical bar covers the head, commencing just behind the mouth and reaching upward through the eye, ending in a point at the edge of the dorsal.

Corydoras metae — Bandit Catfish or Masked Corydoras

This is one of the more recent importations from British Guiana. More chunky than most *Corydoras,* the Bandit Catfish resembles *arcuatus* in ground coloring. However, the stripe which on *arcuatus* follows the line of the back, extends only from the base of the tail to the dorsal fin in the *metae.* In addition, there is a vertical bar across the head through the eyes, giving it its popular name.

Corydoras punctatus — Spotted Corydoras.

GENE WOLFSHEIMER

Corydoras punctatus — Spotted Corydoras

Superficially, this fish resembles the Leopard Catfish and the Blackspotted Corydoras. However, the spot markings on *punctatus* are much larger.

Hoplosternum thoracatum — Hoplo Cat

Heavily armored, *Hoplosternum* is found throughout the Amazon Basin and northern South America. Hoplo Cats, as they are commonly known, reach a length of seven to eight inches in nature, but seldom attain that length in the aquarium. Usually, they breed when between three to four inches. Like *Callicthys callicthys* they are bubble-nest builders, the male caring for the eggs and young.

A. VAN DEN NIEUWENHUIZEN

Hoplosternum thoracatum — Hoplo Cat. (Male.)

They are rather drab in color, a dark olive-brown with a lighter stomach, the young being covered with numerous black dots which make them quite attractive. As the young grow, the dots rearrange themselves so that they finally appear as narrow bands on the adult.

Chanda ranga — Indian Glassfish. (Male)

Family CENTROPOMIDAE

Glassfishes

While there are several glassfishes known to science, only one of this family is commonly seen in the aquarium, and that is *Chanda ranga,* or Indian Glassfish. A slow-moving, gentle fish, it has struck the imagination of aquarists and writers with its transparent glasslike body. In spite of this apparent delicacy, it is quite hardy. The males seem to reflect the light with a gold-to-orange-to-purple hue, making them quite attractive.

Family CHARACIDAE

The Characins

From the point of view of variety, the Characins contribute the greatest number of species to our aquarium, varying from the lovely and peaceful Neon Tetra to the vicious Piranha. Most Characins are found in South America, where they range south almost to the tip and northwards through Central America up into Mexico and Texas. A few Characins are also found in Africa. There have been none found in Asia, Europe or Australia.

Many of the Characins are similar in appearance to barbs, but no Characins possess the barbels, which are fleshy appendages around the mouth. Most but not all Characins have a small fin called an "adipose fin" between the dorsal and caudal. This, however, is not exclusive with Characins. For the most part, the scales of the Characins are small, mirror-like, and semi-translucent. Many Characins have the addition of the word "tetra" to their name, such as the Cardinal Tetra, Buenos Aires Tetra, Black Tetra, etc. This is a holdover from a time when a group of the smaller Characins were classified as *Tetragonopterus,* or tetra for short. The classification is now reduced to a subfamily, but the name lingers on as applied to the entire family. Two of the genera in the family *Characidae* have now been classified as belonging to the subfamily *Tetragonopterinae,* from which they derive the common name of "tetra." These fishes are distinguished in the most part by being relatively small and deep-bodied, rather than extremely elongated.

For the most part, Characins prefer extremely soft, acid water. While they will tolerate quite a variation in water conditions, they will show their best colors and breed most freely when the pH is below 6.5 and the hardness in the water less than two to three degrees. In common with other fishes from the tropical regions, they are stimulated by frequent partial changes of water. Use of a peat filter or the addition of peat water is recommended.

Most of the Characins are typical egg scatterers with no parental care being assumed. For the most part, they prefer living in groups, rather than pairs, and tend to be carnivorous. The regular feeding of dried food should be supplemented by the addition of live foods such as Tubifex, brine shrimp, or Daphnia to the diet at least once or twice a week

A few species exercise elaborate incubation procedures, notably the Spraying Characin or *Copeina arnoldi.* Other exceptions are *Mimagoniates* and *Corynopoma.* These two genera, although egglayers as are all Characins, are fertilized internally like the livebearers. The difference is that these unique Characins do not hold the eggs within their body until the young have developed.

Among the hundreds of Characins large and small, relatively few are found in our aquariums. This is because some are rare, some are delicate, some are unsuited to life in the community aquarium, and many of them are plain silver fishes not usually considered attractive enough to be worth keeping. Among the thousands of fishes found throughout the fresh waters of the world, relatively few have all the desirable characteristics which enable them to find favor with the aquarist. Those fishes which do achieve popularity do so because of their special qualities. Many Characins are difficult to breed in captivity, but are so desirable that each year hundreds of thousands, possibly millions, are imported for the delight of the aquarists of the world.

While it is impossible to list all of them here, the most desirable Characins are as follows:

Anoptichthys jordani — Blind Cave Fish. (Female above.)

GENE WOLFSHEIMER

Anoptichthys jordani — **Blind Cave Tetra**

This is one of the oddities of the fish world. Believed to be derived from a subspecies of the *Astyanax mexicanus* or Mexican Tetra, it has spent so many hundreds or perhaps thousands of generations in lightless caves of Mexico that the eyes have atrophied and it can no longer see. The fish itself is a light pink and rather attractive. In spite of the handicap of blindness, the fish seems to find its way about the aquarium quite well, seldom bumping into obstacles. Perhaps there is some form of built-in radar with which we are not yet familiar. Observers report that the Blind Cave Tetra seems to sheer off as it approaches obstacles which are placed in its way. One theory is that the small bow wave traveling ahead of the fish bounces back as it encounters the obstacle and the reflexes of the fish are fast enough to allow it to change course in time. Lending credence to this theory is the fact that if you hold a net with the bag open in the water, the restless ever-moving Blind Cave Tetra will swim into it. (Move fast or he will just swing around and swim right out again.) But if you chase the fish with the net it is as difficult to capture as some of the sighted fishes. Obviously, it can sense the current created by the movement of the net in the water.

Unfortunately, the Blind Cave Tetra has been known to nip fins and must be watched when left with smaller fishes.

Aphyocharax rubripinnis — Bloodfin.

Aphyocharax rubripinnis — **Bloodfin**

This is another of the many small delightful Characins. Under good conditions the body gleams with a pearl to silver-white luster while the fins are deep blood red. This small fish, originally from Argentina, grows to about two inches in length. The parents are vigorous breeders, frequently leaping out of the water in their breeding frenzy.

Cheirodon axelrodi — **Cardinal Tetra**

This delightful tetra from Brazil was introduced to aquarists in the 1950's, and closely resembles the Neon with its brilliant green band above the red area. It is easy to distinguish between the two, however,

Cheirodon axelrodi — Cardinal Tetra. (the two upper fish are females, the lower male.)

because the red area covers the entire lower third of the Cardinal Tetra from the lower jaw to the tail. The red of the Neon begins about a quarter of the way back at the pelvic fin, the forward area being white. In addition, the Cardinal is a larger, and especially when mature, heavier bodied fish. Like the Neon, it is an ideal aquarium fish, hardy and inoffensive.

Exodon paradoxus — Buck-tooth Characin

Found from British Guiana to Brazil, this medium-sized (four to six inch) Characin is readily recognized by the large polka dot in the midsection, with a similar one on the caudal peduncle. There is a delicate overlay of pastel colors, which change as the fish moves in relation to the light; and it is a beautiful sight to behold. Unfortunately, this is not matched by the disposition of the fish. Several kept together are usually found circling about, warily eyeing one another. When kept in a community tank they can be vicious fin nippers, and even killers. Frequently imported because of its beauty, it is one of those fishes which had best be kept by itself.

Gymnocorymbus ternetzi — Black Tetra, Blackamoor, or Petticoat Fish

One might gain the impression from the name that this rather small Characin from the Matto Grosso on the Rio Negro is all black. Actually, only the anal fin can really be called black and this primarily is in younger fishes. The black fades to gray as the fish matures. There are also two black vertical bars on the forward part of the body and a black hue throughout. The body is rounded although

Gymnocorymbus ternetzi — Black Tetra, Blackamoor, or Petticoat Fish. (Female above.)

not quite so much so as is the Silver Dollar. The extremely long anal fin which runs from the vent almost to the tail is unusual for this type of small Characin. They breed when approximately one and one-half inches in length. The colors of both sexes are similar, but the mature female is noticeably rounder.

Hemigrammus ocellifer – Beacon Fish, or Head-and-tail-Light Fish. (Female above.)

Hemigrammus ocellifer —
Beacon Fish, or Head-and-tail-Light Fish

Coming from the Amazon Basin in Guiana, this long time favorite is likely to maintain its popularity for many years to come. The most noticeable features are the brilliant eyes (gold below, red above) and the shining spot on the caudal peduncle. These features give the fish its popular name. Viewed under a good light, one can see a fine, almost dotted white line running part way through the center of the anal fin of the male. Otherwise, the sexes may be distinguished by the more robust shape of the female.

Hemigrammus armstrongi — Gold Tetra

The brilliant, burnished appearance of this fish is what gives it its attractiveness, rather than any specific color. Looking more like a newly-minted silver coin rather than the gold color its name would imply, there is an intensely shining spot just above and behind the eye

Hemigrammus armstrongi — Gold Tetras.

as well as another at the base of the body. A school of Gold Tetras chasing each other playfully through the thickets of a well-planted aquarium is a pretty sight, one long to be remembered. Typical for the small tetras, sexing is accomplished by noting the differences in body shape. The gold Tetra attains a length of up to two and one-half inches. Its habitat is Western Guiana.

Hemigrammus caudovittatus —
Tetra from Buenos Aires.(Male)

Hemigrammus caudovittatus — Buenos Aires Tetra

Originally collected from the Plate River near Buenos Aires, Argentina, the Buenos Aires Tetra is one of the oldest of aquarium fishes. However, the aquarium-bred fishes lack much of the color of the newly-imported specimens. It grows fairly large, up to about three inches in length, and is known as a fin nipper and plant chewer. In spite of these drawbacks, it is still worth keeping, particularly with larger fishes, as it is hardy and attractive and requires no special conditions.

Hemigrammus erythrozonus —
Glowlight Tetra. (Male above.)

Hemigrammus erythrozonus — **Glowlight Tetra**

This fish, also often called the Red Neon, was originally collected in British Guiana and is truly one of the jewels of the aquarium world. Similar in shape to but slightly larger than the Neon, the outstanding feature is a golden band which runs from the gill cover to the base of the tail where it broadens out into a gleaming spot. Apparently there are local color variations, as Glowlights collected in different areas of northern South America display varying shades of color ranging from a brassy-gold to a brilliant-red. Habits and care are similar to that required for the other small tetras. However, their breeding behavior is distinguished from similar fishes by the fact that the male and female clasp fins and do a barrel roll while the eggs are being extruded. It grows to two inches. Its habitat is British Guiana.

Hemigrammus pulcher — **Pretty Tetra**

Coming from the middle Amazon, the pulcher is quite similar in shape and appearance to the Head-and-tail-Light, but the pulcher

Hemigrammus pulcher — Pretty Tetra. (Both fish appear to be females.)

can grow to almost two and one-half inches compared to the one and three-quarter inches of the Head-and-tail-Light. Also, the "light" in the eye is not as prominent. There is a rectangular black patch on the caudal area, just below the golden spot. This spot has also caused the fish to be called the Rasbora Tetra.

A. VAN DEN NIEUWENHUIZEN

Hemigrammus rhodostomus — Red or Rummy Nosed Tetra. (Male, left — female, right.)

Hemigrammus rhodostomus — Red or Rummy Nosed Tetra

Coming from the lower Amazon, the Rummy Nosed Tetra is instantly recognizable because its bright, red nose is exactly like the nose of a confirmed drunkard! In fact, in a favorable situation this fish could put *"Rudolph"* to shame. The tail is striped, somewhat like that of the Scissors-tail Rasbora, (*Rasbora trilineata);* although the lobes aren't as long, the black and white striping is more intense. The red coloration is present in both male and female, which are otherwise indistinguishable except for the shape. *H. rhodostomus* grows to about two inches, making it an ideal aquarium fish.

Hyphessobrycon flammeus — Tetra von Rio, or Flame Tetra

A long time favorite in the aquarium, and deservedly so, this rather small, one and one-half to two inch fish is ideal in all respects. Like many characins, it tends to lose color when crowded or disturbed.

However, in soft, acid water and well-fed, particularly with live food, it fairly glows with a bright reddish-orange color from which it

Hyphessobrycon flammeus — Tetra from Rio, or Flame Tetra. (Female above, male below.)

derives the nickname, Flame Tetra. The ventral and anal fins of the male are bordered in black. Very hardy and easily bred, its habitat is the vicinity of Rio de Janeiro.

Hyphessobrycon heterorhabdus — Flag Tetra. (Upper female, lower male.)

Hyphessobrycon heterorhabdus — Flag Tetra

This is named the Flag, or Belgian Flag Fish because a lateral stripe running down its body is bordered with red, yellow, and black, the colors of the Belgian national flag. Although there are no obvious sex distinctions, the female profile is so much more rounded than that of the male that its sexing is not difficult. Its habitat is the lower Amazon.

Hyphessobrycon innesi — Neon Tetra

This is a rather small fish which is adult when approximately one and a half inches in length. Like most characins it prefers a temperature of 70° to 80° F. The Neon Tetra derives its name from the brilliant blue-green band of iridescent color running along the mid-section. This line is not actually fluorescent as it has no internal light of its own, but shines by reflecting overhead light. In the dark, this line

Hyphessobrycon innesi — Neon Tetra.

fades to white, and the red area below which extends from the pelvic fin to the tail fades to a pale pink. The color is regained shortly after the lights are turned on. The Neon is an extremely peaceful fish, but should not be kept with fishes large enough to swallow it. Breeding is difficult and seldom accomplished. However, success has been reported by using extremely soft, acid water. Its habitat is Brazil.

Hyphessobrycon pulchripinnis — Lemon Tetra. (All three fish appear to be males.)

A. VAN DEN NIEUWENHUIZEN

Hyphessobrycon pulchripinnis — **Lemon Tetra**

The Lemon Tetra was imported from South America many years ago, and has proved so adaptable and breeds so freely in captivity that for many years no one has bothered to import wild specimens. Like the Tetra von Rio, the Lemon Tetra is one of those fishes which requires favorable conditions before it will display its delicate and lovely lemon-yellow and black coloration.

One of the outstanding features is its large eyes, the upper half of which are a bright-red. The anal fin of the male is decorated with a broad black margin. The Lemon Tetra grows to about two inches in length.

Hyphessobrycon rubrostigma — Bleeding Heart Tetra. (Male below, female above.)

Hyphessobrycon rubrostigma — Bleeding Heart Tetra, or Tetra Perez

Imported in the 1950's, the Bleeding Heart is similar in shape to the Serpae Tetra. However, it does grow considerably larger, up to three inches; it is also distinguishable from the Serpae by the prominent red marking on the shoulder which gives it its name. Because it is so much larger than the Serpae, an adult Bleeding Heart Tetra may be kept in a mixed community tank of larger fishes. The coloration of the male and female is identical; sexing is done by the differences in the dorsal and anal fin shapes. In the male these are elongated and pointed.

Hyphessobrycon scholzei — Scholze's Tetra, or Blackline Tetra

Originally imported from Brazil, the Blackline Tetra has bred so readily in captivity that today, imported specimens are seldom seen. Unlike some of the other tetras which we have described, the Blackline has no vivid coloration. There is a line which, commencing at the gill cover, runs along the lateral area and terminates in a blotch at the base of the tail, from which the name is derived. However, its neat appearance, good habits and hardiness have earned for it a permanent place in the aquarium. A rather small characin, the Blackline grows to two and one-half inches in length.

Moenkhausia oligolepis — Glass Tetra

This medium-sized characin (up to four and one-half inches in length) is notable particularly for the brilliant eye coloring (which is red above and gold below) and from which the name is derived. The Glass Tetra is extremely hardy and breeds readily. An albino variety, which is also extremely attractive, has been developed with a light-

Moenkhausia oligolepis — Glass Tetra.

pink body and red eyes. This tank-bred development is only semi-albino, as it still retains, although faintly, the shoulder blotches of the normal variety.

Silver Dollars

These are a number of genera of disc-shaped characins, primarily silver in color, from which they derive their popular name. They are found in various parts of South America and some of them grow quite large. *Mylossoma duriventris,* for example, reaches eight inches in diameter.

These are a number of genera of disc-shaped characins, primarily aquarium fishes. Growing to the size they do, they may be kept with some of the larger, more belligerent fishes such as some of the cichlids. There are a few reports of their breeding in captivity but no general sex distinctions are known. It is probable that if more live adult specimens were kept, sex distinctions would be recognized.

Superficially, the Silver Dollars resemble the Piranha because of their ovate shape. However, they may be easily distinguished from their bloodthirsty cousin because they lack the heavy lower·jaw of the Piranha. The principal genera and their distinguishing features are as follows:

Mylossoma species — Silver Dollar. Because of their immaturity it is difficult to determine whether these are *aureum* or *argenteum.*

Metynnis species — Red Spot Silver Dollar.

Myloplus rubripinnis — Red Hook Silver Do

Micralestes interruptus — Congo Tetra. (Male above, female below.)

Metynnis: This is the largest genus, containing about twenty-two species. The adipose fin is more elongated than that of the other Silver Dollars.

Myloplus: The anal fin of *Myloplus* is elongated, forming a distinctive sickle shape. The adipose is small, the dorsal elongated.

Mylossoma: The two principal species are *argenteum* and *duriventris.* The anal fin is rounded, the outer edge forming almost a half-moon shape; the adipose fin is small.

Micralestes interruptus — Congo Tetra

This is the African characin most commonly imported and offered for sale, although occasionally *Alestes longipinnis* or Longfinned Characin and *Alestopetersius caudalis* or Yellow Congo Characin are seen.

It is a medium-sized (to about three inches) fish, commonly found throughout the Congo Basin. Unfortunately, the smaller specimens lack the delicate green-gold of the adult. Given soft, acid water and an ample supply of live or high-protein food, it will bloom and reveal itself as one of the most beautiful of our aquarium fishes. The male is particularly beautiful, with pronounced coloring and elongated dorsal fin. The center rays of the male's tail also extend to form a spike, suggesting yet another popular name, "the spike-tail characin."

Rooseveltiella (Serrasalmo) nattcreri — Red-breasted Piranha. (Immature specimen.)

Piranha or Piraya

There are several genera, notably *Rooseveltiella, Serrasalmus,* and

Pygocentrus, with a number of species in each. These are all deep-bodied, sturdy, bulldog-headed fishes whose jaws contain rows of triangular, deltoid teeth. These sharp teeth are set in powerful jaws, enabling the Piranha to shear flesh away with a bite. Traveling in large schools as they do, they are an ever-present danger in the rivers and streams of tropical South America. Most aquarists familiar only with the small specimens usually imported are unaware that some species will grow to eighteen inches in length and several pounds in weight. At this size they really can be dangerous. Even small specimens are quite capable of giving a painful and bloody nip. Several people who have been bitten by Piranhas have reported to the author that they felt no more than a shock at the moment; it was only after they saw the blood that they realized that they had bitten. In an aquarium, a Piranha is a rather dull and uninteresting fish. Surprisingly enough it tends to be timid. Foreign objects introduced into the aquarium such as a net or ornament frequently send it into a panic. It is at such times that a Piranha can be dangerous, as it will frantically bite at anything. It is also dangerous because the degree of tameness which it acquires may cause the owner to become careless. Then one day, perhaps while feeding his fish, he trails his finger in the water only to lose a tip as the Piranha rises to the lure.

On a number of occasions efforts have been made to curb the importation of the Piranha because of the fear on the part of legislators that the fish might escape and become established in the warmer areas of our country. This concern is unrealistic. There is no area of the continental United States which is warm enough all year round for the Piranha to survive.

Needless to say, the Piranha had best be kept one to a tank. Small specimens may be fed the standard live foods, while larger fishes will eat strips of meat and fish. Some Piranha owners make it a practice to purchase sick or dying fishes to feed to their pets. Very little is known about their breeding habits.

Pristella riddlei, albino variety — X-ray Fish, or Water Goldfinch. (Female above male below.)

Pristella riddlei — X-Ray Fish or Water Goldfinch

This is a fish which, in spite of the fact that it does not have particularly bright colors, is so neat and nicely put together that it is very pleasant to keep. In addition, it is easily bred and quite hardy. Originally imported from British Guiana, the Pristella tetra grows to approximately two inches. There is also an albino version with faint gold stripes on the dorsal fin and brilliant red eyes. Habitat: British Guiana.

Thayeria boehlki — Penguin Fish. (Male left, female right.)

GENE WOLFSHEIMER

Thayeria obliqua and *Thayeria boehlkei* — Penguin Fish

Like some Pencil Fishes, these two swim at a tail-down forty-five degree angle. Unlike the Pencil Fishes, however, which tend to be slow moving, the Penguins are alert fishes which actively dart about in the water. When alarmed, they will assume a normal swimming posture and move rapidly. The two species are similar in coloration and posture, but may be distinguished by the fact that in *obliqua* , a wide black line originates somewhere near the center of the body of the fish and extends down into the end of the lower lobe of the tail. In *boehlkei* the black line is also quite prominent, although somewhat narrower, but begins just above the eye and extends along the entire mid-section of the fish, terminating at the extreme tip of the lower lobe of the tail. Neither fish breeds particularly readily in the aquarium. However, if conditions are ideal they will reproduce. Both are from the Amazon basin.

Symphysodon aequifasciata aequifasciata
— Green Discus.

Family CICHLIDAE

Cichlids

The amount of interest shown in cichlids by students of animal behavior, correctly known as ethologists, and the amount of space devoted to cichlids in aquarium magazines and other publications devoted to fishes is out of all proportion to the number of cichlids actually kept in aquaria. With the exception of the dwarf species, cichlids grow large and many are known as pugnacious plant destroyers. And yet, one cannot criticize this aspect of their behavior, for this is part of their pattern of living and breeding which makes them such interesting subjects for observation and study.

There are two notable exceptions to the generally pugnacious, plant destroying behavior of the larger cichlids, and these are the genera *Symphysodon,* commonly known as Discus, and *Pterophyllum* or Angelfish. In general, the breeding behavior of these two follows the pattern of the majority of cichlids, which may be

GENE WOLFSHEIMER

Aequidens (latifrons) pulcher —
Blue Acara. Female guarding her eggs.

briefly described as follows: usually a male cichlid will set up what is known as a territory; that is, an area of the tank which is out of bounds to all other members of his species, although some types will tolerate other species of fishes swimming by. In extremely large aquaria, this territory may take up only a certain portion, and several male cichlids may establish territories within the confines of the single aquarium. However, in smaller tanks up to perhaps fifty

GENE WOLFSHEIMER

A group of *Astronotus ocellatus* — Oscars.

A. VAN DEN NIEUWENHUIZEN

Cichlasoma biocellatum — Jack Dempsey.

gallons, it is usual for one male to assert himself as master of the entire area. If several males are introduced they will fight each other until one male dominates all, perhaps bullying the others to death. A strange fish approaching the borders of this territory, or introduced to the territory, is greeted by the dominant male whose behavior pattern is characteristic for that species. By the response of the newcomer, the occupant determines whether it is a male which should be attacked, or a female which should be courted. Should it be the latter, a series of signals is given which, if she gives the proper responses, culminates in mating. The signals are characterized by side to side wagging, tailflapping, and locking of the lips in what appears to be a wrestling bout. Preliminaries over, the two proceed to clear an area, usually a large, flat rock, cleaning it carefully with their thick rubbery lips to provide a place for the eggs to be laid and fertilized. Angelfish and Discus follow this pattern in general, preferring however, to lay their eggs on a vertical surface, frequently a plant leaf, rather than on a horizontal surface.

Cichlasoma meeki — Firemouth.(Female)

A. VAN DEN NIEUWENHUIZEN

Both parents stand guard over the eggs, cleaning them with their lips and fanning them with their large pectoral fins. The young are guarded and attended to. The dwarf cichlids deviate only slightly from this procedure. They prefer a more sheltered area, such as an overturned flower pot or a cave formed from a rock, in which to deposit their eggs; the eggs may be deposited on either the bottom, the side, or the surface. Frequently, dwarf cichlids will burrow under a rock, laboriously removing the gravel grain by grain, until they have excavated a cavern deep enough to hide themselves. The female dwarf cichlid is more plainly colored and much smaller than the male; frequently though not invariably, the female alone cares for

:hlasoma nigrofasciatum — Convict Cichlid. *Cichlasoma severum* — Banded Cichlid. (Female right.)

the eggs. This is not usually true of the larger cichlids, where both parents care for the family.

The young, when free-swimming, are quite large and need not be fed infusoria at their first stage, but can be started directly on newly hatched brine shrimp and micro worms.

One interesting group of cichlids is the mouth-breeders. These will excavate a small hollow in the sand into which the eggs are deposited. These are taken up in the mouth of one of the parents after being laid and fertilized. Which parent serves as a living incubator depends upon the species. The eggs, and subsequently the young, are carried in the mouth until they are free-swimming. In some species, the young may continue to use the mouth as a sanctuary for several days after they have emerged, returning there at the first sign of danger.

Apistogramma ramirezi — Ramirez' Dwarf Cichlid or Ramirezi. (Male above, female below.) In the genus *Apistogramma*, the male is usually considerably larger than the female, *ramirezi* being an exception.

For the purposes of the aquarist, we will arbitrarily divide the cichlids into two groups by size, as follows:

167

Aequidens maroni — Keyhole Cichlid.

Cichlasoma festivum — Barred or Flag Cichlid

Larger Cichlids

Aequidens maroni — Keyhole Cichlid
Aequidens portalegrensis — Porthole Acara
Astronotus ocellatus — Oscar or Velvet Cichlid
Cichlasoma biocellatum — Jack Dempsey
Cichlasoma festivum — Barred or Flag Cichlid, or Festivum
Cichlasoma meeki — Firemouth Cichlid
Cichlasoma nigrofasciatum — Zebra or Convict Cichlid
Cichlasoma severum — Banded Cichlid

Apistogramma agassizi - Agassiz, Dwarf Cichlid. (Two males.)

Smaller Cichlids

Apistogramma ramirezi — Ramirez' Dwarf Cichlid, or Ramirezi
Apistogramma pertense — Yellow Dwarf Cichlid
Apistogramma ortmanni — Ortmann's Dwarf Cichlid
Nannacara anomala — Golden-eyed Dwarf Cichlid

Nannacara anomala — Golden-eyed Dwarf Cichlid. (Male above.) Parents guarding the newly laid eggs.

Also among this group of dwarf cichlids, none of which grow to more than three inches, we should include *Aequidens curviceps* or Flag Cichlid. While somewhat larger than most dwarf cichlids (it may reach a length of three and one-half inches) and deeper-bodied than most, it is a gentle, easily kept fish which is not belligerent and does not destroy plants.

A. VAN DEN NIEUWENHUIZEN

Aequidens curviceps — Flag Cichlid. Female guarding her eggs.

Vertical Spawners

Science divided the genus *Pterophyllum* into three species: *altum, eimekei* and *scalare.* However, to the amateur hobbyist they are all known as Scalare or Angelfish, because they all resemble each other markedly in shape and finnage. The largest species is *scalare,* which reaches a vertical height of almost ten inches; the somewhat smaller *altum* may reach close to nine inches, and the *eimekei* between eight and nine inches.

Angelfish have appeared in a number of color variations from the original silver fish with black vertical bands. Today, we have a dark-

An Angelfish guarding its eggs.

hued Angelfish known as a "black lace" angel, an all-black form known appropriately as the Black Angelfish, and a yellow variety known as a "butterball." In addition, there is an all silver type which has only faint indications of the bars and is known as a "ghost" angel. There is also a "blushing" Angelfish which has a ruddy area in the anterior portion of its body. In addition, the fins on the color varieties have been extended through selective breeding to form what is known as the "veiltail" Angelfish.

Usually a strip of slate or, as we explained in the chapter on breeding, a strip of stainless steel is provided in an otherwise bare

Black Angelfish. (Female left, male right.)

tank to receive the spawn. This is removed to a hatching tank when the eggs have been laid. An airstone which produces a fine bubble is set alongside the strip so that the current almost, but not quite, brushes the eggs. The young start to hatch in about 72 hours but cling in long wriggling strings to the slate. When they become free-swimming, feed them brine shrimp nauplii and similar sized foods.

The other group of vertical spawners is the Discus. There is a great deal of doubt as to whether there is one species of Discus and three subspecies or two species with one of the two divided into three subspecies. The two species (including subspecies) considered valid by one ichthyologist are *Symphysodon aequifasciata aequifasciata,* common name Green Discus; *Symphysodon aequifasciata axelrodi,* common name Brown Discus; *Symphysodon aequifasciata haraldi,* common name Blue Discus; and *Symphysodon discus,* common name Discus. All the species interbreed freely, producing fertile young.

Discus spawning. The female (upper fish) is laying the eggs while the male, following closely behind, fertilizes them.

In its breeding, Discus superficially resembles *Pterophyllum.* That is, they spawn on a vertical surface, either a strip of slate or broad-leaf plant, and both parents care for the young. The major difference is that the young Discus, upon becoming free swimming, feed on a substance secreted in the skin cells of the parents. This has been analyzed as a combination of proteins and fats exuded at the surface of the epidermis. After several days of being "nursed," the

Baby Discus feeding from the secretions elaborated by the mother.

young assume more normal eating habits and will thrive on a diet of newly-hatched brine shrimp, sifted Daphnia, micro worms, and so on. Because of the apparent necessity for obtaining their "first foods" from the parents, the eggs cannot be removed for separate hatching as can be done with most other cichlids.

The Discus, and we use the name Discus to include all the various species or subspecies, breed much less freely than do the Angelfish. The majority of Angelfishes seen in our aquaria are tank-raised, whereas the overwhelming majority of Discus are still imported.

Like most cichlids, Discus prefer live food as a regular basic diet. In fact, it is probably mandatory if breeding is to be attempted. Extremely soft, aged, somewhat acidic water is preferred.

The Mouth-Breeders

While a number of species rear their young by carrying the eggs and developing fry in their mouths, there are only two which may be seen with any regularity in our aquariums. There is *Haplochromis multicolor,* the Small or Egyptian Mouth-breeder, and *Tilapia*

Haplochromis multicolor — Egyptian Mouth-breeder. (Male above, female with eggs in her mouth below.)

macrocephala, the African or Blackchinned Mouth-breeder. Of the two, the Egyptian Mouth-breeder is certainly the more suitable for the community aquarium as it reaches a length of only about three inches where the African may reach seven. However, in spite of its small size, the Egyptian Mouth-breeder can become quite pugnacious, particularly during breeding. Therefore, the pair had best be kept separated. The male should also be separated from the female once she has taken up her burden. He may be distinguished by the more colorful markings of his fins.

The male of the Blackchinned Mouth-breeder serves as the incubator, and they have been known to breed when only three to four inches in length. Sexes may be distinguished by the brassy yellow gill-cover of the male whereas that of the female is beige to pink. No food is ingested during the incubation.

Distichodus sexfasciatus — Six Barred Distichodus. (Sex unknown.).

GENE WOLFSHEIMER

Family CITHARINIDAE

This family is confined to the continent of Africa. Many of them grow too large to be considered aquarium fishes, but three in particular, all belonging to the genus **Distichodus,** are worthy of mention. These

173

Distichodus lusosso —
Long-nosed Distichodus.

are: *D. affinis* (Red-finned Distichodus), which is primarily bright silver with a brilliant red and black dorsal fin; *D. lusosso* (Long-nosed Distichodus), and *D. sexfasciatus* (Six Barred Distichodus). These last two are quite similar in appearance, both of them having alternate dark-green and brilliant orange vertical bars. *D. lusosso,* which may be differentiated by its long, tapering snout, reaches a length of approximately fifteen inches in nature. *D. sexfasciatus* is considerably smaller, reaching approximately ten inches in length.

Distichodus affinis —
Red-finned Distichodus.

Family CLARIIDAE

This family is restricted to Africa and southern Asia. There are several genera in this catfish family, but most of them either are uninteresting or grow too large for aquarium usage. These are so-called " naked cats" because they lack the heavy scalation of so many of the other aquarium catfishes.

The only member of the family of interest to us as aquarists is the albino *Clarias batrachus (Clarias).* While there is a normally-pigmented brown *Clarias,* this is one of the few, if not the only species, which has an albino form coexisting in nature with a

Clarias batrachus — Clarias Catfish (albino variety).

normally-colored variety. Small specimens with their pink and white bodies and bright-red eyes are quite attractive in an aquarium. The mature *batrachus,* which is widely distributed from Ceylon to eastern India into the Malayan Peninsula, can reach a length of eighteen inches, although it seldom grows to anywhere near this size in the aquarium. The *Clariidae* have one other interesting feature; through a large, sponge-like organ located in the head they are able to utilize atmospheric oxygen and thus can survive polluted water, and even being removed from the water for a period of time, so long as they are kept wet.

Family COBITIDAE

Loaches and Spined Loaches

Found throughout Europe, Asia and Africa, loaches are all bottom-dwelling fishes. They vary from the worm-like *Acanthophthalmus* to the shark-like *Botia.* The term "shark-like," as used for the *Botia,* refers to the wedge-like shape, high dorsal fin and underslung mouth, and not to their habits, which are usually gentle and retiring.

Even those loaches which are not worm-shaped have flattened bottoms with their mouths on the underpart of the head well adapted for rooting from the bottom. Many of the loaches are nocturnal, spending the day hidden in the plants. For these species, cover in the form of an inverted half-coconut shell, a flower pot or a rock cave should be provided. Many loaches dive headlong into the gravel and with a series of wriggles bury themselves completely when disturbed.

Loaches seem to be responsive to changes in the atmospheric pressure, responding with increased activity. This characteristic is notable particularly in the Japanese Weatherfish *(Misgurnus anguillicaudatus)* of Japan and China. The loaches have been used as scavengers because of their bottom-feeding habits. However, for this purpose *Corydoras* are unquestionably superior. The sexes of loaches are difficult to distinguish, and there is very little report of their breeding activity in the aquarium. Certain genera are active algae eaters.

Acanthophthalmus kuhlii — Coolie (Kuhli) Loach.

TOM CARAVAGLIA

Acanthophthalmus — Coolie (Kuhli) Loach

There are several species of the genus *Acanthophthalmus,* all of which have been imported and sold interchangeably under the name "coolie." The two commonest are *A. kuhlii kuhlii* and *A. myersi.* Both are brick-red and dark-brown banded, but *myersi* is slimmer and has fewer bands. These are worm-like loaches with bristly whiskers about their soft, underslung mounths. Reaching the length of more than three inches, their slender shape makes them easy prey for vicious fishes. They, however, can be kept safely with other small aquarium inhabitants. As they are strictly bottom dwellers, care should be taken to see that adequate food reaches their feeding area.

Botia Genus

A number of members of this genus have been imported for use as aquarium fishes. However, only a few of them are really attractive and worth considering. *Botia* are similar in shape to the *Labeo,* but may be distinguished from them by the *Botia's* spine. This spine, which is found wholly or partly developed in a number of the genera of the loach family, is of two bony spikes located between the nose and eye of the fish and slightly below the level of the eye. Normally, these spikes are folded and barely visible; however, they can be, and are, erected voluntarily by the fish in the presence of danger and lock in position with often disastrous consequences for the predator attempting to, or succeeding in, swallowing the loach.

The following *Botia* are the most generally available aquarium inhabitants:

Botia horae — Skunk Botia.

Botia horae — **Skunk Botia**

From Thailand, this primarily yellowish-green to pale brick-colored fish can reach a length of almost four inches. The distinctive markings are a black stripe along the back, from the snout to the tail, continuing as a comma-shaped marking on the caudal peduncle.

Botia macracanthus — Clown Loach, or Tiger Botia.

Botia macracanthus — Clown Loach, or Tiger Botia

This, the most beautiful and only really popular species of *Botia*, is found in Sumatra and Borneo. During the confrontation between Indonesia and Malaysia, because importation from Indonesia was made only with extreme difficulty, the retail price of this fish rose as high as $15.00, which, because of its desirability, was usually paid. While the shape is typically *Botia*, the coloration reminds one of the Sumatra Barb; alternating deep black and ivory-colored bands with bright red fins and tail. In common with most *Botia* species as well, in fact, as with most bottom-dwelling fishes, they are very susceptible to infestations of Ich. This is because during one stage of the life cycle of that parasite the mature parasite drops off the whole fish, and multiplies on the bottom. When the cyst bursts, releasing the free-swimming stage of the parasites, they of course encounter the bottom-dwelling fishes first and attack them. Coupled with this is the fact that many *Botia* species tend to hide. Therefore, it is necessary to examine them regularly for signs of infestations so that treatment may be started before the disease has reached a serious phase.

Botia pulchripinnis — Red-finned Blue Botia.

Botia modesta — Blue Botia

There are two closely-related species, *Botia modesta* and *Botia pulchripinnis* (Red Finned Blue Botia). Both of them have a blue to pale-green body but, whereas the fins and tail of *modesta* tend to yellow, *pulchripinnis* has bright-orange to red fins. *Modesta* is found from the Malay Peninsula into Thailand and grows to a length of almost four inches. While attractive, it will dig depressions in the sand and has been known to harass other fishes.

Botia sidthimunki — Dwarf Loach.

W. TOMEY

Botia sidthimunki — Dwarf Loach

A fairly recent introduction, the Dwarf Loach from Thailand reaches a length of one and one-half to two inches. It is distinctively marked, and once seen not easily forgotten. A black line extends from the tip of the nose into the caudal peduncle, where it becomes a blotch. The stomach is white, the fins colorless except for a little yellow at the base of the tail and a few chocolate or dark gray marks near the margins of the lobe. Another black stripe extends from the nose through the eye and along the back, also ending at the blotch on the caudal peduncle. These center and upper bars are connected vertically with six irregularly shaped half bars. A rectangular-shaped yellow patch on the head is matched by five thumbprint-shaped yellow blotches between the vertical bars. Peaceful, gentle, and somewhat retiring, the Dwarf Loach is an ideal aquarium fish.

Family CYPRINIDAE

Widely distributed throughout the world, the *Cyprinidae* are found in the United States, Mexico, and southern Canada, all of Africa, and Asia. There are about fifteen hundred species, many of which are desirable aquarium fishes. In fact, the well-known Goldfish (scientifically known as *Carassius auratus*) is a member of this family.

Balantiocheilus melanopterus —
Tri-colored Shark, or Silver Shark.

Balantiocheilus melanopterus — Tri-colored Shark or Silver Shark

There are a number of aquarium fishes which share the name "shark." Many of them are of different genera, even, in fact, of different families. Thus, they are not really closely related but bear the name in common because of resemblance in shape to their namesake.

The back of the Silver Shark is arched and there is a large, triangular dorsal fin. Its body is silvery or bluish-silver, but the fins give the fish its distinction. They are an intense yellow with deep-black margins. These fish tend to inhabit the lower levels of the aquarium, frequently resting on the bottom. The fins are usually kept spread out in a sprightly manner. Found in Thailand, Borneo, and Sumatra, adults can attain a a length of fourteen inches. However, young specimens are very desirable, hardy, and easily-fed aquarium inhabitants.

Barbus Genus

Representatives of this genus are found throughout Asia and Africa. Next to the characins, the genus *Barbus* provides the largest number of species of aquarium fishes. Most of them are large-scaled and hardy, while many, though not all, have the barbels or fleshy appendages on the mouth from which the name is derived.

The barbs do not have an adipose fin. Some ichthyologists have placed the smaller barbs in another genus called *Puntius*. However, as there is no general agreement on the use and limitations of

Barbus titteya — Cherry Barb. (Male above, female below.) Spawning in the side by side manner typical of the genus.

Puntius, in this book we retain the older and more popularly known *"Barbus."* Most of the small barbs prefer being kept in small schools of three to six individuals where they actively spend their time playing and darting through the plants.

An example of the eagerness with which they school is the manner in which one can empty a tank of all, or most of its barbs, in the following manner: a large net is held vertically, perpendicular to and with one edge against the front glass of the aquarium. By using a smaller net like a shepherd's crook, one can herd an entire school of barbs into the waiting net. It is understood that barbs school with others of their own species, although there are exceptions in that barbs of closely related species have been known to school together. The barbs are easily fed, thriving on either live or dried food or a mixture of both. They are mid-stratum fishes, and will feed as readily from the surface as from the bottom. Typical of the adhesive egglayers, the male drives the female vigorously until, assuming a side-by-side position, the eggs are scattered through the plants.

The genus is a large one, but we will describe only the more popular species.

Barbus arulius — Long Fin Barb

This barb is frequently confused with the closely-related and similar *Barbus filamentosus,* the Blackspot Barb. This confusion is caused by the fact that the adults of both species have the ends of the rays of the dorsal fin elongated into threadlike filaments. The adult *arulius* has three prominent spots on its side, as well as a broad zig-zag marking

181

Barbus arulius — Long Fin Barb.

W. TOMEY

from the operculum to the base of the tail. However, just to confuse the picture, young *filamentosus* have three bars on the side also, one just below the leading edge of the dorsal fin, one just behind the dorsal fin, and one covering the caudal peduncle. These bars disappear as the fish matures, leaving it with one broad, black spot just above the anal. Both are larger barbs growing to five and one-half to six inches in length, and both originate in India.

Barbus conchonius — Rosy Barb. (Male)

A. VAN DEN NIEUWENHUIZEN

Barbus conchonius — **Rosy Barb, or Red Barb**

An extremely hardy, medium-sized barb, this species is likely to maintain its popularity for years to come. Ordinarily rather colorless,

182

during breeding season the male turns a brilliant, almost raspberry-red color which must be seen to be appreciated. It is easily bred in captivity and enjoys a varied diet, thriving on either live or dried food. The dorsal fin of the male has a black tip which is lacking in the female. Like so many other of the popular barbs, the Rosy Barb comes from northern India and grows to a length of two and one-half inches.

Barbus everetti — Clown Barb, or Everett's Barb

Found in Singapore and nearby Borneo, the Clown Barb reaches a length of more than five inches. In spite of its large size, it is a relatively peaceful barb and can be trusted with all but the the tiniest species. The name "clown" is due to the large, blue-green splotches, like the polka dots of the circus clown. The fins of the male are bright orange, much paler in the female.

A. VAN DEN NIEUWENHUIZEN

Barbus nigrofasciatus — Black Ruby, or Purple-headed Barb. (Female above, male below.)

Barbus nigrofasciatus — Black Ruby or Purple-headed Barb

Originally imported from Ceylon, this smallish, two to two and one-half inch barb is one of the ideal aquarium fishes. Ordinarily an ivory-colored fish with three to four blackish vertical bars, the color changes dramatically during the breeding season. Then the male is suffused with a purple-red glow particularly brilliant in the head region. The entire fish sparkles with a jewel-like luster. The dorsal fin of the male is solid black, while that of the female is almost colorless.

Barbus oligolepis — Island Barb, Checkered or Iridescent Barb. (Female above, male below.)

Barbus oligolepis — **Island Barb, Checkered or Iridescent Barb**

This lovely little barb, originally from Sumatra, rarely reaches a length of two inches. However, with its bluish-black, checkerboard marked sides and bright orange fins, it is a living gem. Peaceful, hardy, and easily fed, the *oligolepis* barb may be kept in any mixed collection of small fishes. The vertical fins of the male are black-bordered and much more brightly colored than are those of the female.

Barbus sachsi — **Schuberti, or Golden Barb**

Coming from Singapore and the Malayan Peninsula, this smallish

Barbus sachsi — Schuberti or Golden Barb. (Two females.)

barb, up to three inches in length, is distinctive with its bright golden color. There are probably several closely related strains, or subspecies, as the color in different specimens varies in intensity from a pale yellow to a bright orange. This color seems unrelated to the conditions under which they are kept and the various color phases breed true.

Barbus schwanenfeldi — Schwanenfeld's Barb. (Sex is indeterminate in these young specimens, although the upper fish is probably a female and the lower a male.)

Barbus schwanenfeldi — Schwanenfeld's Barb

A fairly recent introduction to the aquarium, this barb reached us via Thailand although it is said to be found also in Sumatra, Borneo, and Malacca. A rather large barb, reaching a length of fourteen inches, young specimens with their brilliant, silvery sides flashing are very attractive in the aquarium. The dorsal and tail are bright red, the dorsal is black-tipped, and the forks of the tail are each defined with a black bar.

The specimens which reach our aquarium are, for the most part, collected in the wild, as there are very few records of this fish breeding in captivity, and the large size at which it matures would preclude the probability that the average aquarist has the tank capacity to encourage breeding. Young specimens should be provided with ample swimming room. They are also heavy feeders and, fortunately, will eat a variety of food.

Barbus tetrazona — Tiger Barb, or Sumatra Barb. (Female left, male right.)

A. VAN DEN NIEUWENHUIZEN

Barbus tetrazona tetrazona — **Sumatra Barb, or Tiger Barb**

One of the most conspicuous and desirable of the barbs, this little fellow from Sumatra, Borneo, and Thailand can reach a length of almost three inches. A deep-bodied barb, the black and ivory-striped sides with their sharply defined bars and the bright red rims waving merrily as the fish sports actively about is a pretty sight to see. The Sumatra has often been accused, unjustly in opinion of the author, of being a fin-nipper, although it is probable that fin nipping does occur when the fishes are kept singly or in pairs. This may be due to the strong schooling instinct of the barb, which can best be satisfied by keeping them in groups of four or more. The Sumatra Barbs are extremely hardy and breed freely in typical egg-scatterer manner. The dorsal fin of the male is edged with a broad red band with the balance being black. The coloring of the female's dorsal is not nearly as intense, but she shows a narrow clear band between the black and the red.

A. VAN DEN NIEUWENHUIZEN

Barbus titteya — Cherry Barb. (Female upper left, center and lower fish males.)

186

Barbus titteya — Cherry Barb

Originally imported from Ceylon, this two-inch barb breeds so freely in captivity that all the specimens which you see today are probably tank raised. The male, when in breeding condition, shows a brilliant raspberry-red hue which is extremely attractive. At other times, they are a rather dull-colored fish with pinkish-brown color and dull, dark red horizontal stripes. The female may be distinguished from the male when not in breeding color by the deeper chest and body area.

Brachydanio rerio — Zebra Danio.
(Male left, female right.)

A VAN DEN NIEUWENHUIZEN

Genera *Danio* and *Brachydanio*

Found throughout the Indian sub-continent, as well as in nearby areas, these fishes, which are all commonly known as "danios," are slim, colorful and active. They include the well-known Zebra Danio *(Brachydanio rerio)* and the Pearl Danio *(Brachydanio albolineatus)*. The related and somewhat similar but darker variety of the Pearl Danio is known as the Gold Danio.

The Giant Danio *(Danio malabaricus)* grows to almost five inches in length, whereas the *Brachydanio* species mentioned above seldom exceed two inches. In an aquarium the danios are constantly in movement flashing back and forth. Unlike most of the *Cyprinidae* they lay non-adhesive eggs. Breeding is accomplished in long, shallow tanks with the bottom liberally covered with material, such as marbles or fine plants, to hide the spawn. Spawning usually takes place in groups of three to five fishes with more males than females. Usually three males to two females is the most satisfactory proportion. Professional breeders use marbles as bottom cover, but *Myriophyllum* or some other fine-fronded plant may be weighted down with glass rods as a satisfactory spawning medium. The

Brachydanio frankei — Leopard Danio spawning.   *Danio malabaricus* — Giant Danio. (Male above

water literally seems to boil as the fishes race back and forth depositing their eggs. Spawning completed, the adults are removed and the young hatch in twenty to twenty-four hours. It takes them about twenty-four to thirty hours more to absorb their yolk sac, after which time they may be fed the finest of live food or finely ground dried food.

Brachydanio albolineatus — Pearl Danio.

Labeo bicolor — Redtailed Black Shark

The deep, velvety black beauty which contrasts so strikingly with the blood-red tail must be seen to be appreciated. Imported in great numbers from Bangkok, Thailand, one of the great fish-shipping ports of the world, the Redtailed Black Shark has found a ready market in America. When first imported, so striking was its beauty that early specimens were quickly snapped up at $ 25.00 apiece.

Today, because of the large numbers in which it has been imported, the price has come down dramatically, but it still remains a very desirable fish. Usually considered peaceful, the Redtailed Black

188

Labeo bicolor — Redtailed Black Shark. (Sex unknown.)

Shark has been known to annoy large, slow-moving fishes such as Discus by sucking at their side. There have been reports of its breeding in captivity, but so far no details are known. This is not one of the larger "sharks," growing only to about four and one-half inches in length. This fish feeds extensively on algae which it sucks up with its underslung mouth.

Morulius chrysophekadion — Black Shark.

Morulius chrysophekadion — Black Shark

This fish is closely related to the Redtailed Black Shark, but the black is not as intense and it grows considerably larger, up to almost two feet. The Black Shark is found in Thailand. As specimens age, the intense color tends to fade with just a golden glint showing through. The black will also fade if the fish are kept in alkaline water or in an environment where they are being continually disturbed. These sharks love to browse on algae and will eat almost any fish-food, live or prepared. The mouth is located underneath, somewhat like that of the suckerfish of the United States.

189

Rasbora heteromorpha — Red Rasbora spawning upside down from the underside of a broad-leafed plant.

Genus *Rasbora*

There are twenty-six or more species of this genus known to aquarists. However, the majority of them are rather plain-colored fish and even when available are not eagerly sought out. There are a few members of the genus, however, which because of their beauty, elegance, and general desirability should be included in this catalogue of those fishes most desirable for the home aquarium.

In general, *Rasbora* are schooling fishes and do best when kept in small groups of from three to four individuals, up to a dozen or more. With the exception of the Red Rasbora (*Rasbora heteromorpha*), the members of this genus are all plant scatterers that lay their eggs more or less indiscriminately, and the eggs, being adhesive, attach themselves to the first object they touch. The rasboras do not spawn as freely as do some of the other fishes, such as the barbs, and, therefore, separate conditioning of the sexes for a period of ten days should precede the actual bringing together of the breeders.

Rasboras, which in general come from clear, flowing streams, should have ample swimming room in acid, aged, soft water. They do not display the hurried activity of some fishes such as the danios, but neither are they lethargic. They swim sedately and daintily about the mid-region of the tank in a characteristic "flashing fins" manner.

Rasbora heteromorpha — Harlequin Fish or (Red) Rasbora

This, the most popular of the rasboras, has been imported from the

Far East in great numbers. Another fish, *Rasbora hengeli* (Red Rasbora), is somewhat similar in appearance, but not nearly as attractive as the *heteromorpha*. Both of them have the blue-black triangle covering the posterior portion of the body. *R. hengeli* is a narrow bodied fish with not as pleasing a figure as the *heteromorpha;* also, hengeli lacks the golden sheen, one of the most attractive features of the *heteromorpha*. The blue-black triangle of *hengeli* is much narrower and less complete than that of *heteromorpha*. Hengeli, which comes from Sumatra, scarcely reaches one and one-quarter inches in length whereas *heteromorpha* (from the Malay Peninsula, Thailand, and eastern Sumatra) may attain a length of two inches.

Sexing the Red Rasbora is difficult for the inexperienced. Close observation will reveal that in addition to the usual differences in body shape, the female being more rounded and heavier, the forward lower corner of the blue-black triangle is pointed and complete in the male, whereas the same corner or angle in the female is rounded.

The water for breeding the Red Rasbora should be about 80°F, extremely soft, and acidic, a pH of 5.3 being recorded by some successful aquarists. Actual spawning takes place with the pair side-by-side in an upside-down position beneath the underside of a broad-leafed plant such as a *Cryptocoryne,* or Amazon sword plant *(Echinodorus).* The eggs are pale amber in color and ignored by the parents. Its is also reported that the parents do not eat their own young.

Rasbora maculata — Spotted Rasbora or Pigmy Rasbora

This is one of our smallest egglayers, adults barely reaching a length of one inch. Imported from the southern Malay Peninsula and Sumatra, the Pigmy Rasbora is quite pretty with clown-like blotches

Rasbora maculata — Spotted Rasbora, or Pigmy Rasbora.(Female)

GENE WOLFSHEIMER

near the head, anal, posterior portion, and at the root of the tail. An overall glow when the fish is in good condition distinguishes this species. Because of its small size, the Pigmy Rasbora had best be kept only with the smallest and gentlest fishes, such as Neons and Glowlights. However, they will do quite well in a baby-rearing tank, enjoying the small-sized food which is fed to the babies and ignoring their tank mates.

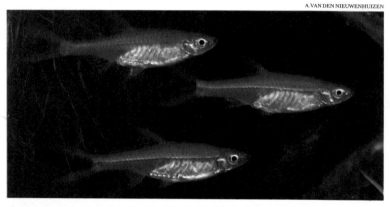

Rasbora pauciperforata — Redlined Rasbora. (These three appear to be females.)

Rasbora pauciperforata — **Redlined Rasbora**

This lovely Rasbora is somewhat similar in appearance to the Glowlight Tetra because it too has a red stripe running horizontally along the mid-section. The Redlined Rasbora, which comes from Sumatra, is larger than the Glowlight, attaining the length of two and three-quarter inches. In addition, the outline is much slimmer and the line tends to a copper or fiery red rather than the paler golden glow of the Glowlight Tetra. Both sexes are identical in markings, sex being distinguished by the shape.

Rasbora trilineata — **Scissorstail or Three Line Rasbora**

This fish has no gaudy colors, does not have an odd or unusual shape, and does not have any unique habits to recommend it. Yet, year after year, it maintains its popularity solely because of its quiet, pleasing manners and neat yet elegant markings. The most outstanding feature of this fish is the distinctive tail markings from which it

Rasbora trilineata — Scissorstail Rasbora

TOM CARAVAGLIA

derives its name. The tail is deeply forked, with the two lobes extended and somewhat rounded. There are two prominent white spots on each lobe, with a distinct black blotch or bar between. As the fish swims, it flicks the lobes open and closed, giving a scissoring impression; otherwise, the fish is predominantly silver. It breeds freely in typical egg-scatterer fashion, and is hardy and gentle. The sexes are identical in color and markings, distinguished only by the greater girth of the female.

Tanichthys albonubes —
White Cloud Mountain Minnow.

Tanichthys albonubes — **White Cloud Mountain Minnow**

Actually, this is a temperate zone fish from near Canton, China, which was collected in the White Mountains, hence its name. Easily bred in captivity, the iridescent stripe which is particularly bright in young specimens at one time caused this fish to be called " the poor man's Neon Tetra." A gentle, easily-fed fish, it can be kept in groups in a well-planted aquarium and will not eat the eggs or young when properly fed. The eggs are laid at intervals over a period of days, with the young being hatched at intervals also.

Nothobranchius rachovi. The male has his dorsal curved over the female in what almost seems a gesture of affection as they spawn.

Family CYPRINODONTIDAE

Killifishes

The egg-laying *Cyprinodontidae* are extremely intersing and varied in coloration. The majority of them are long, slim, torpedo-like fishes, distributed throughout the temperate and tropical areas of the world, and in every continent of the world except Australia.

Most of the killifishes are slow-moving, sluggish fishes, usually inhabiting the upper areas of the aquarium. In this family are found some of the most highly colored of all our aquarium fishes. Where live food is not available, they easily may be trained to take frozen foods such as frozen brine shrimp and frozen Daphnia. Small portions of these may be dropped into the rising stream of air from an aerator, thus imparting motion to the particles.

For those people who specialize in killifishes (and there are thousands of them), the reward is well worth the effort. Many are beautiful and all are interesting to breed.

In breeding habits they can be divided into two groups: the plant spawners and the bottom spawners. Plant spawners lay their adhesive eggs, a few at a time, over a period of days on the fine-leafed fronds of such plants as *Myriophyllum* and hornwort. Commercial breeders use nylon mops and commercial spawning media to receive the spawn. The tank is examined daily and the eggs removed into smaller

Aphyosemion australe —
Cape Lopez Lyretail. (Male.)

Aphyosemion sjoestedti
Roloffia occidentalis —
Golden Pheasant. (Spawning.)

Aphyosemion bivattatum —
Red Lyretail. (Male.)

Nothobranchius guentheri —
Guenther's Nothobranchius.
(Male above, female below.)

containers. Usually, a new container is started every sixth day. These containers, which can be one-gallon jars, are kept in a dimly-lit area until the young hatch. The first few days are spent absorbing the egg yolk. The free-swimming young are large enough to be fed newly-hatched brine shrimp.

An aquarium with a layer of sand, peat moss, or nylon mop on the bottom is provided for the bottom spawners. These can be sub-divided into two groups, those which corkscrew themselves down into the bottom, and those which lay their eggs just below the surface. Bottom spawners also lay their eggs over a period of time, rather than all in one spawning. After removal from the aquarium, the peat moss, if used, is kept moist in a plastic bag in a dimly-lit area. After two to four weeks, depending on the species, water is slowly added to the peat, and hatching usually takes place shortly thereafter.

Feeding is similar for both types: newly-hatched brine shrimp, micro worms, and other fine foods. It is not necessary to feed Infusoria. Growth is rapid, and the young should be separated according to size to prevent cannibalism. Because of the great number of killifishes, and as most of these are recommended only for the more advanced aquarists, a detailed description is beyond the scope of this book, which is intended primarily for the beginner.

However, a list of those most available and most desirable is included for the benefit of those aquarists who would like to try their hand with these most interesting of fishes.

TOM CARAVAGLIA

Oryzias latipes — Medaka.
(Female left, male right.)

Aphyosemion australe australe — Lyretail Panchax, or Cape Lopez
Aphyosemion bivittatum bivittatum — Red Lyeretail
Aphyosemion sjoestedti (*Roloffia occidentalis*) — Golden Pheasant
Aplocheilus lineatus — Panchax Lineatus

196

Aplocheilus panchax — Blue Panchax
Cynolebias belotti — Argentine Pearlfish
Cynolebias nigripinnis — Blackfinned Pearlfish
Micropanchax macrophthalmus — Lampeyed Panchax
Nothobranchius guentheri — Guenther's Nothobranchius
Nothobranchius rachovi — Rachov's Nothobranchius
Oryzias latipes — Geisha Girl Medaka, Japanese Medaka, or Ricefish
Rivulus cylindraceus — Green, Brown or Cuban Rivulus

Cynolebias belotti — Argentine Pearlfish.
(Female above, male below.)

Cynolebias nigripinnis —
Blackfinned Pearlfish. (Male)

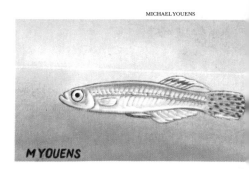

Micropanchax macrophthalmus —
Lampeyed Panchax. (Male)

197

Rivulus cylindraceus —
Green, Brown or Cuban Rivulus. (Male.)

Aplocheilus lineatus —
Panchax Lineatus. (Upper male, lower female.)

Aplocheilus panchax — Blue Panchax.
(Male above, female below.)

Family GASTEROPELECIDAE

In this family, we find three genera of true freshwater flying fishes commonly known to the aquarist as hatchetfishes. Primarily surface

Gasteropelecus sternicla — Silver Hatchetfish. (Sex distinctions unknown.)

swimmers and surface feeders, the hatchetfishes are lovely, odd, and unusual aquarium inhabitants. They are extremely peaceful and somewhat delicate unless kept in soft water and fed a small-sized food. Drosophila, or fruit flies, which are tiny and float on the surface, are an excellent addition to the diet of the hatchetfishes. Hatchetfishes should be kept away from bullying fishes, as they are relatively peaceful and defenseless. Motion pictures taken of the hatchetfishes show that as they leap from the water they beat their fins strongly, adding impetus to their leap or flight. For such tiny fishes (most less than two inches in lenght) to make flights of ten to fifteen feet is truly marvelous.

The three hatchetfishes most commonly kept in the aquarium are: *Carnegiella strigata,* commonly known as the Marbled Hatchetfish; *C. marthae,* the Blackwinged Hatchetfish; and *Gasteropelecus levis,* the Giant Silver Hatchetfish. The Silver and the Blackwinged Hatchetfish are similar in coloration, but the Silver is much the larger of the two. It grows up to two and one-half inches in length, while the tiny, glasslike Blackwinged Hatchetfish barely reaches an inch and one-half. The Marbled Hatchetfish is between the two in size, about one and three-quarter inches.

Another species, *Gasteropelecus sternicla,* is quite similar to, but slightly smaller than the Silver Hatchetfish. It is also seen from time to time. The third genus, *Thoracocharax,* with two species, *securis* and *stellatus,* is seldom seen in aquariums.

Carnegiella strigata — Marbled Hatchet-fish. (Female above, male below.)

A. VAN DEN NIEUWENHUIZEN

Family GYRINOCHEILIDAE

Only one member of this family is of interest to the aquarist, and that is the India Algae Eater *Gyrinocheilus aymonieri*. Actually, this fish should be called the Siamese or Thai Algae Eater, because it is widely distributed throughout Thailand. An elongated, gray-marked fish, the algae eater can attain a length of ten inches but rarely grows anywhere near this size in the aquarium.

Most India Algae Eaters are imported as young specimens

Gyrinocheilus aymonieri — Indian Algae Eater.

approximately two inches in length. They are quite inoffensive. Like animated vacuum cleaners, they move busily about the aquarium, ingesting algae which they rasp off and inhale with their sucker-like mouths.

Both sexes are similar in markings and there are no reports of their having been bred in the aquariums.

Nannostomus marginatus —
Dwarf Pencilfish spawning.

Family HEMIODONTIDAE

Pencilfishes

There are eleven important aquarium species in this group, all included in the genera *Nannostomus* and *Poecilobrycon*. All of these are slow-moving, small-mouthed, gentle fishes. They like a well-planted, brightly-lit aquarium and seem to enjoy sunshine. Because of the small size of their mouths, they must be fed smaller-sized foods. Such live foods as Tubifex and white worms are best chopped or minced with a razor blade and rinsed before feeding. These fishes are all found in central and nothern South America where they inhabit small, slow-moving streams.

One unusual characteristic is the dark, vertical barring which

Poecilobrycon eques — Pencilfish. (Female left, male right.)

appears when the fishes are kept in the dark or frightened. This may be seen when the aquarium lights are turned on after a period of darkness. This dark barring slowly fades away when light conditions return to normal. While the pencilfishes do not breed as freely as do some of the other aquarium egglayers, they will respond to conditioning in soft, acid, peat water. The eggs, which are scattered in fine leafed plants, are eaten voraciously by the parents as well as by any other fishes which are present, and should be removed as soon as possible. In addition to the broader outline of the female, sexing may be accomplished by studying the shape of the anal fin. The anal fin of the male is always rounded below. This is particularly noticeable in those species which have white-edged fins such as *Nannostomus trifasciatus* (Three Banded Pencilfish).

Nannostomus trifasciatus —
Three Banded Pencilfish. (Male)

All species mentioned, with the sole exception of *Nannostomus espei,* are striped longitudinally. *N. espei* is distinguished by four prominent, almost comma-shaped black blotches on the body. All are long slim fishes.

Plecostomus plecostomus — Pluto or Suckermouth.

Family LORICARIIDAE

Heavily armored, the members of this family, distinguished by their sucker mouths, are commonly called "sucker mouth" catfish. Members of this family are useful as aquarium scavengers. Although they have a tendency to hide during the day, they are active at night busily engaged in cleaning algae from the glass, rocks, and leaves of the plants. Here they distinguish themselves, as generally they can clean even the most delicate leaves without harming them. However, some of the larger types, as they approach maturity, are a little too vigorous in their sucking operations, at which time they begin to injure the plant leaves. This is particularly noticeable with broad-leaf plants such as the Amazon sword plant. Overly energetic, *Plecostomus* will literally suck the chlorophyll from the plant leaf, giving a yellowish appearance to what is otherwise a healthy plant. There are several genera in the group, and in the trade they are seldom distinguished by species, being lumped together under the following generic names: *Loricaria, Otocinclus, Plecostomus, Farlowella,* and *Ancistrus.* The genera *Ancistrus* and *Plecostomus* are roughly similar in shape: large heads tapering to a narrow tail, a fairly large dorsal fin which is erected often, heavy armoring, and an underslung mouth with which they cling to various objects. Ancistrus, however, have bristly snouts, that is, "whiskers" which may or may not be forked, protruding from the forward portion of their head. Once seen, these are always recognizable, looking for all the world like pictures of the mythical Medusa. The various species of *Plecostomus* lack these bristles. All of these catfishes are excellent scavengers at the smaller sizes, i. e., up to about three inches.

GENE WOLFSHEIMER

Ancistrus dolichopterus —
Bristlenose Catfish.

Farlowella species — Twig Catfish.

Loricaria parva — Alligator Catfish.
(Female right, male left.)

Otocinclus arnoldi — Sucker Catfish.

Ancistrus dolichopterus, commonly known as Bristlenose Catfish, reaches the length of up to five and one-half inches. In addition to the bristles, there is a peculiar structure—a cluster of spines on either side of its head which can be erected when the fish is alarmed.

Plecostomus plecostomus — (Pluto or Suckermouth), the most commonly imported of this group, may reach up to ten inches in length and sometimes grows to two feet.

All of the above are drab colored fishes, some with spots, and all are found in northern South America.

Farlowella gracilis — Twig Catfish

Here we see protective form and coloration to the greatest degree. Shaped for all the world like an old twig, the camouflage is further heightened by the dark-brown blotched coloration. The fins are transparent, the outer rays of the tail being extended as filaments.

Loricaria parva — Alligator Catfish

A long, slim, gray fish with dark blotches from central South America, it reaches a length of five inches although most aquarium specimens seldom exceed three. It is heavily armored, the male being distinguished by the more pointed shape of its head.

Otocinclus

This is one of the smaller "sucker-mouths," seldom reaching more than two inches in length. The most commonly imported is *Otocinclus arnoldi* (Sucker Catfish), which is usually imported from the southern region of Brazil between Rio de Janeiro and Manaos. Ideal as an algae cleaner, particularly in the smaller aquariums, they prefer being kept in groups and have been bred in the aquarium successfully.

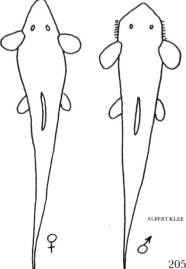

Sexing Loricaria. The male is on the right.

ALBERT KLEE

Family MOCHOKIDAE

All the members of this catfish family come from Africa. As yet, not too many of them have been imported, but several are included here because it is probable that in the future, when collecting facilities and transportation from Africa to Europe and America improve, they will be arriving in increasing numbers.

The *Mochokidae* are largely schooling fishes which prefer dimly lit areas, avoiding bright light. In captivity, they will hide behind large plants, overhanging rocks, or flower pots; or if caves are provided, they can usually be found within. Dimming the lights of the aquarium will bring them out to view. Unlike some members of the *Clariidae,* they are peaceful and will thrive equally well on live or dried foods. All of the *Mochokidae* have three pairs of long barbels, some of which are branched or feathered.

Synodontis angelicus — Polkadot Catfish

One of the most attractive of the catfishes, the Polkadot Catfish derives its name from the numerous reddish-yellow to dark red spots scattered over its purple-gray body. These dots are larger on the head and the rear portion and extend onto the stomach area. First imported from the Congo, this fish can reach a length of eight inches. The young specimens are much more beautiful because the markings, which are white to light-yellow, stand out distinctly.

Synodontis nigriventris —
Upside-down Catfish.

Synodontis nigriventris — Upside-down Catfish

Not particularly colorful, this catfish from the central Congo, which is mostly a mottled light and dark-brown or gray, is worth including in the aquarium collection because of its peculiar habit of swimming upon its back. Young Upside-down Catfish swim quite normally but as they mature, the swim bladder which enables a fish to maintain its level in the water gradually shifts position with result that it is easier for the fish to swim upside-down than right side up. Normally, a fish is darker on its back than on its stomach. This is a protective arrangement which helps to camouflage it. In the Upside-down Catfish, this pattern is reversed and the stomach, which is held uppermost, becomes darker with the back lighter. It can, if it so desires, turn right side up and swim quite speedily in a most normal manner. Left undisturbed, it prefers to hide under an overhanging leaf or ledge, in the famous stomach-up position.

Monodactylus argenteus —
Mono or Singapore Angel.

Family MONODACTYLIDAE

The deep, compressed silvery form of these fishes has given at least one, *Monodactylus argenteus,* the common name of Singapore Angel. In the trade it is also known as the Mono. There is no real relation to the Angelfish, genus *Pterophyllum,* however.

In nature, Monos are found in both fresh and salt water, from Malaya to East Africa. A fast moving, hardy fish, in nature it may reach a vertical length of ten inches. In the aquarium it prefers brackish water, is not a choosy feeder, prefers to school with others of its own kind, and is quite peaceful. Aquarium raised specimens seldom exceed four inches. No sex distinctions are known, nor has it ever been bred.

Family POECILIIDAE

Livebearing Tooth Carps

Those livebearers which are commonly kept as aquarium fishes are, with one exception (which is the Halfbeak), the *Poeciliidae* which range from southern United States to Central and South America. They are excellent community fishes, rarely belligerent and able to

Poecilia reticulata — Red Deltatail Guppy.

A. VAN DEN NIEUWENHUIZEN

live under a varying range of conditions. If given a choice, however, they prefer to be kept in neutral to slightly alkaline water with the addition of a teaspoon of salt to every five gallons of aquarium water. While salt is harmful to aquarium plants in large quantities, this low level will not affect them and will be beneficial to most fishes.

Most livebearers lean heavily towards "vegetable" in their diet and will browse for hours on the algae growth in the aquarium. This is particularly true in the case of the mollies. However, they all, including the mollies, appreciate some live food and a varied diet.

Breeding Characteristics

Young livebearers all resemble females. It is only as they mature, usually between three and six months, that secondary sexual characteristics, which distinguish male from female, appear. These

Poecilia latipinna —
Black Lyretail Sailfin Molly.(Male)

include such features as the high color of the guppy male and extended finnage, such as the large dorsal of the male sailfin molly and the sword of the male swordtail. During the early stages when these secondary characteristics first begin to appear, there is a noticeable change in the form of the anal fin. Rounded and fan-like in the juvenile livebearer, it begins to roll and forms the stick-like tube called the gonopodium, which is the organ used by the male livebearers for fertilization. Until this organ is fully developed, the young male is incapable of mating. Those breeders who are desirous of keeping their strains of fishes pure should bear in mind that the young male can mate once this organ has formed, even though the secondary characteristics, e.g., the sword of the swordtail, have not yet appeared. There are other features used to distinguish the male from the female livebearer. One is the so-called "gravid spot." This is a darkened area in the rear lower portion of the abdomen. Actually, this is not always accurate as a determinant of sex. The gravid spot is actually the peritoneum, the sac-like membrane containing the internal organs. In later stages of pregnancy, because the developing young take up so much room in the abdominal cavity, this sac is pressed against the outer walls. However, in this author's opinion, the "gravid spot" is an inaccurate method of determining either the degree of pregnancy or even the very fact of pregnancy itself. Male livebearers which have eaten heavily frequently show this gravid spot and they certainly are not pregnant.

A more accurate method of determining the state of pregnancy is to view the female from above. Everyone is familiar with the normally streamlined shape of a fish. Pregnancy, especially in the

As a rule, extensive finnage is the prerogative of the male fish. However, many of the modern platies and swordtails are being bred with both sexes having tremendous finnage. This is a pair of Black True Hi-Fin Lyretail Swordtails. The male is on the left

later stages, interferes with this streamlining by causing a "side to side" bulge in the midsection. Experience will enable the aquarist to determine by the degree of the convexity the extent of pregnancy.

At present, we do not know definitely at how young an age a female livebearer can be fertilized. This is because it is possible for a female to store sperm within her body. This sperm remains viable for varying periods of time and thus is available to fertilize the eggs which may develop later. Female guppies can give birth when three months old, while mollies and swordtails do not mature until six to eight months of age. The number of young may vary from as few as six or seven to several hundred.

It is recorded frequently in the scientific literature and popularly believed that the young livebearing fishes must manage to reach the surface and gulp a mouthful of air in order to actuate the mechanism of their swim bladders. However, many of the breeding traps which are designed to automatically segregate the young from their mother at birth are so constructed that the young cannot reach the surface. Nevertheless, somehow or other they do find a means to actuate their bladders and swim perfectly normally.

Guppy

Its correct Latin name is *Poecilia reticulata* although for many years, the guppy was known as *Lebistes reticulatus*. This latter name since then has been shown to have been given to the fish in error. The guppy or Millions Fish is probably the most popular of all the aquarium fishes and, in fact, the name "Guppy" (it rhymes with puppy) to many people is almost synonymous with tropical fishes.

Originating in Trinidad, several other nearby islands, and parts of northern South America, the guppy fitted all the essential requirements for achieving this popularity. It was small, peaceful, hardy, and in the early days of the aquarium hobby when the selection of fishes available was much smaller than it is today, the original male guppy was considered a highly colored fish. The female was a drab gray. Today, through selective breeding, the size of the original guppy has been doubled and, in some cases, almost tripled while the fins of the highly-bred guppy have attained magnificent colors and proportions. Even the female today is coming into her own with some strains showing red, gold, blue, and black in certain body areas and particularly in the tail.

While not considered a salt water fish, guppies, by the gradual addition of salt to their aquarium, can be brought to a degree of tolerance at which they can exist and breed in a marine aquarium. This is practiced frequently by those hobbyists who keep sea horses. Sea horses, which are marine fishes, will eat only live moving food. The young of those guppies kept and bred in the salt water tank provide a ready diet.

Poecilia reticulata — Gold Veiltail Guppy. (Male)

Poecilia latipinna — Green Sailfin Molly. (Male in foreground.)

Mollies

The genus *Mollienesia*, from which the name *molly* was derived, has recently been vacated. So today, mollies in scientific nomenclature are known as *Poecilia* and are considered to be in the same genus as the guppy. For years it had been noticed that the guppy will, under certain circumstances, interbreed with the molly, and now the close relationship of the two has been confirmed.

Poecilia sphenops — Sphenops Molly. (Male)

There are three species of molly which are important to the aquarist. These are *Poecilia sphenops, Poecilia latipinna,* and *Poecilia velifera.* The latter two are known as the sailfin mollies, while the former is popularly called the sphenops molly. The name sailfin derives from the dorsal fin of the male which, developing as he matures, becomes greatly enlarged in adult specimens. Both *latipinna* and *velifera* are quite similar, the primary difference being the number of rays in the dorsal fin, *velifera* having eighteen whereas *latipinna* has only fourteen. In nature, both of these fishes are graygreen, although occasionally melanistic black specimens have been found.

A.VAN DEN NIEUWENHUIZEN

Poecilia latipinna — Green Lyretail Mollies. (Male above, female below.)

The original sphenops molly, which is still popular with aquarists, is mottled black and silver. The posterior edge of the tail of the male is usually bordered with yellow or orange. The dorsal fin of the *sphenops* does not achieve the size of the sailfin dorsal. One easy way to distinguish *sphenops* from young *latipinna* is by observing the placement of the dorsal. The dorsal of the *sphenops* molly originates behind the high point of the back, while the dorsal of the sailfin originates in front of the hump.

213

All of the molly species have been interbred, resulting in many different color varieties and finnage shapes. To mention a few, we have solid black mollies, both sailfin type with an orange-bordered dorsal fin and *sphenops*. The latter in known as the Yucatan molly and usually has silver-rimmed eyes, whereas the sailfin molly's eyes are almost indistinguishable from the rest of the body because of their darkness. There are other black aquarium fishes, but none approach the soft, deep, velvety color of the molly. Albino forms, with red eyes, have also been developed, and a good specimen is magnificent. More recently, a molly has been developed with the outer rays of the tail elongated to form a lyre shape. The ventral fins are prolonged with tassels and it has a well-developed dorsal fin. The lyretails are available in black, the original gray-green, albino, and even a chocolate as well as an orange color. Mollies like guppies, can be acclimated to full strength sea water. They also enjoy an algae growth in the aquarium on which they browse constantly. Lacking this, they should be provided either with a special molly food, or occasional feeding of chopped boiled spinach.

Mollies are found from the southern United States down into Central America. They frequent both fresh and, in the coastal area, salt water. It is not unusual to find the sailfin molly, *Poecilia latipinna*, happily swimming and flaunting his magnificent dorsal fin in the ocean off the Florida Keys.

Xiphophorus variatus — Redtailed Black Variatus. (Male) A. VAN DEN NIEUWENHUIZEN

Swordtails and Platy Fishes

There are three species in the genus *Xiphophorus* which are of special interest to aquarists. These are *Xiphophorus helleri,*

Xiphophorus variatus, and *Xiphophorus maculatus.* In addition, *Xiphophorus montezumae* has been used for hybridizing. The generic *Xiphophorus* means "sword bearer" and refers to the gonopodium. It does not refer to the swordlike extension of the lower rays of tail of the *X. helleri,* which is also present, but to a lesser extent, in males of *X. montezumae.* Platyfishes originally occupied a separate genus known as *Platypoecilus,* but in recent years studies have shown that the differences between *Xiphophorus* and *Platypoecilus* were not sufficient to warrant a separate genus. All platies and swordtails hybridize freely. As a result, many new and highly colored fishes have evolved, with a variety of fin formations.

In general, those hybrids in which the swordtail persists are called "swordtails" while the other are known simply as platies. The platies themselves are further divided; the deeper-bodied being called *maculatus* platies, while the slimmer platies are known as *variatus.* The original *X.variatus* was a blue fish with a red tail and a yellow or orange dorsal fin. A yellow-tail variety was also found in nature and

Xiphophorus maculatus — Cherry Red Platies. (Female above, male below.)

GENE WOLFSHEIMER

Xiphophorus variatus — the original wild Platy Variatus (male).

these two were known individually as Redtail Variatus and Yellowtail Variatus. Today, the Yellowtail is seldom seen, but the Redtail with its shimmering blue body is still popular and is known simply as platy *variatus.* Through crossings with other types of platies and swordtails they have developed such color varieties as the following:

Sunset variatus — this has a yellow, almost sweet potato colored body with an orange tail.

Xiphophorus maculatus — Red Wag Platy. (Two females.)

Marigold variatus—similar to the sunset, from which it was developed, with a bright orange body. The males in particular are extremely colorful.

Black variatus — the body is black with a yellow or colorless tail.

Tuxedo variatus—similar to the black variatus but the head and throat are yellow.

Xiphophorus variatus — Sunset Platy Variatus. (Female above, male below.)

This is the topsail variety of the Sunset Variatus. (Male)

Redtail Black Topsail Variatus Platy. (Male.)

Xiphophorus variatus — Hi-Fin Platy Variatus. (Male.)

Xiphophorus maculatus — Gold Crescent Platy.(Female upper, male lower.)

Redtail-Black variatus—this fish has a black body with a red tail and a yellow dorsal.

White variatus—the body is ivory with a red tail and yellow dorsal fin.

Albino variatus — this is a fairly recent development. It is similar to the white variatus but as is characteristic of albinos, the eyes are red.

In addition to the various color varieties, a "hi-fin" variatus has been developed. This is an extremely attractive fish. It is similar in coloration to the other varieties of variatus, but the dorsal fin of the male has been broadened and elongated.

Platy maculatus—the original *X. maculatus* was a dull colored fish with a few black spots. Hybridization with the *X. helleri* resulted in the early color varieties of platies. The development of the color varieties in the variatus did not take place until the late 1940's and 50's, whereas colorful maculatus platies were produced in the 30's.

Wag platies—the term "wag" refers to the fact that the fins, particularly the dorsal and the caudal, are black. For example, a red platy with black fins would be called a red wag platy, a gold platy with black fins would be called a gold wag platy, and so on. A black platy

Xiphophorus maculatus — Gold Wag Topsail Platy. (Male.)

with colorless fins which is known simply as a black platy would be called a black wag if the fins were dark.

Moon platies—early platies had a dominant characteristic called "the moon" which was simply a crescent-shaped black marking on the caudal peduncle, which is the base of the body on which the tail is set. In fact, an early name for the platy was moon, or moonfish. This factor has been largely bred out, but it still persists in certain color varieties, notably the gold crescent, red crescent, and blue crescent, which are solid colored fishes except for this marking.

Xiphophorus maculatus — Blue Crescent Platy.

In addition, there is tuxedo maculatus. The tuxedo marking is a darkened area of the body beginning approximately at the gill cover and extending to the tail. The head, neck and throat can be any one of a number of colors, and the fins usually are colorless. For example, the red tuxedo would have the forward portion red and the rear half black. If the fins were also dark the fish would be known as a red tuxedo wag platy.

The "hi-fin" sport has also appeared among the maculatus platies and is being eagerly developed.

Xiphophorus helleri — the original color variety of the *helleri* or, as it is more popularly known, the swordtail, was predominantly green with a red stripe along the caudal fin. The swordlike extension of the lower rays of the tail was usually yellow lined with black; altogether a graceful, hardy and extremely attractive fish. Two judicious crossings with the above resulted in first, the brick red sword, which is an orange-red fish with a pattern of lines on its body, and the velvet red sword, a bright solid red colored fish.

Xiphophorus helleri — Green Swordtail. This is the original color variety.

X. montezumae, which is a larger, heavier, and shorter-tailed fish than the *helleri,* was used in these crossings. In addition to green, red, gold, and black swordtails we have the tuxedo and wag pattern developed in the swordtail in the various color varieties. There is also a Berlin or hybrid sword which is red with black blotches. One popular variety is the albino, which is a clear gold with a red eye.

A six inch male *Xiphophorus montezumae* — Montezuma Swordtail.
The fish below, shown for contrast, is a red *Xiphophorus helleri*, or common Swordtail.

The hi-fin has been affixed to the swordtail, this variety being known as the Simpson hi-fin sword in recognition of its developer. The Simpson is being produced in a variety of colors and is a most attractive fish.

There is no doubt that as time goes on you will see many more new and colorful varieties of platies and swordtails being developed. Peaceful, hardy, and attractive, the swordtails make ideal aquarium fishes. At times, the male swordtail has been accused of being a bully. It has been said that an adult male swordtail would not tolerate another male in his territory. However, this problem can be avoided by having a number of male swordtails in the aquarium rather than

Xiphophorus helleri — Hi-Fin or Simpson Swordtails courting.

Xiphophorus helleri — Berlin Swordtail.

two or three, provided an adequate number of females are present, of course.

One word of caution — swordtails are notorious jumpers, so make sure that the aquarium is well covered.

Xiphophorus helleri — Gold Wag Swordtail.

Xiphophorus helleri — Brick Red Swordtails

Xiphophorus helleri — Black Swordtail. (Male right, female left.)

Family SCATOPHAGIDAE

These fishes are probably catadromous, that is, they live in fresh water and return to the sea to spawn.

The one species commonly kept in aquaria is *Scatophagus argus,* commonly called scat. This includes a **geographic** variety which has lovely patches of red on the back and **head, know**n as ruby scat or,

Scatophagus argus — Scat.

sometimes incorrectly, *S. rubrifons.* The *argus* is common throughout the Indo-Pacific region, both in fresh coastal waters and in the sea. The name *Scatophagus* means eater of ordure, and this gives us some idea of its eating habits. In an aquarium, scats enjoy the addition of some sea salt — about one teaspoon to five gallons. They are quite peaceful but will eat plants or anything else edible. Grows to twelve inches in nature. Aquarists have been unable to determine sex distinctions in this fish or to breed it in captivity.

Family SILURIDAE

These are all Old World catfishes, only one of which particularly interests the aquarist. This is the *Kryptopterus bicirrhis,* the Glass Catfish. This unusual catfish from India and the Greater Sunda Islands reaches a length of almost four inches in the aquarium. The unique feature is the translucence of its knife-shaped body. The ribs and sac enclosing its internal organs are clearly visible when a light is held behind it. There are two large feelers extending from the head. This is a schooling type of fish and one of the few catfishes which does not inhabit the bottom area. Rather, it hovers in mid-aquarium, the body moving with a wavelike motion characteristic of the species.

Kryptopterus bicirrhis — Glass Catfish.

A. VAN DEN NIEUWENHUIZEN

The Glass Catfish does not take kindly to dry foods, and if it is to be kept in good health it must have an ample supply of live food which it eats gluttonously, the stomach sometimes blowing up to the size and shape of a marble. At times, when fed heavily, the Glass Catfish ingests so much that is seems impossible for him to survive, but apparently it does no harm as he is back again at the next feeding, darting rapidly in to seize his share.

The Last Word!

Faced with the vast array and variety in the dealer's tanks the beginner tends to become overly enthusiastic when choosing fish. At times he lets this enthusiasm carry him away, and as a result he overstocks.

At first, it is much better to introduce just a few fish to the newly set-up tank after allowing it to settle for at least a week to show up any weaknesses or malfunction of equipment.

Don't overstock at any cost.

Brachygobius nunus — Bumblebee Fish. (Male left, female right.)

Rarities

Though technically not rare because they can be purchased from the aquatic store from time to time, the following species do add that little touch of exotic intrigue to the aquarium, creating a talking point for the viewers:

Brachygobius nunus — Bumblebee Fish or Golden banded Gobie: Striped like its insect counterpart, this two inch fish is well named.

Gnathonemus petersi — Elephant-nosed Fish.

Pantodon buchholzi — Butterfly Fish.

Gobies will select a portion of the tank as "territory" and defend it against even large fishes. If not fed a diet of live food they tend to become fin-nippers. There are several species, all from the Far East.

Gnathonemus petersi — Elephant-nosed Fish: As the name suggests, this fish from Western Africa has a long snout which it uses to good effect in rooting out food. At lengths of up to nine inches, they have a reputation for aggressiveness, but I have kept quite large specimens with small fish without any of the latter coming to harm.

Toxotes jaculator — Archerfish (preparing to shoot at *Tubifex* worms on the aquarium glass).

Prefers a live food diet. There are a number of species with the length and shape of the nose varying considerably.

Pantodon buchholzi — Butterfly Fish: This bizarre creature from Africa looks like a marine Flying Fish and, like it, can skim over the water in prodigious leaps. In the aquarium it spends most of its time at the surface waiting for food and can be trained to take food from the fingers. Can reach a size of five inches.

Toxotes jaculator — Archerfish: The Robin Hood of the aquarium. It can " squirt" small droplets of water with unerring accuracy and hit small flies at rest on overhead vegetation, knocking them into the water. Surely the most unusual way of obtaining food displayed by any fish! Small specimens can be kept in the community tank, although they do prefer some salt in the water — about one teaspoon to five gallons. Adults reach nine inches. Normal temperatures are ideal.

Xenomystus nigri — Black Knife Fish: The distinguishing feature of this fish is the complete absence of a dorsal fin. Growing up to eight inches, this African species moves through the water by undulating movements of an anal fin that stretches all along the lower portion of the body. The wavy action is similar to when you give a coil of rope a shake and the loop moves along in a rolling action. It is generally nocturnal, but it will appear during daylight if tidbits of food are offered.

W.TOMEY

Bleeding Heart Tetras, *Hyphessobrycon rubrostigma*, infected by Ich.

XIII   Diseases

When the beginner is first confronted by the fearful sounding array of fish diseases, he tends to become a little concerned not only for his fish but for his family. Most fish deseases are not transmissible to human beings, and if the aquarist takes normal hygienic precautions he has nothing to fear from his hobby.

The adage that an ounce of prevention is better than a pound of cure applies also to animals kept in the aquarium. Most of the diseases and parasitic infestations come about when the tank and its occupants are neglected, improperly fed, maintained at the wrong temperature, or have a surfeit of carbon dioxide; if in short they are generally mismanaged. Therefore, the first and obvious step in preventing health problems is to keep things as clean as possible.

Recognition of general disease symptoms is of the utmost importance, but don't jump to hasty conclusions. For example, loss of appetite (anorexia) for a short time is very common among most species of fish, but is does not necessarily indicate disease. Healthy fish have clean-looking plump bodies, with erect fins. The first symptom indicating something wrong is persistently clamped fins.

Other symptoms are listlessness, staying on the bottom, hanging at the surface, shimmying, sunken stomachs, torn or ragged fins, spots, marks or blemishes. An experienced, observant aquarist familiarizes himself with the normal behavior and appearance of his fishes. Any deviation from this norm is his first clue to possible trouble.

ALBERT KLEE

Some symptoms of illness. From right to left: spots on the fins and body, indicating a parasite; wasting away or "fish consumption", suggestive of an internal disease; forward fins, a general indication that something is wrong; whitish growth on fins or body, indicating fungal attacks or bacterial diseases of the "fin-rot" type; protruding scales, indicating dropsy.

The "Bends"

Tanks lacking in filtration and aeration may become supersaturated with oxygen. This is especially true if the aquarium is over-planted. Oxygen accumulates in the fish tissues and creates bubbles of gas in the skin and blood which is not unlike the bends — a condition experienced by divers. This can become so severe that bubbles appear under the skin and if the fish is removed from the water it emits a sound not unlike the crumpling of paper. The remedy is to keep the water on the move, promoting a better exchange of gases at the water surface.

Alkalinity

Very alkaline conditions (over pH 8) can cause the eating away of the skin of the fish especially around the gills. The remedy is to find out what is creating the excess alkalinity and re-adjust the pH gradually (see *pH*). The usual culprits are lime-bearing gravel, improperly cured cement ornaments, or large pieces of coral.

Fungous Infection

Mycology is the word the scientists use when talking about the study of fungi. Fishes are susceptible to several forms of fungous parasites; the most common are found among the *Saprolegnia* species. Spread by air or water-borne spore-bearing mycelia, they penetrate the tissues of the fish, where they feed and grow. They thrive on protein. Evidence of this is seen on portions of uneaten food which, when left in the tank, become covered with a hairy fungous growth. Most of these parasites do not attack healthy fish, so this kind of infection usually follows some injury, other disease or bad tank condition.

If the cottonlike growths of fungous infection are apparent, a cure can be effected by bathing the patches with a solution of commercial Mercurochrome. Commercial cures are available and some have proved excellent. The fish can be immersed in either saline solutions or one of the dyes such as malachite green. On no account must the fungus be pulled from the body of the fish. A dilute solution of potassium permanganate (1 grain to 10 gallons of water) is also effective.

Ichthyophonus hoferi (Ichthyosporidium) is one of the more widely distributed species of fungous infection. Fish are infected through their digestive systems by eating contaminated material. The spherical parasite feeds and multiplies on the fish, and, entering the mesenteric blood vessels, the *hoferi* is carried around the system, even into the brain. Treatment is mainly of a prophylactic nature. There is no known cure.

Viral Infection

Because a virus requires extraordinary magnification and is not visible through an optical microscope, our knowledge of viral infections is still in its infancy. One that we do know about is *lymphocystis*, which takes the form of growths not unlike small cauliflowers on the skin of the fish, notably on the dorsal fin. No cure is known and the fish usually succumbs to secondary fungous infection. Fish thus affected are best destroyed.

Protozoan Infection

The lowest and simplest form of animals, these are unicellular forms which multiply by fission. Under this heading comes the one disease that almost every aquarist has to deal with during his fishkeeping career, white spot or *Ich*. This disease is caused by a protozoan parasite whose scientific name is *Ichthyophthirius multifiliis*, but don't let that tongue twister frighten you; translated it simply means "fish louse with many children"! Every year lots of would-be hobbyists are lost to the aquarium hobby because their fish tanks are decimated by Ich, yet the disease is easy to control once you understand its pathology.

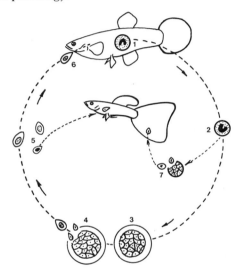

Life cycle of the Ich parasite. 1 — Parasite feeding off fish tissues. 2 — Cyst erupts and the parasite falls. 3 — On the bottom, the parasite multiplies by dividing. 4 — The cell erupts, liberating the parasite. 5 — The free-swimming form now searches for a fish host. It is at this stage that Ich is most responsive to treatment. 6 — By means of its pointed end it burrows into the fish tissues. 7 — Dislodged parasites break open before encystment.

Ich shows itself as tiny white spots, like grains of salt, on the fins and skin of the fish. The parasite must be introduced to the aquarium, usually by new additions of an infected fish or plants or live food. Once introduced, it swims about until it finds a fish host. Using its pointed end to good effect it quickly bores its way under the skin. The fish tissues, resenting this intrusion, react by throwing a protective cyst around the parasite. In this "dome" it lives, feeds and gets fat. This increase in size plus its own excreta swells up the cyst until, like some over-filled balloon, it bursts and the parasite, now loaded with nourishment, falls to the floor of the tank. Here it rests and multiplies. It has been calculated that up to 2,000 young parasites may be produced, and now you know why this disease spreads so rapidly. The cyst, full of young, ruptures and up swim the young Ich seeking a fish host to repeat the life cycle. The period of this cycle varies with tank temperature, but in the average tank at 75°F it would take about four days.

Treatment: We cannot kill the encysted bug without also killing the fish, so treatment consists of dosing the water with a chemical that kills the free swimming bug. Salt, quinine hydrochloride, malachite green, methylene blue, Mercurochrome, have all been used with success. Effective commercial remedies are available.

Velvet *(Oodinium):* Has a similar life cycle to Ich, but the fish looks as if it has been sprinkled with tan powder, hence the common name, Rust Velvet Disease. Copper — in either the sulphate or metallic form — is the treatment.

Fish lice *(Argulus):* Small parasites (about ¼ inch long), they can be observed adhering to the skin and fins of affected fish. With a sharp proboscis they pierce the skin and cause great discomfort; the punctured spot often develops a reddish inflammation. Lice are usually introduced into the tank with new fish or plants. Treat fish by giving them a short bath in potassium permanganate (one grain to ten U.S. gallons of water) for about thirty minutes. Potassium permanganate may be purchased in grain tablets. Most aquarium stores also carry it in solution.

Flukes: Flat, wormlike parasites, hermaphroditic (both male and female in the same body), fitted with suckers and hooks, they stick to the fish. The two main forms are *Gyrodactylus* (Body Flukes) and *Dactylogyrus* (Gill Flukes), the latter being the more dangerous. Adult forms can be seen with a magnifying glass. Body Flukes look like elongated pillows, clinging to one end of the fish; the end portion of Gill Flukes may be seen protruding from the gill covers. To the naked eye, Body Flukes may be recognized by the slimy patches they form, usually near the dorsal fin. Red gills are a warning of possible Gill Fluke infection. Dip fish in a strong saline solution to make the parasites loosen their hold. Potassium permanganate and copper treatment are also effective.

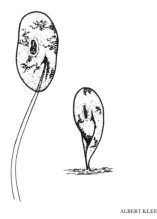

One of the common skin parasites, *Costia necatrix*. Left: swimming position. Right: the parasite attached to a fish.

ALBERT KLEE

Costia: Infested fish have a cloudy look about them. In severe outbreaks even the water can appear cloudy from their colonies, though the latter conditon is rare in the aquarium. This tiny flagellate doesn't like high temperatures. It is so small that special staining techniques and a magnification of about X 300 are required to observe *Costia*. Treatment is as for Flukes. Adding a teaspoon of salt to each five gallons of aquarium water and raising the temperature to 85° F is also effective.

Bacterial Infections

Before the introduction of sulfa drugs and antibiotics into the arsenal of the aquarist, few bacterial conditions could be successfully treated. However, we must exclude penicillin, because most bacteria pathogenic to fish are in the gram-negative range and penicillin is relatively ineffective against these. Aureomycin and Terramycin are effective but have the disadvantage of discoloring the water. Chloromycetin (chlortetracycline) and Bacitracin are preferred. Because diagnosis requires growing the suspected infested tissue in the laboratory, followed by microbiological techniques, this group of diseases is difficult to diagnose.

Chondrococcus columnaris: Characterized by white fungus-like growths in the mouth region. Described first in 1922, this disease, bacterial in nature, is often wrongly called mouth fungus. It is highly contagious to other fish, and if treatment is delayed it can eat away the frontal portion of the head. Swab the infection with malachite green.

An antibiotic such as Chloromycin or Terramycin will effect a rapid cure. These are usually dispensed in 250 milligram capsules.

Use one of these for each ten U.S. gallons to be treated. The capsule is opened and the powder emptied and dissolved in a few ounces of warm water poured into the aquarium.

Often, one of the first indications of mouth fungus is the fish hanging near the surface with gills distended. Close inspection will reveal the whitening of the lips characteristic of the disease.

Mycobacterium piscium: Fish tuberculosis — not to be confused with the human kind. Symptoms are emaciation and frayed fins accompanied by skin lesions. This disease is so similar in appearance to *Ichthyophonus* that one is often mistaken for the other. Fish maintained in optimum conditions and kept on a good diet may never contract this disease. Should it appear, either isolate or dispose of the infected fish. One or two drops of formalin (the standard 40% solution) per U.S. gallon has been recommended as a treatment.

W. TOMEY

A Brick Red Swordtail infected with tail rot.

Tail and Fin Rot: Fins become frayed and torn either through bacterial action or from fighting or being attacked by other fish. Treat as if for fungous infection. If the rotting becomes severe, cutting away the infected parts is necessary. Swab the torn fin afterwards with a mild antiseptic.

The way to distinguish between fins damaged by infection and wounds caused by other fishes is to examine the ragged edges carefully. Infections show a fine white or gray edge while ripped fins are clear.

Dropsy: For a long time *Pseudomonas punctata* was blamed for this infection, which produces a blown up, bloated effect with protruding scales. New developments have indicated that *Pseudomonas* is merely a secondary infection. The main causation is probably viral, although there are several possible causes of dropsy. The strange thing about dropsy is that it strikes at individual fish and rarely assumes epidemic proportions. Death occurs in a matter of weeks, so destroy infected fish. In the larger species temporary relief is affected by tapping the fish with a hypodermic needle, but this is not for the beginner.

Eye Diseases: Mechanical or chemical damage to the cornea of the eye usually results in some form of fungous infection. It is more dangerous here than on the body because the spores may penetrate the eye and enter the brain. Treat by bathing the eyes with a 1 % solution of silver nitrate in distilled water. Neutralize the silver nitrate immediately with a 1% solution of potassium dichromate. Repeat the treatment until the fungus disappears.

Pop-Eye: In this the eye swells up and is known as exophthalmus or pop-eye, caused by *Pseudomonas punctata* bacteria. Though no sure cure is known, relief is given when the affected fish is moved to very "aged" water.

Gray Cataract *(Cataracta traumatica)*: Eye takes on whitish "boiled" appearance.

Worm Cataract *(C. parasitica)*: Similar in appearance to above; examination of the affected eye with a magnifying glass reveals the tiny dots, the ends of worms in the eye. Not contagious to other fish. Treat with silver nitrate as above.

Fish Enemies

Although very few aquarists will doubt the value of feeding live foods, there are certain hazards inherent in their use, notably the possible introduction into the tank of harmful creatures. A well-known poster during the war instructed us to "Know your Enemy," and this you must do if you are to know what should be kept out of the aquarium.

Bloodworms: Small, free swimming worms colored like Tubifex worms. But unlike the latter, they move about the tank in a characteristic figure eight movement. Belonging to the genus *Chironomus,* they are the larvae of a midge. Bloodworms are sold as live food and have excellent nutritive value. As I stated earlier, cases have been reported of this worm eating its way back out of a fish that had eaten it. (Ed. note — in many thousands of bloodworm feedings I have never seen this happen.)

Water Bugs: Most of these creatures like water boat bugs (*Corixidae*) and water scorpions (*Nepidae*) kill their prey by grasping and sucking. Even small specimens must be kept out of the tank.

Planaria: These are repulsive looking flatworms that are actually large protozoans. They are harmless to fully grown fish but can attack fish fry and eggs. Don't attempt to kill these creatures by crushing or cutting; the parts will regenerate. They thrive under foul conditions, and if they are seen in the tank it must be cleaned. Keep the tank clean and the planaria will disappear. For faster results use potassium permanganate.

Leeches: Though the members constitute a large family they all resemble long, flat, narrow worms. They move about in the tank by an undulating movement. Only a few species are known to be dangerous to fish, but take no chances and remove any you see. However, because of their nocturnal and burrowing habits they often infest a tank before they are seen. Usually carried in on new plants, this is an additional reason for thoroughly washing them.

Hydra: In Greek mythology, the Hydra was a nine-headed sea monster — in the tank it looks like a miniature sea anemone. It is a simple polyp with a cylindrical body from which grow tentacles. These wave about in the water attempting to catch prey such as Daphnia or newborn fry. They move about by a tumbling action. Disturbed, they retract into formless blobs. They are dangerous only to small fish but they look unsightly. As they are carnivorous, the simplest way to eliminate them is to eliminate all live food. Avoid feeding Daphnia and similar foods until they disappear.

Whirligig: This torpedo-shaped creature is the larval form of the *Dytiscus* Beetle. Its head is armed with sharp pincers which reach out and grasp their prey — which may even be fish many times their size. Both beetle and larva are taboo. They are quickly noticeable in the aquarium so net them out.

A Pinch of This . . . A Drop of That?

Dispensing drugs by measuring a pinch of this or a lump of that just won't do; it gives rise to sloppy treatment with a hit-or-miss chance of success. Most druggists will be only too glad to help make up your prescriptions. Be sure to explain what the drugs are for and that they are to be used in a fish tank. In Britain some years back, chemists dispensed two kinds of the drug methylene blue — medicinal quality and the coarse industrial or technical grade. I wonder how many aquarists condemned the use of this dye because when asking for it they neglected to explain to the chemist that it was for treating sick fish. Consequently they had been given the industrial quality, unsuitable for the job.

Diagnosis

Before attempting to make a diagnosis, check that the disorders in your fish are not due to bad tank conditions. Do this by siphoning off some of the old water and replacing it with fresh water — it may work wonders! If this has no effect, then check the symptoms displayed and see if you can recognize the ailment. In any event, if you buy the ready-made cures, don't go in for the wonder medicines that claim they cure everything; like the medicine man's snake oil, they appear to be the ultimate deterrent in the fight against disease. Although the antibiotics have improved the situation tremendously, don't despise the old and tried remedies.

If you keep a drug cabinet, label all chemicals with the date of purchase or the date they were dispensed. Some drugs change their state and become stronger with age. Others lose their effectiveness when exposed to the action of light — although these are usually kept in dark bottles. *If in doubt, throw the chemical out!* Above all, keep all medicines out of the reach of children.

Most of the remedies mentioned here may be purchased at your local aquarium shop, ready mixed and with instructions for dispensing. An eye dropper, by the way, is not exact enough when the prescription requires the dose in drops. Purchase a dropping bottle. This allows only one drop of liquid to be dispensed at a time.

For the benefit of those hobbyists who are of a scientific turn of mind, here are instructions for mixing the drugs and the proper dosage.

Salt: the coarse form is preferred. Up to one teaspoon for each five gallons of water may be added to a planted aquarium for a mild treatment. Remember that salt does not evaporate, so keep a careful record and do not add any additional salt unless you have first replaced some water. By treating the sick fish in a bare container, the amount of salt can be gradually increased by the addition of a teaspoon for each five gallons every 24 hours, up to a maximum of one teaspoon per gallon for most fish. Several partial changes of water are required before replacing the fish in its own aquarium. A heroic treatment involves using or making up a solution of one teaspoon of salt for each quart of water. The fish is dipped into this for five minutes and removed. Salt is a very good general remedy to be used when all else fails, or when in doubt as to what specific disease you are treating.

Malachite Green: dissolve one gram of pure drug in 40 ounces of water for stock, or ask your druggist to make up a ¾ of 1 % solution. Use five drops per gallon.

Potassium Permanganate: available in ½ grain and 1 grain tablets. Dissolve one grain in a little warm water, and add this to each ten gallons of water to be treated.

Quinine Hydrochloride: dissolve and add one teaspoon of the powder to each ten gallons of water to be treated.

Methylene Blue: for a stock solution, dissolve five grams of pure powder in one liter of distilled water. Use three drops for each gallon of water.

Mercurochrome: the standard form available is a 2% aqueous solution. Use two drops for each gallon of water.

Copper Sulfate: dissolve one gram of pure copper sulfate in one liter of distilled water. Use one teaspoon for each gallon of water.

Antibiotics (Aureomycin, Terramycin, Chloromycetin, Tetracycline, etc.): these are dispensed in 50 milligram, 100 milligram and 250 milligram size capsules. The largest is the most economical. Open the capsule, dissolve the contents in lukewarm water, and add directly to the aquarium. 250 mgs. will treat ten to fifteen gallons.

Formalin: this is actually a 37 ½ % solution of formaldehyde. Use one drop to each gallon of water. For a 30 minute dip, which is effective against many parasites, use 32 drops per gallon in a separate tank. Watch the fish, and if there is any sign of weakness remove them immediately.

Equivalents:

> One liter = approximately one quart
> 28.350 grams = one ounce
> 30 cc = approximately one fluid ounce
> four cc = one teaspoon

Where possible, treat all sick fish in separate tanks and keep these hospital aquaria devoid of plants.

If the manufacturer of a cure prescribes a specific dosage per gallon of aquarium water, remember that rocks and gravel will displace quite an appreciable amount of water and that this must be taken into account when making any calculation.

Many facilities are available to the fishkeeper for accurate post mortem examination of their fish. Professional bodies, museums and aquarist clubs will all help. Fish sent for examination must be packed correctly in preservative and a full description given. It isn't a bit of use sending a fish for post mortem if it is too far desiccated to allow for accurate investigation.

Disease in the average well-kept aquarium is rare. Take suitable quarantine precautions and isolate all fish and plants before introducing them to the community tank. Disinfect new plants as previously described. Live foods, either bought or collected from the wild, should be tipped into a shallow tray (a photographer's white developing dish is ideal) and examined for unwanted creatures before being fed to the fishes.

Killing Fish Painlessly

This is not an action most of us relish, but something that everyone in the hobby has to face. Fishes can be killed instantly by immersing them in strong alcohol. If alcohol isn't available, they can be anesthetized in a 5% solution of urethane or chloretone in water, then thrown hard against a stone floor.

Preserving Specimens

Ethyl or grain alcohol is ideal, but because of certain legal restrictions in force in many states and countries of the world, possession of this chemical is prohibited; instead, formalin is used.

To preserve large specimens (over nine inches long), inject the body cavity with a 10 % formalin solution, which your druggist will make up for you. Place the specimen to be preserved on a piece of cork or soft board and correctly position the fins, holding them in place with pins. For smaller specimens immerse in a 5 % formalin solution.

Commercial formalin is apt to decompose when stored. It produces free acid in this state and will damage specimens placed in it. The chemical takes on a yellow color changing to red-brown as it ages.

Warning: Formalin is both corrosive and poisonous, so treat it with respect and don't leave the bottle lying around where children can reach it. Frequent contact with this liquid often causes a painful eczema on the fingers. To prevent this, wear rubber gloves when handling it or cover the hands and fingers with a good barrier cream. A thin layer of Vaseline, while messy, is suitable for this purpose.

XIV Toxins

Metals

There are five toxic metals likely to be encountered by aquarists: copper, zinc, lead, silver and aluminum.

Copper: The toxicity from the metallic salts of copper and its zinc alloy, brass, even in relatively small amounts, may be fatal to fishes; wet corrosion from these metals is rapid and intense, and the water soon contains concentrations strong enough to render it poisonous to both animal and plant life. If the water in your domestic supply is run through copper or stored in a copper storage tank, be sure to run the tap for a few minutes before drawing any water. Copper sulphate is recommended as a cure for certain *Oodinium* parasites, but unless used in the prescribed amounts this chemical can kill. Coins in the fountain at Trevi might be fine but not in the home aquarium.

Zinc: Galvanized iron is highly poisonous as the zinc coating is very dangerous when dissolved in water. Soluble zinc salts are powerful precipitants of protein matter.

Lead: This metal is usually considered safe and only becomes harmful when dissolved in solution. Avoid the over-use of lead strip as a plant weight in soft, acid water because it will slowly dissolve and could become toxic.

Silver: Certain filter materials contain silver granules. These kill harmful micro-bacteria present in water. Though dissolved silver is toxic, the tiny amounts liberated by this medium are not sufficient to be harmful. Prolonged use of silver, however, can turn fish eggs sterile.

Aluminium: Wet corrosion of pure aluminum is a minor danger since the formation of protective coatings of oxide prevents further corrosion. Due to this, the darkening of aluminum reflectors, while unsightly, should not be scoured because the coating protects the metal.

Poisons

The book "Silent Spring" by the late Rachel Carson awakened us to the dangers of man's pollution of nature's domain. Many poisons find their way into the aquarium by accident. In the home, fly sprays, air fresheners and polishes--the majority dispensed in fine droplet form by aerosol sprays--drift about the room and can be drawn into the tank by the air pump. Even a close fitting reflector is no defense here. Sprays containing DDT or other chlorinated hydrocarbons are deadly to fishes. If these sprays are used in the vicinity of the tank, turn the pump off and cover the tank with a tight fitting sheet of plastic fastened down by string. Leave it in place until the fine mist from the spraying has had time to disperse.

Never paint a tank containing fish or plants nor, for that matter, paint even in the near vicinity. Many of the vapors given off as the paint dries can cause trouble. If you have to decorate and it is impossible to move the tank, open as many doors and windows as feasible, stop the air pump, and cover as described above.

If cleaning fluids are used to to clean the front glass, see that none splashes into the tank. Never clean a reflector or cover glass with these cleaning fluids since water can drip back into the tank as condensation and carry toxins with it.

Nicotine is highly poisonous and, obviously, cigarette butts are out. When you have guests in your home and the air in the room develops a smoke fog, stop the pumps.

Symptoms of Poisoning in Aquatic Animals

The symptoms exhibited as the result of poisoning vary with the poison and the dosage received. To further complicate matters, many of these symptoms are also common to other fish ailments. Generally, the fish display erratic movement or lie on their sides gasping for breath. Shimmying, convulsions and loss of natural color are all signs to make one suspect poison. An immediate transfer of the fish to fresh water usually brings relief, but if the poison is far advanced no cure exists.

Copper and zinc kill by coagulating the mucous covering of the body, especially in the gill area, where they clog the fine membranes. The fish dies by suffocation. Fish suffering from metal poisoning will usually hang gasping at the surface, where they cruise aimlessly about. One way to differentiate between diseases and this type of poisoning is that where disease may effect only certain fishes, poisoning affects *all* the fishes, all of them usually reacting within a short time of exposure.

Build Up of Poisonous Wastes

During the normal processes of excretion, the fish void nitrogenous wastes as urine from the kidneys. Decaying food and plants in the aquarium are attacked by bacteria. Both of these actions produce ammonia, a deadly poison. Normally, ammonia is converted by bacteria into nitrites and then nitrates, which are materials used by the plants to help them grow. If artificial plants are used or if the tank is overcrowded or improperly cared for, then ammonia may build up to toxic levels. Therefore, change about one third of the tank water every few weeks.

The importance of carbon dioxide has already been covered-- the poison symptoms displayed by the fish being very similar to those of ammonia poisoning. Because carbon dioxide develops mainly under acid conditions, a pH check of the tank will help to distinguish between carbon dioxide and ammonia poisoning. Watch out for the fish gulping in atmospheric air at the surface.

Fouling of an aquarium produces hydrogen sulfate; this gives rise to a smell characteristic of rotten eggs. A tank in good order has very little or no odor at all.

Chlorine and Fluoride

The addition to the home water supply of chlorine and sodium fluoride has caused some aquarists much concern. The control of both of these additives is simple. Let the water stand in open containers for at least 24 hours. The chlorine gases will dissipate naturally. A small percentage of fluorine doesn't appear to affect the fish. The process of dissipation may be hastened by aeration and filtration and rise in water temperature. This is necessary only when large amounts of water are changed. The small amounts involved in replacing the condensation losses can be ignored, as they are quickly diluted to the point of harmlessness by the rest of the tank water.

An aerial view of the largest tropical fish hatchery in the world. It is located on the west coast of Florida.

XV Professional Hatcheries

Breeding fish commercially is one venture, I can assure you, that demands knowledge, capital and a sense of adventure. Since the turn of the century when dealers first began to endeavor in earnest to supply the hobbyists' ever increasing demand for more and more fish, breeders have attempted to balance "supply and demand" by either producing the fish on their own "farms" or importing them from abroad. Today the commercial breeding of fish is big business.

In other trades when a dealer buys a load of goods that is either damaged on arrival or proves to be a poor seller, he can always recoup some of his money by selling cheaper. Not so the commercial fish breeder. If a fish dies it is worthless — nothing is deader than a dead fish; it is even useless as food.

Add to this hazard those of pilfering (from outdoor pools), losses from predators such as birds and snakes, bad debts, delayed freight, the ravages of nature from storms, hurricanes, floods, frost and drought, and the reader will quickly realize that, though at first

247

glance fish breeding looks pleasantly profitable, difficulties like these make it a very risky business indeed.

As far as the more common species of fish are concerned, it is very important to breed only those fish which are ready sellers; otherwise, disposal of one's stock becomes a major problem. The longer the fish remain unsold, the more they eat — and the higher the food bill grows.

Let us take a hypothetical case of a breeder wishing to supply just one hundred fish per week of an egglaying species.

One of the first surprises to the "beginner" is the number of tanks required! Breeding these fish can be condensed into the stages of:

[a] conditioning the parents;
[b] the spawning;
[c] rearing the resultant fry.

To insure maximum results the adult fish are kept separate while they are conditioned, males in one tank and females in the other; then they are brought together for the mating. After spawning, the adults are removed. The fry remain for about two weeks. So far, that has meant three tanks are required.

After two weeks the growing fish are transferred to larger tanks, because crowding then would be fatal. We'll probably need a further three tanks to insure the brood has room to grow. After two months, they will be of salable size.

A grand total of *six* tanks to produce just a hundred fish! And remember — it is easy to spawn fish, the task is to raise them. The amateur who raises 25 young from a spawn of several hundred is delighted. When one realizes that a commercial venture would have to produce many more fish than this if it were to succeed, one can visualize just how many tanks one would need. No wonder the perpetual gripe of the indoor hatchery owner is that he never has enough tanks!

To make a commercial hatchery pay requires certain conditions. The first is a plentiful supply of suitable water. The public water supply is usually doctored with chemicals to protect the public's health and is totally unsuitable for fish breeding. This means that to obtain the right kind of water either a well must be sunk or a good supply of untreated water must be on hand.

Climate also plays its part in deciding the location of the hatchery.

The temperature of the tank is critical, and unless one wants to cut the profits with huge fuel bills, warm climates are preferred. This is probably why the State of Florida is such a favored spot, comprising the world's largest aquarium fish farm. Although a few fish farms are operated in California and Arizona, their output is much smaller than Florida's.

Outdoor Hatcheries

Outdoor hatcheries construct large pools by using excavating machinery to scoop out long trenches which are then filled with water and seeded. Certain topographical conditions are required for this type of construction.

The hatcheries which depend on pools bulldozed out of the raw earth are known as "dirt farms" and are found primarily on the west coast of Florida, in the Tampa, Palmetto, Bradenton, St. Petersburg areas. Here the temperature seldom drops too low in the winter and there is a constant water table temperature. This means that when the pools are excavated there is a certain amount of natural seepage of water which tends to maintain its level. Also, wells are sunk which can bring water to the surface at a constant temperature above 70° F.

When cold weather comes as it does every so often to Florida, the spigots are opened up on the pools. It is not an uncommon sight during these cold weather spells to see all the fishes in the pools clustered in the current of warm water entering the pool.

It is rare for Florida to see more than one or two really cold days during the winter season. Usually, for the short duration of the cold spell, no extra precautions are necessary. The fishes become torpid and sink to the bottom. Fishes intended for shipment are trapped out of the pools before these brief cold periods since the fish then are too sluggish to enter the trap.

Fishes are raised in these pools, in a more or less natural condition, although they are fed regularly. Hatcheries, of course, requiring tremendous quantities of food, do not use the little shaker top cans with which we are so familiar. Each hatchery has its own "secret" formula which is jealously guarded. In general, however, a mixture of oatmeal, fish-meal, shrimp and egg yolk is the basic diet. This can be supplemented by such items as meat meal and rice polishings. Great vats of salt water are constantly maintained for the continuous hatching of brine shrimp eggs.

While separate strains of livebearers are kept in each of the pools to propagate, a certain amount of selection must take place. Fishes which are trapped out of the pool are hand-divided by a skilled employee into several groups; one group is retained for breeding, another group — usually the largest in numbers — is set aside to be shipped, undersized fishes which are otherwise of good quality are returned to their respective pools to continue growing, and the unsuitable, or culls, are destroyed. This is necessary in order to maintain the strain.

Every fish hatchery has, in addition to its outside pools, extensive indoor facilities where egglayers are bred, and new, delicate and imported species are conditioned. These so-called fish rooms are more like our conception of a standard hatchery. There are rows and rows of tanks, while the floor is usually lined with shallow form concrete pools. The balance of the floor is concrete, sloping for a run-off. Most of the hatchery workers are barefooted and in shorts, or wear rubber boots. How we hobbyists, who must keep our fishes in the living room and dread a drop of water on the carpet, must envy this! Aquariums which are to be emptied are just siphoned onto the floor and water runs off to the drain by itself.

Under these favorable conditions, egglayers are spawned and their young reared to a size preparatory to being placed in outdoor pools in order to achieve full growth.

The hatcheries on the east coast of Florida, primarily in the Miami area, usually have their pools made of concrete blocks which are set on concrete bases and coated with a water-proofing material. These are called "vat farms." One of the principal reasons the pools in the hatcheries in the Miami area are mostly above-ground varieties, is that the coral layers just below ground make digging trenches out of the question. Each pool has a drain near the bottom so that it can be completely emptied, dried and sterilized. This must be done periodically as otherwise the accumlation of parasites, and the possible deterioration of strains of fishes, would make the inhabitants of the pools unusable.

Because the pools on the west coast of Florida cannot be drained, another method of sterilization — chemical — is practiced. Every so often, usually every two or three years, everything in the pool is killed by a chemical such as muratic acid or copper sulphate. The pool is allowed to remain empty for a period of time and then is restocked, hopefully, for the next few years.

Another method of renewing the pool is to pump it completely dry using a powerful portable pump. Chemicals, such as hydrated lime, are spread over the area and the pool allowed to refill itself naturally. It will stand empty for a period of weeks while the natural cycle, aided by the addition of soy bean meal or fertilizer, re-establishes itself.

With all those problems, it is hard to imagine why so many persons running commercial hatcheries are such enthusiasts. The introduction of fast jet air services has eased their burden a little. In the past, fishes were shipped by rail, often requiring four or five days to make the trip. Today a shipment can reach almost any part of the United States within 24 hours. As all shippers now guarantee that their fishes will be delivered alive, you can see what a difference speedy transportation makes.

Local conditions have compelled many hatcheries to specialize. The available water determines which species of fish they can produce with a minimum of preparation; some specialize in breeding only livebearing fish, while others devote the whole of their tanks and pools to the production of rare and common aquatic plants.

With due deference to the many wonderful professional hatcheries I have visited throughout the world, I would like to clear up a couple of small points that seem to bother most new visitors to a hatchery. In the large commercial fish farms devoted to the production of hundreds of species, feeding, sorting, capturing and packing take up a large amount of time and don't leave much room for cleaning and maintaining tanks at the standard conditions of home aquaria. Please don't expect the clinical appearance one expects from the hobbyist's one tank. Also, because the breeder is usually very busy, don't expect the " red carpet" to be put down for your visit. While you are enjoying yourself, the wholesaler must make his living!

The Professional and the Amateur

Since 1900, the hobbyist and the dealer have worked hand-in-hand to solve mutual problems. However, the record shows that on some occasions interference by the amateur in the commercial field has spelled ruination for the professionals involved.

One such case occurred in 1955 in the Philippine Islands. When the improvement of air freight reduced the time of the air shipping journey from Manila to San Francisco to 12 hours, a handful of enthusiastic professionals started shipping marine fishes to the

United States. At first, huge losses occurred but, with the accumulation of knowledge and cooperation between an American dealer and his Philippine contact, these difficulties were largely overcome. Healthy fish were soon available to hobbyists all over America.

The Filipinos learned that after capture the fish had to be kept in tanks and acclimatized before they were shipped out. The commercial hatcheries did just that, but many amateurs, seeing the rich pickings from the business, "muscled in" and started to ship unacclimatized specimens. As the demand increased they even shipped questionable fish to the United States. The fish died in great numbers and brought problems to all. The genuine commercial dealer suffered because of the interference of amateurs who, in most cases, actually didn't know any better.

The Philippine trade started to die and by 1957 had been almost laid to rest. It was a long time before the original dealers were able to live down the stigma and resume trade.

Breeders, collectors and exporters of aquarium fish are found throughout the world, though because of environmental conditions they concentrate on different aspects of the trade.

Hong Kong, Singapore and Bangkok

Hundreds of thousands of tropical fishes, perhaps millions, are raised each year in each of these cities for shipment all over the world. They are raised primarily by small Chinese breeders, each of whom contributes his output to a larger hatchery which acts as a shipping agent.

In the Colony of Hong Kong, over 100 people are regularly employed just in collecting live fish food to supply the many commercial establishments. Because of the waters, conditons on the mainland are slightly on the acid side and very suitable for the fish bred. Most of the farms are found in the portion of the mainland called "The New Territories." Here, breeding is done, for the most part, in small wooden or brick buildings lined with shallow (five to ten inch) concrete vats and housing rows of tanks. Because the Hong Kong territory is relatively small in area and only semi-tropical, there is no fish collecting carried on.

Singapore, however, which is on the Malay peninsula, and Bangkok in Thailand, supplement the shipments of fishes which they breed with many locally collected species. Such favorites as *Rasbora heteromorpha, Monodactylus argenteus, Gyrinocheilus aymonieri,* and many others are collected in great quantities. Because the weather is more favorable in these last two places, a great deal of breeding takes place in large concrete pools out-of-doors.

The Chinese are very clever breeders, but they have not originated anywhere near the number of new strains and species that the Florida farmers have, nor does the combined total output of fishes bred in the three areas equal the production in Florida.

Moving on to India, the comercial trade goes back to the year 1930. When the rest of the aquatic world was still amazed at the breeding of livebearing species commercially, a Bombay pioneer was already producing Angelfish by the bucketful!

Shipping Fish

Early distributors used to send their fish in metal cans. In addition to the drawback of weight, the fish in these containers were bounced against the hard sides of the can during shipment and on arrival at their destination were prone to infection. Their anterior portions which took the brunt of this were very affected indeed and the term " mouth fungus" became synoymous with newly arrived specimens.

Plastics and expanded polystyrene altered all that and today's travelers are shipped out in plastic bags (usually doubled for strength) filled a quarter full of water and then inflated with oxygen. Tranquillizing drugs are sometimes introduced into the water to sedate the fish and restrict their movement during transit. They revive quickly when placed in fresh water, none the worse for their experience. The fish bags are packed with paper and placed in cardboard or styrofoam boxes. Airline companies were quick to see the expanding market and now special sections of their flights are devoted to the handling of live fish.

Training Personnel

Is it possible for the amateur enthusiast to make commercial breeding a career? If the actual owning and running of hatchery is intended then the qualifications (finance, etc.) are no different than starting up in any self-employed, commercial venture, but for employment in an established fish farm there are other standards.

For many years the staff of fish hatcheries consisted of a core of experienced personnel. Others had to learn the job in the hard school of trial and error. Though many suitably qualified people graduate from schools and colleges, the lure of the professional fish farm with all its attendant risks isn't a very attractive financial proposition and they wander into other fields.

Thanks to the efforts of many farm owners, training courses do now exist to educate those who seek employment. One large commercial establishment in Western Germany actually runs a course that enables the student to take up paid employment with the company as well as allowing him to attend suitable instruction at a local school. After 12 months of this, the trainee is interviewed and his progress reported on by the regular staff. Together with the employer they decide which branch of the business the student is best suited for. If the commercial aptitude is evident, then the pupil goes back to school to study selling techniques, bookkeeping, and all the paraphernalia of selling and shipping fish. If, on the other hand, the student shows a natural bent for the hatchery and its work, then he takes up biology and aquarium know-how.

At the end of four years of study, students take examinations set by the local authority. With this proof of ability they can be assured of employment in a professional fish hatchery.

The aquarium hobby has held second place in the list of recreational pursuits for many years, and is still growing. With this growth of interest have come increased demands for more and more fish. After a period of trial and error, the professional fish farmer today is more ready than ever to meet these demands.

Although the chances of the hobbyist, with his limited set-up, becoming a "big man" commercially are slight, recent years have seen some amateurs producing varieties of fish that have commanded a ready market. When time is not a limiting factor, the amateur can experiment. If he is successful, he will soon find that no matter where he lives, the world will beat a path to his door. This is particularly true in the field of supply breeding, where the production of new and finer strains is a highly competitive avocation. Because of intensive attention required, this is one area in which the amateur can compete with the professional. In the specialist fields, many amateurs have proved by their prowess that turning professional is still a possibility, and many a set-up started modestly in a garage or living room now boasts expanded premises.

XVI Things to Come

New Species

It seems hard to imagine that even though there are 40,000 or so living species of fish known to man, there could be even more. Yet, even as you sit reading these words, someone — somewhere in the world — is out searching for new specimens, some of which may be suitable for keeping in the aquarium. About 168 families, representing some 3,000 species of fish, are known to inhabit the North American continent alone! Yet experts tell us that many more species have yet to be discovered. Small wonder that the current press devoted to aquarium keeping is constantly tantalizing us with news of some hitherto unknown specimen.

And they aren't all " new." Some specimens, known to have existed milleniums ago, but believed to have become extinct as the Dinosaurs, have come to light — the Coelacanth *(Latimeria chalumnae)*, for instance.

Who knows what weird and wonderful specimens future collectors will keep in their aquaria?

Aquarium Clubs

Most major cities today have at least one aquarium society while some of the specialist societies boast a world wide membership. Hobbyists meet at regular intervals to discuss their problems, and through films, tapes and lectures learn more about tropical fish.

In addition to their normal programs, many groups organize social events and expeditions to collect specimens for their aquaria; others help maintain tanks in schools, hospitals and homes for the aged. In so doing they perform a great service by bringing joy into drab lives.

An aquarium teaches children quite naturally about nature and her world. Seeing something other than themselves creates in children an unselfish spirit. Further, the many facets of aquaristics can encourage them to explore the limitless worlds of zoology and botany.

Owning large numbers of tanks filled with thousands of fish is not a prerequisite to membership in an aquarium society. If your interest in fish — rather than your decorative taste — prompted you to purchase an aquarium, then I suggest that you contact your local aquarium society and go to their next meeting. Remember that many of the new varieties of fish now available to aquarists were developed in a single community aquarium. Be the pioneer of your family — buy some fish; go to a meeting — discover a world!

Shows

Why do fishkeepers go to a lot of time and trouble just to exhibit their fish? The hope of being among the winners is only one answer — for as mountains that have to be climbed and records that have to be broken, there are men who enter any competition to attain a sense of achievement.

Fish shows vary from large public shows to small "Table Shows" held on meeting night among the members of a club. In the large "Open Shows," competition is much stiffer and the gains higher. These are not only competitions but great social occasions as well.

The trouble hobbyists take to compete in these shows was exemplified when an avid aquarist from the west coast of Canada traveled over 2,000 miles overland, just to show his Guppies!

Schedules giving the various classes where fish can be shown are published. The fish are exhibited in drum bowls for the smaller species, and in tanks for the larger. There are classes for the "Aquarium Beautiful," where the exhibitor sets up a completely furnished aquarium at the show; and classes for "novelty," in which the competitor uses artificial figures and ornaments to create an unusual picture within the confines of a tank.

Entrance fees are not expensive and every opportunity and inducement is given the hobbyist to participate — some clubs have elaborate facilities to look after the comfort of both visitors and exhibitors alike — even to the point of arranging overnight accomodations for two-day events.

Vacation and the Aquarist

Each year vacation time rolls around and the pet keeper has the problem of finding someone to look after his pets during his absence. Though instruction on what to do about your aquaria during such an absence might seem ambitious for a "beginner's guide," it will have to be faced sooner or later, so here are a few pointers:

One of the hardest things to learn about keeping a sparkling tank is learning how to feed the fish. If you do have a friend or neighbor willing to come in and see to the tank during your absence, don't rely on their knowing how much food to use, for unless they, too, are aquarists they will invariably overfeed.

Play safe, place sufficient fish food for one daily feed in either paper cups or paper spills; tell your "caretaker" to empty just one of these into the tank each day, and no more. Hide any other fish food!

Starting a few weeks before you leave, gradually lower the temperature of the aquaria. At lower temperatures the metabolism of the fish is slowed down and they become less active; this short period of reduced activity will do them no harm. At high temperatures fish eat more and excrete more which means cleaning the tank more often.

Place a "do not touch" notice on the lines bringing electricity to the tank. Once during our absence, a well-meaning friend disconnected the tank heater to plug in a vacuum cleaner. The house was *spotless* on our return, but the fish had more spots than I care to mention; the drop in temperature had reduced their resistance to disease and Ich had struck.

In planted tanks, cut back the growth. Otherwise, you will return to a jungle. Another reason to cut down the plants is that during the hours of darkness plants reverse the gaseous exchange and give off carbon dioxide. If your tank is going to be in the dark for a long period, it is always wise to reduce the plant growth.

Check all electrical appliances and connections, and renew those that are worn or faulty.

Fill your tanks to allow for evaporation. If the weather is warm, this could be a considerable amount. See that the heater/thermostat is well down in the water.

If available, pour a liberal amount of live Daphnia into the tank last thing — they will live on and provide a change of diet.

Don't overfeed with dried food just before you leave in the mistaken belief it will tide the fish over — it will simply be ignored by the fish and foul the tank. Fish can go long periods without food. If you cannot get someone to visit, leave the tank alone. It will be quite safe for a week or two if you have carried out the above precautions.

Finally, why spoil your vacation by worrying about the aquarium? Over the years we have left many tanks for long periods. On our return they were minus quite a lot of water through evaporation, but the water left was crystal clear and the fish healthy and happy.

Have a good holiday and don't forget, if your cat is a fish lover too, board him out — it's safer!

Index to Fishes (by Common Name)

(See the Index by Scientific Name on page 266 for page numbers.)

Blue Discus	*Symphysodon aequifasciata haraldi*
Blue Gourami	*Trichogaster trichopterus var.sumatranus*
Blue Gularis	*Aphyosemion gulare caeruleum*
Blue Panchax	*Aplocheilus panchax*
Blushing Angelfish	*Pterophyllum scalare*
Bristlenose Catfish	*Ancistrus dolichopterus*
Bronze Corydoras	*Corydoras aeneus*
Brown Discus	*Symphysodon aequifasciata axelrodi*
Bucktooth Characin	*Exodon paradoxus*
Bumblebee Fish, or Golden-banded Gobie	*Brachygobius nunus*
Butterball	*Pterophyllum scalare*
Butterfly Fish	*Pantodon buchholzi*
Cardinal Tetra	*Cheirodon axelrodi*
Cherry Barb	*Barbus titteya*
Chocolate Gourami	*Sphaerichthys osphromenoides*
Clarias	*Clarias batrachus*
Clown Barb, or Everett's Barb	*Barbus everetti*
Clown Loach, or Tiger Botia	*Botia macracanthus*
Coelacanth	*Latimeria chalumnae*
Congo Tetra	*Micralestes interruptus*
Convict or Zebra Cichlid	*Cichlasoma nigrofasciatum*
Coolie (Kuhli) Loach	*Acanthophthalmus myersi*
Coolie Loach, Leopard Eel, Prickly Eye, or Striped Loach	*Acanthophthalmus kuhlii kuhlii*
Deep Angelfish	*Pterophyllum altum*
Deep-bodied Hatchetfish	*Thoracocharax stellatus*
Discus	*Symphysodon discus*
Dwarf Gourami	*Colisa lalia*
Dwarf Loach	*Botia sidthimunki*
Dwarf Pencilfish	*Nannostomus marginatus*
Dwarf or Pigmy Corydoras	*Corydoras hastatus*

Elegant Corydoras	*Corydoras elegans*
Elephant - nosed Fish	*Gnathonemus petersi*
Firemouth Cichlid	*Cichlasoma meeki*
Flag Cichlid	*Aequidens curviceps*
Flag Tetra	*Hyphessobrycon heterorhabdus*
Geisha Girl Medaka, Japanese Medaka, or Ricefish	*Oryzias latipes*
Ghost Angelfish	*Pterophyllum scalare*
Giant Danio	*Danio malabaricus*
Giant Gourami, or Striped or Banded Gourami	*Colisa fasciata*
Glass Catfish	*Kryptopterus bicirrhis*
Glass Tetra	*Moenkhausia oligolepis*
Glowlight Tetra	*Hemigrammus erythrozonus*
Gold Tetra	*Hemigrammus armstrongi*
Golden Pheasant	*Aphyosemion sjoestedti*
Golden-eyed Dwarf Cichlid	*Nannacara anomala*
Goldfish	*Carassius auratus*
Green, Brown or Cuban Rivulus	*Rivulus cylindraceus*
Green Discus	*Symphysodon aequifasciata aequifasciata*
Green Kissing Gourami	*Helostoma temmincki*
Green Sailfin Molly	*Poecilia latipinna*
Guenther's Nothobranchius	*Nothobranchius guentheri*
Guppy, or Millions Fish	*Poecilia reticulata*
Halfbeak	*Dermogenys pusillus*
Head-and-tail-Light Fish, or Beacon Fish	*Hemigrammus ocellifer*
Honeycomb Gourami	*Colisa chuna*
Hoplo Cat	*Hoplosternum thoracatum*
Indian Algae Eater	*Gyrinocheilus aymonieri*
Indian Glassfish	*Chanda ranga*
Island Barb, Checkered Barb, or Iridescent Barb	*Barbus oligolepis*
Jack Dempsey	*Cichlasoma biocellatum*
Japanese Weatherfish	*Misgurnus anguillicaudatus*

Keyhole Cichlid	*Aequidens maroni*
Kissing Gourami	*Helostoma rudolfi*
Lampeyed Panchax	*Micropanchax macrophthalmus*
Lemon Tetra	*Hyphessobrycon pulchripinnis*
Leopard Corydoras	*Corydoras julii*
Leopard Danio	*Brachydanio frankei*
Lesser Angelfish	*Pterophyllum eimekei*
Long Fin Barb	*Barbus arulius*
Long Fin Hatchetfish	*Thoracocharax securis*
Longfinned Characin	*Alestes longipinnis*
Long-nosed Distichodus	*Distichodus lusosso*
Lyretail Panchax, or Cape Lopez	***Aphyosemion australe australe***
Marble Headstander	*Abramites microcephalus*
Marbled Hatchetfish	*Carnegiella strigata*
Mexican Tetra	*Astyanax mexicanus*
Molly, or Sphenops Molly	*Poecilia sphenops*
Montezuma Swordtail	*Xiphophorus montezumae*
Moonlight Gourami	*Trichogaster microlepis*
Mosquito Fish, or Dwarf Top Minnow	*Heterandria formosa*
Neon Tetra	*Hyphessobrycon innesi*
Opaline or Cosby Gourami	*Trichogaster marmoratus*
Ortmann's Dwarf Cichlid	*Apistogramma ortmanni*
Oscar or Velvet Cichlid	*Astronotus ocellatus*
Panchax Lineatus	*Aplocheilus lineatus*
Paradisefish	*Macropodus opercularis*
Pearl Danio, or Gold Danio	*Brachydanio albolineatus*
Pearl Headstander	*Chilodus punctatus*
Pearl or Mosaic Gourami	*Trichogaster leeri*
Pencilfish	*Poecilobrycon eques*
Penguin Fish	*Thayeria boehlkei*
Penguin Fish	*Thayeria obliquua*
Peppered Corydoras	*Corydoras paleatus*
Piranha	*Pygocentrus piraya*
Platy	***Xiphophorus maculatus and X. variatus***
Pluto, or Suckermouth	*Plecostomus plecostomus*

Polkadot Catfish	*Synodontis angelicus*
Porthole Acara	*Aequidens portalegrensis*
Pretty Tetra	*Hemigrammus pulcher*
Puffer	*Tetraodon fluviatilis*
Rachov's Nothobranchius	*Nothobranchius rachovi*
Ramirez' Dwarf Cichlid, or Ramirezi	*Apistogramma ramirezi*
Red Lyretail	*Aphyosemion bivittatum bivittatum*
Red or Rummy Nosed Tetra	*Hemigrammus rhodostomus*
(Red) Rasbora, or Harlequin Fish	*Rasbora heteromorpha*
Red Rasbora	*Rasbora hengeli*
Red-breasted Piranha, or Natterer's Piranha	*Rooseveltiella (Serrasalmo) nattereri*
Red-finned Blue Botia	*Botia pulchripinnis*
Red-finned Distichodus	*Distichodus affinis*
Redlined Rasbora	*Rasbora pauciperforata*
Redspeckled Killy	*Aphyosemion cognatum*
Redtailed Black Shark	*Labeo bicolor*
Robert's Tetra	*Hyphessobrycon roberti*
Rosy Barb, or Red Barb	*Barbus conchonius*
Rosy Tetra, or Black Flag Tetra	*Hyphessobrycon rosaceus*
Sailfin Molly	*Poecilia velifera*
Scat	*Scatophagus argus (rubrifrons)*
Scholze's Tetra, or Blackline Tetra	*Hyphessobrycon scholzei*
Schwanenfeld's Barb	*Barbus schwanenfeldi*
Schuberti or Golden Barb	*Barbus sachsi*
Serpae Tetra	*Hyphessobrycon callistus*
Siamese Fighting Fish	*Betta splendens*
Silver Dollar	*Mylossoma argenteum*
Silver Dollar	*Mylossoma duriventris*
Silver Hatchetfish	*Gasteropelecus sternicla*
Silver Hatchetfish (Giant)	*Gasteropelecus levis*
Singapore Angel, or Mono	*Monodactylus argenteus*
Six Barred Distichodus	*Distichodus sexfasciatus*

Skunk Botia	*Botia horae*
Skunk Corydoras, or Arched Corydoras	*Corydoras arcuatus*
Slender Catfish	*Pimelodella gracilis*
Small or Egyptian Mouth-breeder	*Haplochromis multicolor*
Spotted Corydoras	*Corydoras punctatus*
Spotted Rasbora, or Pigmy Rasbora	*Rasbora maculata*
Spraying Characin	*Copeina arnoldi*
Striped Anostomus	*Anostomus anostomus*
Sucker Catfish (Algae Eater)	*Otocinclus arnoldi*
Sumatra Barb, or Tiger Barb	*Barbus tetrazona tetrazona*
Swordtail	*Xiphophorus helleri*
Talking Catfish, or Spiny Catfish	*Doras (Acanthodoras) hancocki*
Tetra from Buenos Aires, or Buenos Aires Tetra	*Hemigrammus caudovittatus*
Tetra von Rio, or Flame Tetra	*Hyphessobrycon flammeus*
Thick-lipped Gourami	*Colisa labiosa*
Three Banded Pencilfish	*Nannostomus trifasciatus*
Three Line Rasbora, or Scissorstail	*Rasbora trilineata*
Three Spot Gourami	*Trichogaster trichopterus trichopterus*
Tri-colored Shark, or Silver Shark	*Balantiocheilus melanopterus*
Twig Catfish	*Farlowella gracilis*
Two Spot Barb, or Tic-Tac-Toe Barb	*Barbus ticto*
Upside-down Catfish	*Synodontis nigriventris*
Variegated Platy	*Xiphophorus variatus*
Veiltail Angelfish	*Pterophyllum scalare*
White Cloud Mountain Minnow	*Tanichthys albonubes*
X-ray Fish, or Water Goldfinch	*Pristella riddlei*
Yellow Congo Characin	*Alestopetersius caudalis*
Yellow Dwarf Cichlid	*Apistogramma pertense*
Zebra Danio	*Brachydanio rerio*

At a Glance

The following Index is in tabular form to provide maximum information in minimum space. It is comprehensive and easy to follow. The fishes are listed alphabetically by their scientific names. These can be looked up in the preceding list which is also alphabetical but by common names.

The vertical columns are identified by capital letters, the key to which is given below:

A. *Suitability for the community aquarium.*
    1. Recommended.
    2. Not suitable.
    3. Can be kept only with fishes of the same size.

B. *Average adult length.*
    1. Two inches or less.
    2. Two to three inches.
    3. Three to four inches.
    4. Over four inches.

C. *Range.*
    1. Southern North America and Central America.
    2. South America (except the extreme south).
    3. Africa and the Near East.
    4. India and Southeast Asia.
    5. Indonesia and Australia.

D. *Temperament.*
    1. Shy and retiring.
    2. Peaceful.
    3. Aggressive.

E. *Temperature requirements.*
    1. 68 - 73⁰ Fahrenheit.
    2. 73 - 78⁰ Fahrenheit.
    3. 78 - 80⁰ Fahrenheit.

F. *Breeding habits.*
    1. Gives birth to live young
    2. Scatters eggs — provides no parental care.
    3. Provides care of the eggs and young.
    4. Mouth-breeder.
    5. Builds bubble nest.
    6. Sub-stratum burier.

G. *Aquarium strata usually occupied.*
    1. Surface swimmer.
    2. Middle of the tank.
    3. Bottom.
    4. Ubiquitous.
H. *Beginner's breeding rating.*
    1. Easy to breed.
    2. Intermediate
    3. Relatively difficult.
    4. Not spawned in captivity.
I. *General diet.*
    1. All foods (see Chapter VII).
    2. Live foods preferred (can be trained to take prepared).
    3. Vegetable.
    4. Mainly animal protein.

Because characteristics frequently overlap and new knowledge becomes available daily, the characteristics given for each species are average or predominant.

For example: looking at our first fish, *Abramites microcephalus,* column "D" (Temperament) says "peaceful," yet "A" tells us to keep with fishes of their own size. At first glance this seems contradictory, but if we look in column "B" we see that it grows to more than four inches. Because a fish this size, regardless of its peaceful nature, tends to overpower smaller fishes, particularly at feeding time, it had best be kept with larger-size fishes.

One further reminder: under "H" sub-catergory 4, "not spawned in captivity": this means up to the present time and to the best of the author's knowledge. It is probable that by the time this book appears in print quite a few species listed as "H = 4" will have been bred.

Index to Fishes (by Scientific Name)

SPECIES	CHARACTERISTIC									Page no.
	A	B	C	D	E	F	G	H	I	
Aphyocharax rubripinnis Bloodfin	1	2	2	2	2	2	1/2	1	1	**150**
Aphyosemion australe australe Lyretail Panchax, or Cape Lopez	1	2	3	2	3	2	1	2	2	**196**
Aphyosemion bivittatum bivittatum Red Lyretail	1	1	3	1	2	2	1	2	2	**196**
Aphyosemion cognatum Redspeckled Killy	1	1	3	2	2	3	4	2	2	**123**
Aphyosemion gulare caeruleum Blue Gularis	2	3	3	3	1	6	3	2	4	
Aphyosemion sjoestedti Golden Pheasant	2	3	3	3	3	6	1	3	4	**196**
Apistogramma agassizi Agassiz' Dwarf Cichlid	1	3	2	2	2	3	2	2	2	**168**
Apistogramma ortmanni Ortmann's Dwarf Cichlid	1	2	2	2	3	3	3	2	4	**168**
Apistogramma pertense Yellow Dwarf Cichlid	1	2	2	2	3	3	3	2	2	**168**
Apistogramma ramirezi Ramirez' Dwarf Cichlid, or Ramirezi	1	2	2	2	2	3	2/3	2	1/2	**167**
Aplocheilus lineatus Panchax Lineatus	3	3	4	3	3	2	1	2	4	**196**
Aplocheilus panchax Blue Panchax	1	3	4	3	3	2	1	2	4	**197**

SPECIES	A	B	C	D	E	F	G	H	I	Page no.
Astronotus ocellatus Oscar or Velvet Cichlid	2	4	2	3	2	3	2	3	4	**168**
Astyanax mexicanus Mexican Tetra	3	3	1	3	1	2	2	2	1	**149**
Balantiocheilus melanopterus Tri-colored Shark, or Silver Shark	3	4	5	2	2		2	4	1	**180**
Barbus arulius Long Fin Barb	1	4	4	2	2	2	2	3	1	**181**
Barbus conchonius Rosy Barb, or Red Barb	1	4	4	2	2	2	2	1	1	**182**
Barbus everetti Clown Barb, or Everett's Barb	1	4	4	2	2	2	3	2	1	**183**
Barbus filamentosus Blackspot Barb	1	4	4	2	2	2	2	2	1	**181**
Barbus nigrofasciatus Black Ruby, or Purple-headed Barb	1	2	4	2	2	2	2	1	1	**183**
Barbus oligolepis Island Barb, Checkered Barb, or Iridescent Barb	1	2	5	2	2	2	2	1	1	**184**
Barbus sachsi Schuberti or Golden Barb	1	2	4	2	2	2	3	2	1	**184**
Barbus schwanenfeldi Schwanenfeld's Barb	1	4	4	2	3	2	3	3	1	**185**
Barbus tetrazona tetrazona Sumatra Barb, or Tiger Barb	1	2	5	2	2	2	2	1	1	**186**

SPECIES	A	B	C	D	E	F	G	H	I	Page no.
Barbus ticto Two Spot Barb, or Tic-Tac-Toe Barb	3	3	4	2	2	2	2	1	1	**123**
Barbus titteya Cherry Barb	1	2	4	2	2	2	2	1	1	**187**
Betta splendens Siamese Fighting Fish	1	2	4	2*	3	5	1/2	1	1	**131**
Botia horae Skunk Botia	1	3	4	2	2		3	1	2	**177**
Botia macracanthus Clown Loach, or Tiger Botia	1	4	4	1	2		3	1	2	**178**
Botia modesta Blue Botia	1	3	4	2	2		3	1	1	**178**
Botia pulchripinnis Red-finned Blue Botia	1	3	4	2	2		3	1	1	**178**
Botia sidthimunki Dwarf Loach	1	2	4	1	2		3	1	2	**179**
Brachydanio albolineatus Pearl Danio, or Gold Danio	1	1	4	2	1	2	1	1	1	**187**
Brachydanio frankei Leopard Danio	1	2	4	2	2	2	1/2	2	1	**188**
Brachydanio rerio Zebra Danio	1	2	4	2	2	2	1/2	1	1	**187**
Brachygobius nunus Bumblebee Fish, or Golden Banded Gobie	1	1	5	2	2	3	3	3	2	**227**

* single males only

SPECIES	A	B	C	D	E	F	G	H	I	Page no.
Callichthys callichthys Armored Catfish	3	4	2	2	1	5	3	2	1	**143**
Carassius auratus Goldfish	1	4		2	1	2	4	2	1	
Carnegiella marthae Blackwinged Hatchetfish	2	2	2	1	1	2	1	4	4	**199**
Carnegiella strigata Marbled Hatchetfish	1	2	2	2	2	2	2	3	1	**199**
Chanda ranga Indian Glassfish	1	2	4	2	2	2	2	3	4	**147**
Cheirodon axelrodi Cardinal Tetra	1	1	2	2	2	2	2	3	1	**150**
Chilodus punctatus Pearl Headstander	1	3	2	2	3	2	3	3	3	**140**
Cichlasoma biocellatum Jack Dempsey	3	4	2	3	2	3	4	2	2	**168**
Cichlasoma festivum Barred or Flag Cichlid, or Festivum	3	4	2	3	2	3	4	2	2	**168**
Cichlasoma meeki Firemouth Cichlid	3	4	2	3	2	3	4	2	2	**168**
Cichlasoma nigrofasciatum Convict or Zebra Cichlid	3	4	2	3	2	3	4	2	2	**168**
Cichlasoma severum Banded Cichlid	3	4	2	3	2	3	4	2	2	**168**
Clarias batrachus Clarias	1	4	4	2	1	3	3	4	1	**174**

CHARACTERISTIC

SPECIES	CHARACTERISTIC									Page no.
	A	B	C	D	E	F	G	H	I	
Colisa chuna Honeycomb Gourami	1	2	4	2	3	5	4	3	1	**135**
Colisa fasciata Giant Gourami, or Striped or Banded Gourami	1	3	2	2	3	5	4	2	1	**133**
Colisa labiosa Thick-lipped Gourami	1	3	4	2	3	5	2	2	1	**134**
Colisa lalia Dwarf Gourami	1	2	4	1	3	5	2	1	1	**134**
Copeina arnoldi Spraying Characin	1	2	2	2	2	3	1	3	2	**148**
Corydoras aeneus Bronze Corydoras	1	2	2	2	2	2	3	2	1	**143**
Corydoras agassizi Agassiz' Corydoras	1	2	2	2	2	2	3	3	1	**168**
Corydoras arcuatus Skunk Corydoras, or Arched Corydoras	1	2	2	2	2	2	3	2	1	**143**
Corydoras elegans Elegant Corydoras	1	2	2	2	2	2	3	3	1	**144**
Corydoras hastatus Dwarf or Pigmy Corydoras	1	1	2	2	2	2	3	2	1	**144**
Corydoras julii Leopard Corydoras	1	2	2	2	2	2	3	2	1	**144**
Corydoras melanistius Blackspotted Corydoras	1	2	2	2	2	2	3	3	1	**145**
Corydoras metae Bandit Catfish, or Masked Corydoras	1	2	2	2	2	2	3	3	1	**146**

SPECIES	A	B	C	D	E	F	G	H	I	Page no.
Corydoras paleatus Peppered Corydoras	1	2	2	2	2	2	3	3	1	**143**
Corydoras punctatus Spotted Corydoras	1	2	2	2	2	2	3	3	1	**146**
Cynolebias adolffi Adolff's Cynolebias	2	2	2	3	1	6	3	2	4	
Cynolebias belotti Argentine Pearlfish	2	2	2	1	2	6	2	2	2	**197**
Cynolebias nigripinnis Blackfinned Pearlfish	2	2	2	1	2	6	2	2	2	**197**
Danio malabaricus Giant Danio	3	4	4	2	2	2	1/2	2	1	**187**
Dermogenys pusillus Halfbeak	1	2	4	2	3	1	1	2	2	**124**
Distichodus affinis Red-finned Distichodus	2	4	3	2	1	2	2		2	**174**
Distichodus lusosso Long-nosed Distichodus	3	4	3	2	1	2	4	4	2	**174**
Distichodus sexfasciatus Six Barred Distichodus	3	4	3	2	1	2	4	4	2	**174**
Doras (Acanthodoras) hancocki Talking Catfish, or Spiny Catfish	3	4	2	3	2/3		3	4	1	**124**
Exodon paradoxus Bucktooth Characin	2	4	2	3	3	2	2	3	2	**151**
Farlowella gracilis Twig Catfish	1	4	2	1	3		3	4	3	**205**

Header: CHARACTERISTIC

SPECIES	A	B	C	D	E	F	G	H	I	Page no.
Gasteropelecus levis Silver Hatchetfish (Giant)	2	2	2	1	1	2	1	4	4	**199**
Gasteropelecus sternicla Silver Hatchetfish	2	2	2	1	1	2	1	4	4	**199**
Gnathonemus petersi Elephant-nosed Fish	3	4	3	1	2		2/3	4	2	**229**
Gymnocorymbus ternetzi Black Tetra, Blackamoor, or Petticoat Fish	3	2	3	3	3	2	2	2	1	**151**
Gyrinocheilus aymonieri Indian Algae Eater	1	4	4	2	2		3	4	3	**200**
Haplochromis multicolor Small or Egyptian Mouth-breeder	3	2	3	2	2	4	2	1	1	**172**
Helostoma rudolfi Kissing Gourami	1	4	4	2	3	2	4	3	3	**135**
Helostoma temmincki Green Kissing Gourami	1	4	4	2	3	2	4	3	3	**136**
Hemigrammus armstrongi Gold Tetra	1	2	2	2	2	2	2	2	1	**152**
Hemigrammus caudovittatus Tetra from Buenos Aires, or Buenos Aires Tetra	3	2	2	3	1	2	2	1	1	**153**
Hemigrammus erythrozonus Glowlight Tetra	1	1	2	2	2/3	2	2	2	1	**154**
Hemigrammus ocellifer Head-and-tail-Light Fish, or Beacon Fish	1	2	2	2	2	2	2	1	1	**152**

SPECIES	A	B	C	D	E	F	G	H	I	Page no.
Hemigrammus pulcher Pretty Tetra	1	1	2	2	3	2	2	3	1	**154**
Hemigrammus rhodostomus Red or Rummy Nosed Tetra	1	2	2	2	2	2	2	4	1	**155**
Heterandria formosa Mosquito Fish, or Dwarf Top Minnow	3	1	1	2	2	1	2	1	1	**125**
Hoplosternum thoracatum Hoplo Cat	1	4	2	2	1	5	3	3	1	**146**
Hyphessobrycon callistus Serpae Tetra	1	1	2	2	2	2	2	1	1	**125**
Hyphessobrycon flammeus Tetra von Rio, or Flame Tetra	1	1	2	2	2	2	2	2	1	**155**
Hyphessobrycon heterorhabdus Flag Tetra	1	1	2	2	2	2	2	1	1	**156**
Hyphessobrycon innesi Neon Tetra	1	1	2	2	2	2	2	3	1	**156**
Hyphessobrycon pulchripinnis Lemon Tetra	1	1	2	2	2	2	2	2	1	**157**
Hyphessobrycon roberti Robert's Tetra	1	1	2	2	2	2	2	3	1	**125**
Hyphessobrycon rosaceus Rosy Tetra, or Black Flag Tetra	1	1	2	2	2	2	2	2	1	**125**
Hyphessobrycon rubrostigma Bleeding Heart Tetra, or Tetra Perez	1	3	2	2	2	2	2	2	2	**158**

SPECIES	A	B	C	D	E	F	G	H	I	Page no.
Hyphessobrycon scholzei Scholze's Tetra, or Blackline Tetra	1	1	2	2	2	2	2	3	1	**158**
Kryptopterus bicirrhis Glass Catfish	1	4	5	1	2		2	4	1	**226**
Labeo bicolor Redtailed Black Shark	1	4	4	2	2		3	4	1/3	**188**
Leporinus fasciatus Banded Leporinus	3	4	2	2	2	2	2	3	3	**141**
Loricaria parva Alligator Catfish	1	3	2	2	1	3	3	3	3	**205**
Macropodus opercularis Paradisefish	3	2	4	3	2	5	2	2	1	**136**
Micralestes (Phenacogrammus) *interruptus* Congo Tetra	3	2	3	1	2	2	2	3	2	**161**
Micropanchax macrophthalmus Lampeyed Panchax	1	1	3	2	2	2	2	3	2	**197**
Misgurnus anguillicaudatus Japanese Weatherfish	1	4	*	2	1	2	3	4	2	**126**
Moenkhausia oligolepis Glass Tetra	1	4	2	2	2	2	2	5	1	**158**
Monodactylus argentcus Singapore Angel, or Mono	1	4	4	2	2		2	4	1	**207**
Morulius chrysophekadion Black Shark	3	4	5	2	2		3	4	1/3	**189**

* Northeast Asia into China

SPECIES	A	B	C	D	E	F	G	H	I	Page no.
Mylossoma argenteum Silver Dollar	1	4	2	2	2		2	4	3	**161**
Mylossoma duriventris Silver Dollar	1	4	2	2	2		2	4	3	**161**
Nannacara anomala Golden-eyed Dwarf Cichild	1	2	2	2	2	3	3	2	2	**168**
Nannostomus marginatus Dwarf Pencilfish	1	1	2	2	2	2	2	1	1	**201**
Nannostomus trifasciatus Three Banded Pencilfish	1	2	2	2	3	2	2	3	1	**202**
Nothobranchius guentheri Guenther's Nothobranchius	2	2	3	3	3	6	3	3	2	**197**
Nothobranchius rachovi Rachov's Nothobranchius	2	2	3	3	3	6	3	2	2	**197**
Oryzias latipes Geisha Girl Medaka, Japanese Medaka, or Ricefish	1	1	4	2	1	2	4	1	1	**197**
Osteoglossum bicirrhosum Arowana	2	4	2	3	2/3	4	4	3	4	**126**
Otocinclus arnoldi Sucker Catfish (Algae Eater)	1	1	2	2	2	3	3	3	3	**205**
Pantodon buchholzi Butterfly Fish	2	4	3	3	2		1	4	2	**230**
Pimelodella gracilis Slender Catfish	3	4	2	1/2	3		3	4	2	**126**

SPECIES	A	B	C	D	E	F	G	H	I	Page no.
Plecostomus plecostomus Pluto, or Suckermouth	1	4	2	2	2	3	3	4	3	**204**
Poecilia latipinna Green Sailfin Molly	1	4	1	2	2	1	2	1	1/3	**213**
Poecilia reticulata Guppy, or Millions Fish	1	2	1	2	2	1	2	1	1	**210**
Poecilia sphenops Molly, or Sphenops Molly	1	2	1	2	1	1	4	1	1	**213**
Poecilia velifera Sailfin Molly	1	4	1	2	3	1	2	1	1/3	**213**
Poecilobrycon eques Pencilfish	1	2	2	2	2	2	2	3	1	**201**
Pristella riddlei X-ray Fish, or Water Goldfinch	1	2	1/2	2	2	2	2	2	1	**163**
Pterophyllum altum Deep Angelfish	1	4	2	2	2	3	4	2	2	**169**
Pterophyllum eimekei Lesser Angelfish	1	4	2	2	2	3	4	2	2	**169**
Pterophyllum scalare Angelfish, or Scalare	1	4	2	2	2/3	3	2	1	1	**169**
Pygocentrus piraya Piranha	2	4	2	3	3		2	4	4	**162**
Rasbora hengeli Red Rasbora	1	1	4	2	2	2	2	3	1	**191**
Rasbora heteromorpha (Red) Rasbora, or Harlequin Fish	1	2	5	2	2	2	2	1	1	**190**

SPECIES	A	B	C	D	E	F	G	H	I	Page no.
Rasbora maculata Spotted Rasbora, or Pigmy Rasbora	1	1	4	1	3	2	2	3	1	**191**
Rasbora pauciperforata Redlined Rasbora	1	1	4	2	2	2	2	3	1	**192**
Rasbora trilineata Three Line Rasbora, or Scissorstail	1	4	5	2	2	2	2	2	1	**192**
Rooseveltiella (Serrasalmo) nattereri Red-breasted Piranha, or Natterer's Piranha	2	4	2	3	3		2	4	4	**161**
Rivulus cylindraceus Green, Brown or Cuban Rivulus	1	2	1	2	1	2	1	2	2	**197**
Scatophagus argus (rubrifrons) Scat	1	4	4	2	1		4	4	1	**225**
Sphaerichthys osphromenoides Chocolate Gourami	1	2	5	1	3	4	4	3	1	**137**
Symphysodon aequifasciata aequifasciata Green Discus	2	4	2	2	3	2	4	3	2	**171**
Symphysodon aequifasciata axelrodi Brown Discus	2	4	2	2	3	2	4	3	2	**171**
Symphysodon aequifasciata haraldi Blue Discus	2	4	2	2	3	2	4	3	2	**171**
Symphysodon discus Discus	1	4	2	2	3	3	2	2	4	**171**

SPECIES	A	B	C	D	E	F	G	H	I	Page no.
Synodontis angelicus Polkadot Catfish	3	4	3	2	3		3	4	1	**206**
Synodontis nigriventris Upside-down Catfish	1	3	3	1	3		1	4	2	**206**
Tanichthys albonubes White Cloud Mountain Minnow	1	1	4	2	2	2	2	1	1	**193**
Tetraodon fluviatilis Puffer	3	4	4	3	1	2	4	3	1	**82**
Thayeria obliquua Penguin Fish	3	3	2	3	2	2	2	3	1	**163**
Thayeria boehlkei Penguin Fish	1	2	2	2	2	2	2	3	1	**163**
Thoracocharax securis Long Fin Hatchetfish	2	2	2	1	1	2	1	4	4	**199**
Thoracocharax stellatus Deep-bodied Hatchetfish	2	2	2	1	1	2	1	4	4	**199**
Tilapia macrocephala African or Blackchinned Mouth-breeder	2	4	3	3	2	4	4	1	1	**172**
Toxotes jaculator Archerfish	3	4	5	2	3		1	4	4	**230**
Trichogaster leeri Pearl or Mosaic Gourami	1	4	5	2	3	5	1/2	1	1	**137**
Trichogaster marmoratus Opaline or Cosby Gourami	1	3	4	2	2	5	4	2	1	**139**

SPECIES	CHARACTERISTIC									Page no.
	A	B	C	D	E	F	G	H	I	
Trichogaster microlepis Moonlight Gourami	1	3	4	2	2	5	4	2	1	**138**
Trichogaster trichopterus var. sumatranus Blue Gourami	1	3	4	2	3	5	5	2	1	**138**
Trichogaster trichopterus trichopterus Three Spot Gourami	1	3	4	2	2	5	4	2	1	**138**
Xenomystus nigri Black Knife Fish	3	4	3	1	2			4	2	**127**
Xiphophorus helleri Swordtail	1	4	1	2	2	1	4	1	1	**214**
Xiphophorus maculatus Platy	1	2	1	2	2	1	4	1	1	**214**
Xiphophorus montezumae Montezuma Swordtail	1	4	1	2	1	1				**214**
Xiphophorus variatus Platy, or Variegated Platy	1	2	1	2	2	1	4	1	1	**214**

Picture Index of Fishes